75422089 X

Africa
Reimagined

Africa Reimagined

Reclaiming Prosperity for the Continent

Hlumelo Biko

AMBERLEY

To my mentors:
Mamphela, Jeremy, Tonderai, Steve Phelps and Blessing

This edition published 2021

Amberley Publishing
The Hill, Stroud
Gloucestershire, GL5 4EP

www.amberley-books.com

British Library Cataloguing in Publication Data.
A catalogue record for this book is available from the British Library.

ISBN 978 1 4456 9972 1 (print)
ISBN 978 1 44569 973 8 (ebook)

1 2 3 4 5 6 7 8 9 10

Design and typesetting by Martine Barker
Set in Baskerville/Optima
Printed in the UK.

Contents

Foreword

HLUMELO BIKO has done something very special in this book, something that Africa sorely needs. He has woven together many strands of scholarly research into the origins of race and identity with the aim of reconceptualising the African reality. It is a complex combination that embraces primeval African values and a holistic worldview, and calls for a reimagination of Africa's future from a positive trajectory of African socio-economic evolution. His ideas are a corrective to the harmful self-deprecation sustained by what he calls 'black mental boxes and the conceptual chain that holds the boxes shut'. These 'mental boxes' arise from the failure to democratise knowledge as a means of empowerment; the acceptance of other societies' myths as gospel truths instead of recognising these myths for what they are; the privileging of other people's social agendas above the preservation and development of African culture; and the acceptance of a mentality of scarcity over that of abundance.

In *Africa Reimagined*, Hlumelo combines the meaning of the Ugandan proverb, 'If you cut your chains you free yourself, if you cut your roots you die' with the words of the American historian David McCullough: 'History is who we are and why we are the way we are'.[1] For, as Biko points out, not only do these chains bind Africa; they also form the social and psychological wall that holds Africa within the confines of misery and decline. He makes bold suggestions on the ways African governments and peoples can and should reimagine the life and fortunes of the continent. He laments the failure of Africa to transition from oral history into codifying knowledge and historical achievements.

Biko argues that, above all, Africa needs psychological liberation. In this sense, the book extends his father's ideas of Black Consciousness. Steve Biko argued that 'the most potent weapon in the hands of the oppressor is the mind of the oppressed'. Hlumelo Biko unpacks this in its practical import, in the sense that it is not only individual self-worth that comes with psychological liberation, but also the social, economic, political and holistic ownership of a person's being.

Biko ends with a ringing call for a United States of Africa, balancing 'state power and local authority while allowing for the construction of a new African federal political economy' – a reimagined future for Africa, where the worth of the self translates to all that is worthwhile for positive living. In this regard, he echoes a stanza from the 1908 poem by renowned Xhosa poet Samuel Krune Mqhayi, who wrote:

Kuz'imihla ayikude, Esiya kuti sifunde
Imiqondiso yexesha, Ubudenge sibuqhwesha
Sithande ibala lethu, Sithand' amasiko ethu.
Sithande iinkosi zethu, Sithande uhlanga lwethu.
Sizingce ngentombi zethu, Nangemithi yezwe lethu,
Sizidle ngeentaba zethu, Sizidle ngo Thixo wethu.

These days are not far, When we will learn,
Understand the signs of the times,
When ignorance will be gone.
On that day we will love our colour;
On that day we will be proud of our culture;
On that day we will respect our kings;

On that day we will love our people.
On that day we will be proud of our young women;
On that day we will admire the trees of our land;
On that day we will delight at the sight of our mountains;
On that day we will be proud of our religion.[2]

This book should be more than a bedside reader, and I hope that African academics, social scientists, economists, politicians and analysts will feed on it as they craft new ideas of an Africa reimagined. And Steve Biko's hope will hold true not just for South Africa, but for the whole continent: 'We have set out on a quest for true humanity, and somewhere on the horizon we can see the glittering prize … In time we shall be in a position to bestow upon [South] Africa the greatest gift possible – a more human face.'[3]

Malusi Mpumlwana
Bishop of the Ethiopian Episcopal Church
February 2019

Introduction:
Why African culture matters

SOME YEARS AGO, I was in the beautiful city of Hamburg for the wedding of a childhood friend of mine and her German fiancé. On my second day there, as I was rushing back to the hotel after a tour, I left my phone in the taxi, which was driven by an African. As a sign of the times, the phone was a brand-new BlackBerry I had just bought on my way to the wedding. As I walked into the hotel, my sense of dread must have been written all over my face, causing an employee at the concierge desk to ask me what was wrong. I frantically explained to him that I had left my phone in the taxi, and we both dashed outside to see if, by some miracle, the driver was still there. He was nowhere to be seen. I raised my arms in dismay, signalling to the concierge that I fully expected never to see my phone again. He looked at me with a puzzled expression, and calmly said that my phone would be back in no time. I immediately assumed he knew the taxi driver, and said so. Again he flashed me a puzzled look and said he didn't, but, as far as he knew, no one steals things left in German taxis. Lo and behold, my phone was returned a few hours later after the taxi driver noticed it, called the last dialled number and figured out that it belonged to me. I am sure many people have had similar experiences.

What struck me about my experience was the fact that here were two African fellows in Germany acting in a way completely congruent with how we would both have been raised (never steal, and treat others the way you would want them to treat you), but that if we were both anywhere in Africa we would scarcely have expected either of us to return one another's phone. It might happen that we would both have done so, but the *expectation* would not have been there. What is it about my German experience that sums up our expectations of social obligations? It is not that there is anything special about Germany or German people, but rather, in this case, that my expectations were shaped by an alignment in German society between long-held values reflecting fundamental beliefs about right and wrong, what the country's laws spell out as obligations and punishment for breaching those values, and the personal obligations placed on the individual (an African taxi driver, in this case).

This book has a simple goal: to call attention to the fact that, at the core of Africa's many different development challenges, there is a misalignment between her people's understanding of citizenship, her laws, norms and values, and her culture. This lack of alignment makes us act unpredictably towards each other, based on a general lack of faith that rules are being followed consistently in society.

I feel that now, two decades into what most of us hope will be Africa's century, is a good time to champion the cultural realignment needed to ensure that African institutions reflect shared African norms and values. This realignment can transform the lived experience of Africans by changing their expectations of each other.

To achieve such a realignment, we need first to reimagine Africa without the current dominant psychological constraints and debilitating stereotypes. Future leaders on the African continent, free from old constraints and empowered by this realignment towards a different future, will help turn the dream of an African century into a reality. Evidence that this goal has been met will be when Africans in the workplace, at places of worship or at schools and universities are free to be individually successful, socially predictable and culturally themselves. This simple requirement baffles too many of us who live in Africa in 2019. Our misalignment of norms, values and laws is most obviously reflected in the weakness of the African family structure.

This book is an exploration of the role of identity in providing us with the platform to make contributions to, and demands from, society as a whole. More importantly, it is an exploration of how identity and identities shape our socio-economic preferences. According to one definition, 'Identities are the traits and characteristics, social relations, roles, and social group memberships that define who one is.'[1] Simply put, our identities are the predominant ways that we think of ourselves. Who we say we are, what friendships we form, what groups we associate ourselves with are all expressions of identity. Our choice of identity is the most important choice we will ever make. Being comfortable and secure in our identities turns out to be one of the biggest preconditions for a successful lifelong learning journey. This is an important milestone to reach if African citizens are to further develop the type of patriotism necessary to enable them to act more intentionally in shaping the societies they live in. Secure identities that are spiritually, morally and culturally aligned within a contextual awareness of the historical development of these norms shape socially conforming individual behaviour.

The book's simple goal is supported by research that shows how no society can be run successfully if the rules it adopts are not supported by old wisdom. This old wisdom, passed down from generation to generation, is what is commonly referred to as culture. In other words, our constitutions and our approach to the rule of law are nothing without the legitimacy derived from both active and tacit cultural approval. As a 'historical reservoir',[2] culture is an important factor in shaping identity. We draw on our cultural cues to give us feedback about sameness with and difference from others. These cues have the power to make us feel secure or insecure within our identities. Individuals with insecure identities find it difficult to bond, to trust and to be accountable to others. These tenets – trust, the

3

ability to bond and one's accountability to others – are the bedrock of social capital.

In almost all African countries, critical, formal institutions do not reflect African culture. African attitudes to the rules and regulations governing their countries reflect the failure to enable individuals to personally identify with them. We need to reimagine Africa's systems of governance, her approach to culture and her adoption of norms, values and laws.

What follows is a framework for asking fundamental questions designed to remind us to put indigenous[3] African interests first. This framework seeks to test the tension between the collective, community-oriented focus of many Africans and the imperative to foster self-confidence within individual citizens to accomplish their personal goals. Psychologist Albert Bandura describes the latter as 'self-efficacy'.[4]

In my view, any new or proposed policy needs to be put to a test to measure the extent to which it will promote individual African self-efficacy and collective social-capital maximisation. Without both self-efficacy and social capital, wealth creation is difficult to achieve. So, the challenge is to navigate between acting collectively and acting in one's own self-interest. Reimagining[5] Africa has to be guided by a desire to amplify those ideas that are freedom-maximising and to nullify those that detract from the collective and individual freedoms of Africans. The resolution of conflicts between freedom-enhancing and freedom-minimising policy choices is complex and subjective. It is for this reason that all the recommendations in this book assume that the constituency most affected should make the majority of such policy choices. Up until now, however, politics in most African countries has not worked this way. We have internalised the centralised decision-making tendencies of our colonial masters.

In addition to thinking about the creation of rules in a centralised way, the construction of post-liberation African societies has had a dual bias towards all things urban and foreign. The nature of that bias insinuates itself into the ways Africans construct their communities, teach their young and conduct their parliaments and senates. This has been accelerated by the fact that African popular culture is deeply aspirational towards urban and foreign symbols of modernity. We are captured by the desire to keep up with modernity as described and prescribed by our Western counterparts.

This type of psychological capture affects the internal narratives that shape our identity. DP McAdams's life-story model of identity asserts, 'People living in modern societies provide their lives with unity and purpose by constructing internalised and evolving narratives of the self.'[6] Once this internalised model is captured by a desire to conform to a foreign construct of modernity, individuals find it difficult to meet the designation of being both themselves and successful. They find it even harder to arbitrate between their individual and collective agendas.

I believe we need a framework that asks questions about the realignment of our historical narrative, our sense of identity and our self-image. This framework could shape an approach towards collective cooperation, how we balance formal versus informal institutions, and our attitude towards building social capital.

Africa Reimagined is therefore guided by the following foundational principles:

1. Core individual confidence is in part an outcome of the possession of a positive collective historical narrative.
2. The most important decision an adult makes is to choose their identity.[7]
3. Nurturing our self-image requires a successful battle against both categorisation and stereotyping.
4. Placing our culture at the centre of our life is essential to being free to be self-affirming.
5. An individual approach to collective cooperation requires the acquisition of both human and social capital.
6. Our professional effectiveness is determined by our internalisation of the legitimacy of formal institutions and their alignment with our working memory of the old wisdom we grew up with.

7. Making social capital count requires a different way of thinking about scarcity and abundance.

Ever since the first Europeans returned to the African continent on a colonial mission, beginning in the Ptolemaic period in 332 BCE, Africans have been psychologically dominated by their impressions of Westerners and Islamists as saviours of the continent. Beginning in 332 BCE, Africans worshipped a foreign deity, spoke a foreign language, accepted a foreign ruler and adopted a different spiritual belief system. This combination of foreign cultural offensive weapons changed Africans' internalised impressions of reality. These internalised impressions challenged and eventually replaced the traditional African understanding of reality. Despite being fore-warned by the likes of Frantz Fanon, Marcus Garvey and Chief Albert Luthuli, modern Africans have allowed this subtle process to reach the point of cultural genocide. It is only by reflecting on the way we currently see the world that we notice how our colonial history has transformed us.

We have ignored or discarded the urgings of Kwame Nkrumah, Julius Nyerere and Patrice Lumumba that we seek alternative ways to organise African societies. In many African universities, social scientists have underplayed the psychological effects of this cultural genocide based on their bias towards the study of so-called objective reality. The restriction of discussion and analysis to only those things that we can conclusively prove to exist creates constraints to radical change. Much of the cultural genocide involved the unquantifiable effects of knowledge lost through the destruction of African knowledge systems, most crassly displayed in the destruction of the Royal Library of Alexandria and the Malian library in Timbuktu. Even though I am aware of the postmodern approach to social science as a study of objective thinking, I believe this approach misses the critical importance of subjective ideas and how they shape human beings. This book is singularly concerned with individual Africans' subjective understanding of our own reality, and how this understanding shapes our beliefs about concepts such as freedom, religion, community, institutions, economic growth, social capital and human development.

Our reality is what we perceive it to be. Racism, oppression and stereotyping are all subjective experiences that each of us internalises slightly differently according to the personal history that has shaped our individual identity. Collectively, these subjective ideas both shape and are shaped by culture. Conceptions of self or identity are crucial building blocks upon which the idea of citizenship is constructed. When the cultures of the majority of citizens are constrained and marginalised in a society and their history is systematically destroyed, identities are compromised and the society goes into a tailspin. The idea of citizenship fails to take root because the individuals are unable to connect their sense of ownership with a country that feels like it is still very much in foreign hands.

This marginalisation process impacts countless African societies. Perhaps no country has been more influenced by this process than my own home country of South Africa, given the sheer number of European settlers, and the length of time that imperialism, colonialism and apartheid lasted. Since writing my first book, *The Great African Society*, I have come to understand the huge gulf created by identity crises that stand in the way of progress. How we see ourselves relative to others greatly impacts on how we prepare to engage and compete with them. Our ability to compete is immeasurably impacted by how efficient society is at removing obstacles to maximising our productivity as citizens. Our productivity as citizens is influenced by the presence or absence of a sense of ownership of our workplaces, our places of worship and the cities and countries we reside in.[8] The more empowered workers are, the more they feel a sense of ownership. We feel more empowered as workers if we can express ourselves and our talents more freely in the workplace.

It seems obvious that one of the defining attributes of a great society is the extent to which it enables citizens to self-actualise, that is, to achieve their potential. Those societies that stifle self-actualisation will have trouble retaining the best talent. One has to realise that self-actualisation takes place within a context of beliefs about how the world works, and how we believe we fit into this world. In other words, our impressions of the world have a major influence on the ways in which we act. I have become fascinated by the formation of impressions that lead people to act on new ideas. We use these impressions to construct our own reality.

In researching this book, I have been guided by two related questions: how do ideas, beliefs and norms form?, and what happens in society to let these beliefs shape our actions? I think it is important to ask these questions because it has become obvious that, in attempting to run their countries and the organisations within them, Africans don't believe in the rules of the game they have chosen to adopt. High crime rates, chronic vote-rigging in both national and local elections, rampant corruption and widespread governance failures underscore this lack of belief in the prevailing rules. The critical thing to understand is why we find it so hard to internalise these rules. Additionally, it is important to understand why we as Africans feel beholden to rules that obviously don't resonate with us intimately. Understanding our informal institutions better, and, for us young people, learning more about old cultural wisdom, can help us to reimagine how better to organise the societies we are part of.

Conducting research guided by these questions has helped me to understand much better how myths form, and how narratives weave together over time, only to be occasionally cemented by the seal of authority and thereby become heralded as history. I have had to relearn a key research principle, that any reader should be sceptical of the subjectivity inherent in all humans who construct written or spoken narratives. What has been an entirely new learning is the way in which groups of people can co-author present reality by explicitly or implicitly agreeing on an interpretation of a set of facts. Narratives, in other words, matter a great deal.

Humans experience three types of reality, two of which are well understood and a third that we often forget to recognise. The first is objective reality, exemplified by our shared experience of life as oxygen-breathing inhabitants of this planet. The second is subjective reality, such as how attractive we perceive our environment to be and the way we perceive ourselves in it. The third is intersubjective reality,[9] which is a group's commonly held set of myths or beliefs – for instance, a belief in God, Amen Ra or Allah.

Specifically within the African construct, our documented intersubjective reality begins with Africa's 'discovery' by Europeans. African history predating the Berlin Conference of 1884–1885 is almost wholly devoid of our own story of human development. We have been reduced to a one-dimensional anthropological study, within which events happen to African people while they passively conform to the results of these events.

There is a set of facts commonly agreed on by historians and ordinary citizens alike. We have the second-largest and second-most-populous continent. We speak close to 3 000 different languages, and are commonly believed to have the world's greatest genetic diversity. We are the cradle of global civilisation. Beyond this common understanding is where the deviations in our subjective realities occur.

This diversity of Africa's subjective reality has not prevented a dominant narrative from emerging. The media has settled on a common negative narrative about Africa. Somehow, history portrays us as a stagnated collection of foraging and hunter-gathering societies civilised by contact with the outside world. Almost all of our history books begin the in-depth analysis of our history in the 19th century, as a soon-to-be-colonised continent. Popular culture has dramatised this narrative in a variety of ways, from movies such as *The Gods Must Be Crazy* (1980) to the infamous 2007 cover of *The Economist* magazine titled 'The Dark Continent'.

We are described in the language of subjects who are usually other than the author. These descriptions move from wonder to awe and swiftly towards pitying patronisation as the authors describe a succession of military defeats, with some dramatisation of a handful of pyrrhic victories. African people are described in paternalistic tones, complimenting the intriguing nature of their historical

customs while framing their current cultures as reflective of ideal-
istic and naive norms and values. Historians typically explore our
history through the lens of colonialism. They compare and contrast
each African country's experience and implicitly question where
Africans would be without Western civilising contact.

This 'traditional' body of history usually ends with the struggle
for independence and the perils of post-colonial self-government,
and the ineptitude of indigenous people's management. This leaves
the reader wondering if the Africans in question would not have
been better off being permanently colonised. At some point the common understanding is that Africans are both unlucky and incapable
of independently managing their affairs. As Africans, we outwardly
reject this interpretation of our history. However, a lack of compelling
alternative narratives, together with a depressing set of negative
present-day images, seems to confirm some of our worst fears, namely,
that this view of Africans may be right.

This defeatist construction of reality leads African leaders and
citizens to rely on many psychological crutches. We are crippled
by two opposing narratives that sit side by side in conflict with one
another. One is that we are proud of our history as the cradle of civilisation. This pride is often affirmed by our day-to-day observations of
examples of African ingenuity that give us hope for the future. The
second is that, as a recently liberated continent, Africa trails the rest of
the world in the race to modernise. These opposing realities give rise to
a form of cognitive dissonance that weakens core confidence among
African people. This makes it difficult for the majority of African
professionals to have a strong sense of self-confidence and self-efficacy
when competing against their global counterparts.

There has to be a different way of thinking about Africa. We
have to re-examine our history in all its glory and depression, just
as any other continent would do. We have to make African history
ours again. History has to become Our Story. We have to reassert the
historical fact that Africans birthed the world's first great civilisation
over 3 000 years before the birth of Christ.[10] It must be acknowledged

that this Egyptian civilisation was mothered in 4000 BCE by Sudan and Ethiopia,[11] and that these societies taught the Egyptians how to build pyramids and understand their universe. Ancient historians such as Herodotus understood and documented that Africans populated many parts of the Near, Middle and Far East. Linguists, sociologists, scientists and historians now openly admit that the first Indus River civilisation was dominated by Africans called Dravidians.[12] That Herodotus and other ancient historians used the word 'Ethiopia' to refer to the inhabitants of the territories east of Egypt all the way to India should be instructive in how we think about African dominance between 3000 BCE and 332 BCE.

We must reassert the fact that Africans from Mali and Egypt arrived in the Americas 700 years before the birth of Christ, not as slaves or hostages, but as explorers who left large statues that were admired by indigenous Americans.[13] This historical fact, having been proven by scholars such as Ivan van Sertima, has been recognised by the United States Congress, which has dropped all reference to Christopher Columbus having discovered America, yet we won't teach it in our African schools. It has to be remembered that Africans, specifically the Moors (Berbers) of the Maghreb, helped the Arabs to both colonise and civilise the Iberian Peninsula, beginning in 711.[14] It is important for both Africans and Europeans to realise that without this gift of civilisation, Europe would not have emerged when it did from the Dark Ages.

There is a demand for a new intersubjective reality. The African continent cannot be a permanent recipient of policy advice, nor can it be a permanent feature on donor lists. It has to re-establish the reality of Africa as a vast continent made up of talented people in search of a development model that works for them in the modern era. This book explores in detail the psychological predilections that make economic development difficult on the African continent, and the space where history, social psychology and political economy meet.

I examine how interpretations of history shape relationships with present-day cultural norms and attitudes towards modern institutions. I look at how these norms impact on people's freedom of thought, their attitude to rules, their approach to leadership and their economic behaviour, and how these choices tilt the advantage from indigenous Africans towards immigrants or non-indigenous Africans. I start by presenting an alternative subjective reality from an Africanist point of view. The purpose of this work is to kick-start the process of socialising this interpretation of reality in the hope that one day it may merge with others like it, espoused by my fellow Pan Africanists, to form a permanent intersubjective African reality able to generate a rich base for patriotism.

I choose to write in this fashion about this topic because I have reimagined the Africa I want to live in. In this Reimagined Africa, my Africanness is fundamental to who I am. It is fundamental to the perspective I bring to any interaction with other human beings. In the Africa I want to live in, my idea of self is encoded in a belief that Africans have the oldest human culture, one deserving of its place among those of the rest of the world. This belief demands that I work towards a realisation of the dream that Africa should be for Africans, that African economies need to be stewarded by Africans, that African culture should sit at the apex of all of the African political economies, that the African child should be educated in the knowledge of their true history. An intimate understanding by Africans of this reality would enable us to feel ownership of an equal share in all the splendour that modernity has to offer.

As a collection of ideas, *Africa Reimagined* is informed by an aspiration towards a deepened consciousness that we are more than our skin tone, our nationality and our ethnicity. We are the initiators of a long continuum of human cultural, intellectual and economic progress. This continuum is informed by the understanding that Africans governed the world's first great civilisation, Ancient Egypt. The Ancient Egyptians were the first civilisation to interpret matter's interaction within the universe using mathematics, philosophy and science. Indeed, the word 'chemistry' is derived from the words 'alchemy' and 'Kemet', the ancient name for Egypt. These Egyptians excelled in medical science and applied mathematics. Egypt's achievements in engineering, astronomy and public administration serve as proof of the level of sophistication this great society reached. That we have, as Africans, successfully governed ourselves for thousands of years prior to any influence by Europeans or Asians provides a basis for believing that we can do so again.

Our long-range perspective therefore can afford to be that of a people rich in all manner of endowments, not least a complex basket of cultures whose proximity to each other is undeniable. The Nubian and the Bantu have migrated all over Africa, creating a genetic connectivity that underpins our overall cultural orientation. There is no more direct description of the most important feature of that culture than the translation of the word Bantu – simply, 'people'. We are a people-oriented culture more concerned with relative gains or losses than absolute ones. We are more concerned with social harmony than individuality. We are more concerned with the extended interpretation of family than a nucleus.

The wealth of African nations lies in our uninhibited expression of ourselves through our culture. In many African countries, migration has created a melting pot of recognisable interpretations of the same culture. We are happiest and least inhibited in each other's company, where we are free to express our cultural identity to its fullest degree. African culture is expressed in many languages, but its essence is universally African.

In this regard, our leaders have failed us. They have, in most African countries, sacrificed our cultures on the altar of economic development. The resulting cultural pacifism has been the hallmark of our engagement with people from both the East and the West. This has produced a timid representation of who we are in our interactions with people of European and Asian descent. We have built nations that are not psychologically owned by their citizens.

Many studies have shown the link between this inhibited, threatened posture and a reduced level of cognitive functionality in the workplace and at school, resulting in lowered productivity. This lowered productivity makes a large but unquantified contribution to the underperformance of many African economies.

We speak of the era of colonialism and imperialism as part of our history. The reality is that cultural imperialism is a very present reality. The promotion of cultural pacifism by our leadership is a central component of the sustainability of the modern cultural imperialist apparatus. This book seeks to promote the unlearning of what Edward Said has called the 'inherent dominative mode'.[15] Unlearning cultural pacifism demands a strengthening of our own cultural muscle memory.

Reimagining Africa requires a new philosophical underpinning of why the African cultural muscle needs to be flexed. Calling it 'muscle memory' invokes precisely the action needed to begin our journey towards becoming liberated Africans capable of being both successful and ourselves. We need to remember when we, as an African people, were strongest, and to understand how our old wisdom entrenched the values, norms and morals that were the pillars of African social construction. We need to remember the source of our cultural strength.

One of the great tools cultural imperialists use is truncating human history. They do so by choosing to start teaching history from periods (relatively short in world history) of European dominance. This anti-historical approach promotes the view that people who regard themselves as white have always been superior to darker-skinned people and, by extension, always will be. Hence, historical knowledge and current power structures drive cultural superiority in ways that deserve analysis.

Indeed, the insertion of race into historical periods during which race was either meaningless or carried the inverted racial connotations of today's pecking order has distorted our understanding of human relationships. For instance, for the first 2 000 years of the Egyptian dynasties, darker-skinned people were more revered for their closer resemblance to the dominant depiction of the gods.[16] Racist colour-coding of the human race is something Africans should fight at every turn.

Africans have historically not thought in race-based terms. Ours was always a tribal worldview underpinned by the belief that all people are the same. That belief has been used against us over time. One of our greatest historical mistakes, made early on by the chiefs, pharaohs, queens and kings who interacted with Europeans, was to elevate foreigners to a level above all other Nubians and Bantu. That blunder opened the way for economic imperialism, colonisation and, ultimately, cultural imperialism. This mistake has been duplicated by many post-colonial leaders, who have insisted on race-based categorisation as the basis for redressing the ills of the past.

For as long as white is a category next to black, indigenous African people will continue to have their muscle memory blocked by a deep-seated racial inferiority complex. Removing racial categories and the language of racism from our lexicon would facilitate important conversations, illuminating what we are beyond our skin tone. I believe this is a necessary first step to the recognition of Africanism as a common denominator. This would begin to shift the burden of recent history off those of us regarded as black, coloured or mixed race. It may even begin to place a longer-range historical burden on those who regard themselves as white to distinguish between their European and African heritages.

In advocating the reimagining of Africa I am, as the African saying goes, chasing the tails of my father's cattle. The work I am proposing Africans do is a logical extension of Black Consciousness, advocated by Stephen Biko and his comrades in the 1970s. Truly believing that all darker-skinned people are the same as, if not better than, any light- or fair-skinned people allows us the freedom to return to an African worldview. If we free ourselves from the need to wage a race-based equality battle, it will allow us to make a far greater claim: that we are part of a long lineage of cultural, intellectual and scientific benefactors dating back to Sudanese antiquity, past the last of the great Egyptian empires, to 2 January 1492, when the Moors were defeated in the Spanish city of Granada. This claim transcends blackness. It claims all of modern-day humanity and is by definition a higher-order form of consciousness.

To make this substantiated claim to all of modern humanity is the most empowering launching pad for our engagement with the rest of the world. It opens the way to a sense of wonder and possibility. It prompts us to read world history from an entirely different point of view. It fills us with both ownership and responsibility to do our part in extending this historical contribution to human intellectual progress. It allows us to engage with philosophy, both ancient and modern, with a clear mind, comforted by the knowledge that our people contributed richly to its fundamental pillars. It allows us to say the words 'our people' both inclusively and exclusively, without any fear of contradiction.

I invite all readers to come around to this way of viewing Africa and its role in the world. Using this alternative philosophy of freedom, the following pages espouse the reimagination of Africa's capability to transform itself into a continent that can take its rightful place in world affairs. I tell this story in ten chapters.

Chapter 1: Normalising abnormality

This chapter describes how Africa's conception of work and play has been reorganised by major global events. The impact of the introduction of Christianity and Islam, the invention of the alphabetic system and the invention of the modern monetary system combined to alter how productivity is judged worldwide. Great as these changes have been for improving the quality of our spiritual, financial and intellectual life, there are unquantified costs that we continue to pay. These changes have conspired to rob Africans of their original unitary and holistic worldview in which everything was connected to everything. This has resulted in Africa's losing its mentality of abundance and swapping it for the mentality of scarcity.

Chapter 2: Sources of Africa's cultural fragility

Studies around the world have explored how important culture is in facilitating society's adoption of rules and following a set of norms. It turns out that the alignment of values to indigenous culture is the single most important variable determining whether rules are adhered to or norms are followed. Because of a desire to make Western people feel at ease and in control, key elements of African culture have been discarded over time. This chapter attempts to unpack what cultural elements have been discarded and to count the costs of their loss. The chapter hints at the knock-on effects of Africa's inability to modernise.

Chapter 3: The evolution of African identity

Anglo-Saxon domination brought with it an era characterised by the quest for reason. Unfortunately for Africa, the age of reason led to an elaborate justification of the global slave trade that birthed racism. This fathered identity crises among Africans that inhibit their ability to optimise their talents. In this chapter, I explore how these inhibitions work and give them historical context. The search for reason and the logical explanation of how the world works has also brought with it a culture of individualism. This cultural shift challenges the construction of African society, which has histori-cally been communitarian. How African communities are affect-ed by a way of life framed through the prism of individualism has defined the post-colonial African experience. Understanding this allows us to design strategies to achieve a better balance between prosperous community-building and well-equipped individuals.

Chapter 4: Thinking differently about African institutions

The essential challenge presented to Africans by the Berlin Confer-ence was the illegitimacy of the borders that demarcated what are now 55 separate countries. The challenges this has posed are fundamental to understanding why Africa struggles to develop rapidly. Small economies with weak institutions and a weak sense of patriotism are the legacy of Berlin. This chapter reimagines Africa as a large economy powered by strong institutions that tap into latent social capital.

Chapter 5: African social capital's triple threats

Making Africa's political economy thrive requires strong institutions, healthy social capital and deliberate human development. To achieve this, Africa has to overcome the current triple threats of migration, unemployment and urbanisation. This chapter seeks to explore how these threats can be neutralised and turned into opportunities.

Chapter 6: Modern African state institutions

The modern African state has been conceived as a top-down locus of control. To succeed in the long term, the African state has to be reconstructed to become responsive to bottom-up pressures from the electorate. These modern states have to find a balance between African traditional political structures and modern democratic institutions. This chapter advocates that this reconstruction incorporate a strong bias towards mimicking the cultural tenets of rural African institutions. It identifies political-party centrality as the chief inhibitor of democratic progress in Africa. Alternative democratic formations are suggested that can approximate what liberation movements in Africa have fought for.

Chapter 7: Case study: how identity affirmation works against Pan Africanism

South African society is fractured by an identity crisis that makes social cohesion impossible. How our identity impacts on our economic choices is critical to understanding how we are to build societies that are supportive of human capital development. Lessons learned in this regard by Africa's most developed country would be instructive for the rest of the continent.

Chapter 8: Liberating human capital

Africa needs a cognitive revolution as the final step towards African liberation. Reconceiving freedom and liberty can help Africans redefine modernity and reorient their development model to focus on policies that are empowering to the citizens of the continent. This cognitive revolution will undoubtedly lead to a stronger sense of self-determination that opens up the individual's responsibility to be a contributing member of society.

Chapter 9: Banking social capital

This chapter advocates an inverted approach to scarcity and abundance. I argue that African economies could move themselves out of poverty by aggregating community savings and spending through large corporations that could dramatically improve cash flow and disposable income in poor communities. This would help merge the formal economy with the informal economy, unlocking hidden economic capacity and greatly increasing taxable income in the process.

Chapter 10: Ten figments of reimagination

The final chapter summarises the lessons learned in this study. It also attempts to weave these lessons together into the beginnings of a coherent philosophy. Rather than make policy suggestions, this chapter attempts to look at a freedom-maximising approach to decision-making. Its ultimate objective is to stimulate a conversation about Africa and its future, rooted in a fundamentally different interpretation of both its history and its strategic assets.

1

Normalising abnormality

EVERY ONCE IN A WHILE, a parent sets up what they think is a teaching moment, only to get a rude awakening themselves, resulting in their learning more than they are teaching. In 2018 I took my son to watch the film *Black Panther*, thinking that I would be exposing him to something that would make him more (as the kids say these days) 'woke'. But I was the one whose eyes were opened. Growing up in townships in South Africa like Lenyenye, Langa and Gugulethu, I did not have occasion to read Marvel comics. Apart from knowing that *Black Panther* was one of the few superhero movies with an African superhero, I went in blind.

I was stunned by the film and what it stood for. Director Ryan Coogler created a new subjective reality in which the most technologically advanced nation in the world is a secretive African one named Wakanda. This nation has managed to harvest the extraordinary powers derived from a mineral resource named vibranium to build a capital city that showcases technology the rest of the world hasn't even heard of yet. Against the backdrop of majestic skyscrapers, vibranium-powered hovering cars fly alongside a magnetic-levitation train zipping along an elevated track.

Once we adjust to the glitz and the glamour that surrounds this mystical world, we notice some interesting details that complete the mind-bending assault on our traditional view of normal. African beads, clothing patterns and traditional weapons sit side by side with space-age artillery and cloth made using nanotechnology. African music plays in the background of a command centre that would make NASA jealous. The generals in the army are dominated by women, whose outfits combine Masai warrior clothing with *Star Trek*-type gear.

This serves to instantaneously challenge the viewer's previously held assumptions about standards and norms. In a 'normal' super-hero movie, the superhero (whether they come from space or if their mutation happened here on earth) is from some small town in the United States of America, has an American accent and is 'white'. We don't think twice about these details. We simply accept, and are indeed primed by society to accept, them as normal. Yet this social priming is hardly benign. The signals we pick up indicate import-ant details about how the world works and what the ethnic pecking order is. From these signals, and from the stylised intersubjective view of white superiority reinforced by popular culture, we start to form hardened views of socially acceptable hierarchies and the limitations they imply for our expectations of certain ethnic groups.

Most of us are constantly alert to the signals that indicate whether what we are doing is socially acceptable or not. This instinct has allowed humans to organise themselves around generally accepted ways of acting, from which come morals, ethics, values and laws. As humans have developed, we have come to use the terms 'normal' and 'abnormal' as shorthand to describe these ways of acting, or behaviour.

We deem something to be normal if it conforms to a standard. Accordingly, whoever creates the standard gets to determine the social acceptability of behaviour. When studying and writing about different social impulses, social scientists often speak of norms and values. We don't always ask who sets the original standard against which such norms are judged. It is only in very rare cases that norms or values are more than loosely defined descriptions that attempt to explain what are often fairly recent practices. More worryingly, our inability to rigorously test norms against the backdrop of historical changes in social structure and the nature of cultural influences on social action leads us to make conclusions about behaviour that are often faulty.

We would do well to remember Emile Durkheim's thoughtful reflection: 'All empirical instances of social action can be said to be shaped and channelled, on the one hand, by social structure, culture and (on the other hand by) collective emotions.'[1] In today's winner-takes-all approach to history, just one side of Durkheim's social equation is satisfied, namely, that norms are what the dominant social power structures say they are. Not enough room is left to consider the enormous role played by collective emotions in legitimising rules and norms.

Africans, who over the last thousand years have not often been the victors in conflicts with people of other continents and religions, have lost their voice in history. Over the last 2 500 years, in particular, Africans have seen their norms and values recede into the social background. This has been exaggerated by the way in which African history has been written. Our history has hidden from us the crucial role that culture and collective emotions play in the long-term sustainability of what elites have pronounced to be modern norms. To put this another way, there have been long periods of history during which the Pharaonic Dynasties of Egypt (3100 BCE to 332 BCE), the Kingdom of Mapungubwe (900–1300), the Kingdom of Mali (1230–1670), the Kingdom of Axum/Abyssinia, both in modern-day Ethiopia (1270–1636), the Kingdom of Kongo (1390–1888) and the Kingdom of Ghana (700–1240) had legitimate claim to being among the wealthiest and most advanced societies in the world. These periods are completely ignored, or presented in a bastardised fashion, by popular African history.

I begin this book with an appeal for the appreciation of cultural identity, because such an appreciation is a prerequisite for our ability to reimagine Africa. The foundation for reimagining Africa has been laid perhaps most substantially by scholars such as Cheikh Anta Diop, Dr Yosef Ben-Jochannan, John Henrik Clarke, Chancellor Williams, Dr Ivan van Sertima and Professor George GM James, who are regarded by many Pan Africanists as the pre-eminent historians of ancient African civilisation. For Cheikh Anta Diop, an approach to the study of norms and values has to be mindful of the following factors: 'For every individual his or her own cultural identity is a function of that of his or her people. Consequently, one must define the cultural identity of a people. This means to a great extent one must analyse the components of the collective personality. We know that three factors contribute to its formation: 1) a historical factor; 2) a linguistic factor; 3) a psychological factor.'[2] Understanding a people requires a keen knowledge of their history, their languages and how they construct reality.

The political struggle of African nations for liberation from colonialism and/or imperialism has been misjudged as a struggle purely for the attainment of liberal democracy. This has led to a severe misreading of the influence of both collective emotions and cultural sentiment on desired popular norms.[3] An alternative way to look at the struggle for liberation in Africa could be as a struggle for self-determination. Looking at the liberation struggle in this way requires faith in the ability of the African masses to self-determine. Self-determination implies the attainment of both political and economic freedom. Defining the objective in this way would also require an admission that post-colonial African societies have failed to carry out the self-determination required by the people, thus the struggle very much continues.

Had the struggle for self-determination been won, the historical, linguistic and psychological factors identified by Diop would have been embedded in African societies in a way that would lead to radically different political economies, dominated by the desires of the majority of African people. In the absence of a concerted attempt to let the people shape post-colonial society, elites have allowed an Anglo-Saxon form of capitalism to become the drumbeat to which Africans march. This march has radically distorted the individual African's ability to enforce the natural balance between work and leisure. The result has been the compromising of the social fabric of modern African families in the process of so-called development.

Since antiquity, societies the world over have structured themselves so as to most effectively coordinate the lives of the individuals who make up the collective with maximum benefit to succeed in the key priorities of a given historical period. Since time immemorial, those priorities have included mating, safely raising offspring, worshipping one's chosen god(s) and efficiently feeding the collective unit (whether a nuclear or a broader conception of kinfolk).

Later, the priorities of societies necessarily shifted as populations grew and the complexity of social coordination intensified. These changes included the development of animal and plant husbandry, collective rituals/ceremonies, environmental challenges such as rising or sinking river levels, and warfare. With each increasing degree of complexity, the individual's welfare became increasingly diametrically opposed to that of the collective. Each stage of development has come with an encroachment on individual leisure time. Africa has moved from the colonial to post-colonial stage without stopping to ask people whether this is the best way to organise their time.

European societies have had the luxury of a much more gradual restructuring. They have migrated from the more easy-going, leisure-oriented lifestyles of Ancient Greek society to the hard-charging work-centric outlook of modern European society. Ancient Greek society, being greatly influenced by the universal outlook of the Egyptians, had a more balanced view of labour and leisure than does modern-day European society. Aristotle puts this distinction into sharp relief: 'The end of labour is to gain leisure.'[4] In fact, Greek philosophers believed very strongly in the unity of mind and body and in the relationship between all forms of human skills and qualities.

This Ancient Greek view of life is most influential in the way human society has woven together education, sports and leisure within our school systems. The towns built by the Romans, themselves greatly influenced by the Egyptians and the Greeks, included amphitheatres, public baths and gymnasiums, all indicating the importance of leisure in their lives. But underlying Aristotle's comment is the resignation to a particular sequence of life: work first, play later. Leisure was seen, even in Ancient Greek society, as a reward for work.

Plato, in *The Republic*, affirms Aristotle's view about what today we call 'work-life balance': 'First duty, then happiness, is the natural order of our moral ideas.'[5] It is interesting that, even as Plato hints at the immorality of the pursuit of happiness, his own reflections on the topic were the result of unrestricted leisure time spent thinking, reading and writing. This is the sleight of hand that elites have used to cement class differences the world over. Upper-class members of society have leisure time that allows them time for reflection, reading and self-improvement. Members of the lower classes, on the other hand, have to work mindlessly for most of their waking hours.

Daniel McLean and Amy Hurd, authors of a standard textbook on leisure studies, suggest that, over time, technological development has tipped the work-life balance in favour of work. However, 'tribal societies do not make the same sharp distinction between leisure and work that more technologically advanced societies do. Whereas the latter set aside different periods of time for work and relaxation, a tribal pre-technological society had no such precise separations. In tribal societies work tends to be varied and creative rather than being a narrow, specialised task demanding a specialised skill as in modern industry.'[6] I agree that economic development, and the increasing specialisation of labour that comes with it, has made the distinction between work and leisure more rigid. I would argue, however, that the technological sophistication of a society is not the leading indicator of the role that leisure plays within it. Ancient Egypt was an advanced society. As a consequence, it was highly socially stratified and had well-defined divisions of labour, together with the first known use of a calendar, astronomy and many other technological innovations. Yet the Egyptians managed to preserve a healthy role for leisure as a core element of life.

The Moors colonised the Iberian Peninsula from 711 to 1492. During that time they transformed this region by introducing advanced drainage systems and irrigation techniques. They built 16 universities and introduced geometry and a modern form of counting.[7] Despite this modernity, the Africans must have influenced modern Iberian attitudes to work and leisure. Consider the way modern Europeans in Spain and Portugal, but also in Greece and Italy (both having been heavily influenced by Egyptian ways of life), arrange their day to best suit their preferred eating, socialising and sleeping times. They distinguish themselves from northern Europeans by choosing to start work a little later, taking a siesta after lunch and working till later in the evening. This is a reflection of their capability for self-determination and how this expresses itself in their prioritisation of a high quality of life.

In fact, a bigger determinant of work-life balance is the attitude to work itself. Modern life has seen a successful encroachment of work on leisure time, leading to a situation in which many people are at work five or six days a week, often for over 12 hours, and have one or two days of leisure per week, if they are lucky. The poorer the labourer, the less leisure time, a position compounded by long average times spent commuting to work during the week, and by the likely high demands of household-related work during weekends.

This encroachment on individual leisure time is driven by broader societal attitudes to work and class, which have necessitated a socially acceptable narrative that serves as a rallying cry in times of war, a lullaby when recuperating from strenuous activity or a soothing hymn when facing imagined or real adversity. These narratives weave together individual beliefs, which are held at first by just a few individuals, but which later, after becoming widely accepted, become norms. These are sometimes enshrined as a society's core beliefs or values. This is what is meant by intersubjective reality.[8]

Max Weber, the founder of sociology, believed that there was a time in human history when the acquisition of material things subordinated the individual to what was deemed to be the main purpose of life – the making of money: 'Man is dominated by the making of money, by acquisition as the ultimate purpose of his life. Economic acquisition is no longer subordinated to man as the means for the satisfaction of his material needs. This reversal of what we should call the natural relationship, so irrational from a naive point of view, is evidently as definitely a leading principle of capitalism as it is foreign to all peoples not under capitalistic influence.'[9] This astonishing perspective, from *The Protestant Ethic and the Spirit of Capitalism*, lays out Weber's case that Anglo-Saxon Protestants have an inherent bias towards ordering their lives around the concept of work. He generalises that they are inclined to think of their work as a manifestation of who they are, and thus to see the completion of tasks as part of their reason for being. The term 'goal orientation' describes this state of mind. Weber postulates that this drive to work is underpinned by a calling, which Protestants believe to come directly from God.

The by-product of the Protestant work ethic is a surplus of capital. Sociologist Anthony Giddens, in the introduction to *The Protestant Ethic and the Spirit of Capitalism*, summarises Weber's view: 'The regular reproduction of capital, involving its continual reinvestment for the end of economic efficiency, is foreign to traditional types of enterprise. It is associated with an outlook of a very specific kind: the continual accumulation of wealth for its own sake, rather than for the material rewards that it can bring.'[10] This 'outlook of a specific kind' is powered by deeply individualistic values and norms that have been cultivated for millennia by Europeans and their fellow Anglo-Saxons residing elsewhere in the world.

The idea of work as an absolute reason for being does not have the same historical basis in African culture. As a consequence, it has largely failed to take root on the African continent. By the time the concept of consumerism was introduced to Africans, it met with a people-centric, community-oriented culture developed over thousands of years that had at its centre the pursuit of leisure. The Dogon tribes residing in Mali have perhaps the longest unbroken record of self-determination anywhere in Africa. They work just as hard as, if not harder than, the average European, but they do so as part of a holistic set of beliefs that break the monotony of the workday into spiritual, community, environmental and family-oriented chores that round their lifestyle out in a manner that is consistent with how their ancestors lived thousands of years ago. According to the classic account of anthropologists Marcel Griaule and Germaine Dieterlen, 'The principles at the base of Dogon social organisation are especially expressed in the classifications, which include all natural manifestations as well as those of their own invention. These classifications constitute a system in which, for example, plants, insects, fabrics, games and rituals are divided into decomposable categories numerically expressed and related to each other. In addition, the religious and political authority of chiefs and also the family and juridical structures (particularly systems of kinship and marriage) are established upon the same principles; all activity of daily life of the individuals depend on these.'[11]

Consumer-oriented societies have a moral compass that is different from what the Ancient Egyptians called Maat, which essentially is a focus on living a life that is morally pleasing to one's ancestors while being cognisant of the karmic consequences of one's actions. Consumerism and individualism were not planted in the fertile soil of organised Western religion in Africa. It took time and considerable coercion for Christianity, and later Islam, to take root. When these religions did take root, they had to exist side by side with (and adjust themselves to) strong communitarian values and norms.

The organic belief system of Africans is anchored on a continuum along which people are who they are because of other people, and they live to please both their elders and those who have lived before them. Within these broad parameters, Africans believe that life is there to be enjoyed, and that leisure is in fact sacrosanct. In contrast, Weber's analysis of the Anglo-Saxon individualistic conception of the purpose of life necessitates that there should be a trade-off between work and leisure.

If African societies were not held together by an overwhelming dedication to work, what held societies such as Kush (modern Ethiopia), Nubia (modern Sudan) and Kemerovo (modern Egypt) together for over 3 000 years? The answer is somewhat uncomfortable for modern liberal society to accept. The common denominator of the most peaceful, organised and prosperous societies to have existed on the African continent seems to have been structured social stratification by way of a caste system. Under this system, you were apprenticed to a role in society based on your parents' profession; unless you showed a special talent for something else, you would follow in their footsteps. This was kept in place by leaders who operated according to African dynastic rules, legitimised by a divine mandate. Further legitimacy was gained by the presence of an intricate social security mechanism.[12]

Europeans studying African history from the perspective of modern values are quick to criticise tribalism and the functionality of the African clan system. These critiques miss the fact that the concept of the individual as a separate entity from the clan or the community did not exist in African society. It is still difficult for modern Africans to separate themselves from their fellow clan members, making the fluid adoption of capitalism in its Western form almost impossible. Given the lack of social materialistic pressure in ancient African society, the social security provided by the clan structure facilitated the preservation of leisure time as a central element of life. Any threat to this delicate balance was met with pushback and/or social instability.

Like their Western counterparts, Africans viewed their vocation as a calling, but a collective calling organised along clan lines and blessed by ancestral mysticism.[13] In the attention paid to preventing unwanted competition over professional roles, one can clearly see that the central emphasis was on social harmony and not individual prosperity. Reducing competition allowed the steady, deliberate approach to one's profession that gave room for the pursuit of leisure. The net effect of this harmony was to achieve balanced lifestyles that left significant opportunities for self-expression through hobbies that were part of leisure time. In the absence of self-determination, Africans have to live according to a double standard. Their employers value leisure but not enough to allow them the time to enjoy it; similarly, their employers value self-improvement but not enough to pay for it. Work equals survival and survival requires total self-sacrifice.

My advocacy for more balanced lifestyles of all African citizens is related to my understanding that without stable institutions like the family unit, this continent will not have its African century. As employers continue to value labour more than leisure in the lives of their employees, so the neglect of the African family unit continues to the detriment of society.

It is important to differentiate between leisure and sloth. Many forms of leisure are extremely strenuous. Sport has been a part of the African lifestyle since humans first walked the earth. Some tasks that might have been considered work, such as hunting and construction, were part of a continuum of work and pleasure that knew no beginning or end. Even the concept of cooking meat over a fire is a ritualised form of both work and pleasure. Time for thinking, reflection and teaching young members of the community were all part of the African conception of leisure. Judged against the backdrop of self-determination, it seems clear that autonomy is one of the leading differentiators between work and pleasure. Hence I define leisure as the permitted exercise of the individual's right to self-amusement. The unbalanced lifestyles of those members of society lower in the social structure represents a long-term threat to the collective cooperation of society as a whole.

According to historian Yuval Harari, we humans wouldn't be able to function successfully in groups larger than 150 people without the use of religion, tribal or customary law and some form of social stratification.[14] If this is true, then we can correctly catalogue religion, law, capitalism, communism, companies, cooperatives, schools and political parties as institutions that are put in place to foster particular belief systems modelled on social narratives designed to manage conflict within the collective. Once this narrative becomes widely accepted, it is adopted as a new shared reality. In *The Social Construction of Reality*, sociologists Peter Berger and Thomas Luckmann describe how this process works as a sort of social sedimentation. In this way, newly introduced ideas take time to brew.[15] Humans experience reality, and later make up stories to make sense of what they have experienced. It is this storytelling part of the mind that accepts and promotes new intersubjective realities. The process described by Berger and Luckmann assumes an organic popularisation of ideas.

In Africa, perhaps much more than elsewhere, society is shaped almost completely by the elite's experience of reality. Ordinary people have a much smaller say in social trends than in most places in the world. The sense of injustice felt by those at the bottom of the African economic pyramid is chiefly responsible for the inability of capitalism to take root. The narrative of what capitalism should be in society as told by those in the upper echelons of society, versus the majority's experience of the harsh reality of both inequality and inequity, accounts for the failure of capitalism to be accepted as part of the common African's intersubjective reality.

The popularity of money is a good example of how this process of social sedimentation plays itself out. In a normal society, as the shared reality of money's place in society increases, the network effect of money reinforces its utility. Norms form over time that allow dominant political actors to respond to the demand for an innovation or to introduce one that gets enacted into law, becomes moralised by the church and later justified in the education system. These processes often take place over several centuries. This slow social sedimentation gives them legitimacy. Once the dominant social actors enact laws, normalise behaviour through the early adaptation of key institutions in society (like the church, for example) and introduce this into educational syllabi, adaptation becomes a necessity for survival. In this way in many developed societies money slowly became the most popular of all collective cooperation mechanisms.[16] The majority of Africans were forced by structural changes (urbanisation, hut taxes, induced labour and slavery) to their economies to accept the dominant preference for this form of currency as legal tender. The slow-brewed social sedimentation was a luxury not afforded to Africans. As a result this 'norm' was forced on society. Today, the rapid adoption of cellphone banking, electronic payments and internet banking is an example of how necessity has further induced social change on many developing countries, including those on the African continent.

What is difficult to discern are the long-term consequences of these structural changes to people's long-term attitudes to capital. Will work be seen as more than the task at hand in Africa as it is in Europe? What will be the consequence of this change or failure to change? Will modern work be seen from the perspective of a communal calling, as it was in the days when social stratification was prevalent? These questions are hard to answer. What we do know is that in almost all Western economies, money and labour create a materialisation of the modern shared reality of work. If one inverts this logic, material goods are how employees in these societies convince themselves that the twin superstition of money and corporate labour are real. In other words, they collectively justify the illegitimacy of leisure. Even those driven by money, in an Aristotelian way, to acquire leisure often find themselves unable to shake the superstition underlying the drive to work.

The Dalai Lama has reflected on what surprises him most about humanity: 'Man. Because he sacrifices his health in order to make money. Then sacrifices money to recuperate his health. And then he is so anxious about the future that he does not enjoy the present; the result being that he does not live in the present or the future; he lives as if he is never going to die, and then dies having never really lived.'[17] Most Africans don't have the time to stop and ask the essential question at the heart of the Dalai Lama's reflection. Their societies have conspired to force them to worry only about money while sacrificing health, spiritual well-being and ultimately their beloved community ties in order to survive.

In a very real sense, materialism is itself a superstition of the privileged minority and a form of psychological torture of the majority. It requires the artificial stimulation of demand for products and services that human beings previously had no use for nor any conception of their existence. Materialism is immaterial without the inception of demand for something. Once that desire for a good or service has been put in place, we all become slaves to the demand to fulfil its resultant wants and needs.

Materialism in the modern world has been turbocharged by the twin engines of planned obsolescence and acute loneliness caused by increasing individualism. The objects we buy are quickly redundant and we are forced by an impulse to keep up with our peers to replace them with the latest versions. What facilitates this process is our attitude to work. The more we believe in the sacrosanct nature of work, the more hours we spend away from friends and family, and the more we purchase material goods and services as emotional consolation for our loneliness. Anglo-Saxons have developed coping mechanisms to dull the impact of rampant materialism. Their approach to charitable giving and their ability to divorce themselves from their capital through trust funds and other investment instruments are learned coping mechanisms developed over hundreds of years. Most importantly, money, materialism and the social pressures they bring were built on the foundation of individualism. This is a social foundation many Westerners take for granted.

The social foundation of African society is communitarian. The dominance of money, materialism and individualism clash head-on with African cultural norms. Africans have not been allowed to choose their own value system to enter the 21st century. If the love of money is the root of all evil, then the induction of labour in Africa has proven to be the square root of all evil. Colonialists and imperialists from all over the world wielded their powers in their new territories with the express purpose of inducing labour to extract raw materials or purify material goods whose demand in their home countries was a direct result of marketing.

In the modern era, marketing can be defined as a coercive force that is utilised by those in control of the means of myth production. In a largely post-slave-labour world, it is the myth of demand that catalyses the coercion of labour, and it is the coercion of labour that facilitates the stimulation of demand for material things. It is these material things that give money its meaning to human beings. This chain of cause and effect continues to give the West power in Africa long after the end of colonialism. The choice for Africans, as they reimagine their societies, is whether to continue to give in to the West's use of marketing to coerce demand for their products or to try and bend its force around the natural contours of African culture. Can you resist the allure of Western culture if you do not know your own?

Is it possible for Africans to consider turning away from materialistic individualism towards leisure-oriented collectivism? To help us towards better answers to this question, we should ask ourselves some deeper questions about the philosophical underpinnings that give birth to an African worldview. Africans have had to grapple with these issues since the beginning of time. African philosophy predates Greek philosophy by 2 000 years. Thanks to the meticulous work of modern scholars, we can now gain some insight into the fundamental thought structures governing the African way of life prior to its interaction with civilisations from elsewhere.

Molefi Asante, Professor of African American Studies at Temple University, offers the following insight: 'To understand African ways of thinking it is necessary to suspend for a while linearity and to consider the entire world, universe or universes, as one large system where everything is connected and interconnected. This is the principal African view of reality … [Whereas] it is the giving up of the ego that is at the core of Asian cultures; in African cultures the ego is real and materiality is concrete but manageable under the influence of custom and tradition based upon human mutuality.'[18] This belief in the interconnectedness of things, that everything is everything, brings with it an abundant view of material wealth. Africans have for thousands of years operated with a mentality of abundance.

The need to save, to plan for the distant future and to forego today's leisure in exchange for tomorrow's rewards is in conflict with the fundamental African belief that, as long as I honour my customs, the world has more to offer me than I need. In contrast, the Anglo-Saxon worldview is shaped by a mentality of scarcity. After thousands of years of living with shortages of space, mineral wealth, sunlight and food, the Anglo-Saxon worldview is primed for hard times. Such priming necessitates planning, sacrifice and an individualistic survival instinct that is fundamentally at odds with the African belief system. Inasmuch as both worldviews can benefit from one another, the point of departure needs to be that there is merit in retaining one's own old wisdom.

A practical way to illustrate how the ancient African belief system worked is to explore how it was taught at the time. An Egyptian manuscript, often called 'The Eloquent Peasant', written between 2040 BCE and 1650 BCE, summarises that society's philosophy around ten core virtues to be taught and followed:

- **Criticality** – the ability to distinguish good from evil and right from wrong.
- **Devotion** – displaying loyalty to others and one's God.
- **Self-control** – human beings are born into order but remain oblivious to this order as chaos seems to penetrate our lives.
- **Discipline** – training that develops self-control and orderly behaviour.
- **Tolerance** – allowing and permitting others to express their views.
- **Forbearance** – possessing freedom from resentment.
- **Steadfastness** – holding firm to one's beliefs and ideas.
- **Faith** – an expression of optimism.
- **Spiritual desire** – showing the will to achieve victory over present circumstances.
- **Initiation** – achieving mastery over self.[19]

These ten virtues are core to the system of values called Maat. Maat is informed by the belief that humans have the ability to attain godliness in their lifetime if they aspire to and live up to higher ideals. Reflected in these ideals is the belief in the abundance of time. Time that allows you to seek and gain redemption. Time that allows you to seek and gain mastery of self. Time for you to be taught discipline, tolerance and a deference towards those older than you. This mentality, underpinned by an abundance of time, is chiefly responsible for a sense of faith-based optimism about the future.

This attitude to the past, present and future, based on the abundance of time, is perhaps *the* core African value. From it flow many norms. The norm of patience with mistakes made by others, based on a belief that time will educate these people to be better. The norm of yielding to the needs of other members of the community, based on the belief that over the long course of time even the wealthiest may one day become needy. The norm of yielding to your elders, out of deference that time has taught them better than you and that one day you will also be an elder.

My belief is that spiritual and material poverty stems from the undermining of this core African value. Embracing Western values has brought an artificial scarcity of time. Losing control over the management of our time has broken our social structure. To reverse this condition, Africans have to look to the past to challenge the standards that underpin today's norms. This is by no means to say that modernity cannot be embraced. On the contrary, the fundamental takeaway here should be that being connected with one's historical culture allows a more sure-footed launching pad into the modern world.

Historians now accept that it was the movement of East Africans, from as far south as modern-day Uganda (then called the Mountains of the Moon) and Central and West Africans from as far west as Nigeria, who came together to settle on the banks of the Nile, that created the great Egyptian civilisation.[20] The norms and values that grew out of that civilisation were formed from a melting pot of micro cultures that fused over time into one. During that time, the popularity of 'The Eloquent Peasant' represented insights into what drove the region's belief system.

The ideas entrenched in the ten virtues are reflected in the common norms that bind African cultures even in the modern era. These norms and values were to serve as part of a preparation for the African child to enter society as a positive contributor to a co-operative machine designed to minimise conflict. The norms reduced distinctions between people through the emphasis on self-control, discipline and forbearance. These norms were designed to maximise teamwork through a focus on relative gains.

The function of the hereditary caste system was to remove intra-caste perceptions of inequity. It was designed to create grit through the emphasis on joint suffering through the amplified value of empathy. The proof that this system worked was in the 3 000 years of relative (to modern history) harmony and prosperity enjoyed by Ancient Egypt. Societies in Mali, Ethiopia, Kongo and Ghana would later use the same value system to govern themselves in relative peace for hundreds of years.

Leisure-oriented collectivism based around hereditary clan-based social stratification was Africa's answer to the challenge of collective coordination faced by every society. As a system, it yielded huge returns, facilitating a balance between individual desires and collective prosperity. It downplayed material possessions and trumpeted the value of harmony. However, as history has shown, such a welcoming, transparent and unsuspecting culture is inherently vulnerable to attack by outsiders. The source of vulnerability may stem from the belief in the interconnectedness of all humanity. The desire to look for commonalities rather than differences also contributed to the vulnerability of this system. In many instances, kingdoms defended by tens of thousands of soldiers were conquered with hardly a shot being fired. The naive deference to the achievements of others, while restraining the desire to brag about one's own achievements, undermined Africa's defences against foreign intrusion. These are all factors hard-coded in African norms and values that, in retrospect, made us sitting ducks for those who knew how to wield global soft power using the prolific global myth-making machines of the media, the law and the church.

Having explored and contrasted African norms and values with those of the Anglo-Saxon world, it is worth noting the irony that what is regarded as the modern norm seems so out of place with how rational humans would organise their day. Working so that you can some day enjoy leisure. Toiling for your individual interests so that you can one day take care of your kinfolk. Erecting myths in abstract concepts (contractual law) and objects (money) so as to cooperate with your neighbours. These are actually manic abnormalities. Civilisation was more balanced, stable and definitely more leisurely before manufactured materialism became the norm. Ancient African wisdom knew well enough to guard against what we have wholeheartedly embraced in the form of money-oriented materialism. Old wisdom tells us that the African system of values constitutes a cultural outlook best suited for a leisure-oriented collectivism. What stops Africans from living these values in modern society is an interesting question that deserves its own chapter.

2

Sources of Africa's cultural fragility

ANYONE WHO HAS HAD A GUEST stay in their house for an extended period of time knows how easy it is for the visitor to disrupt certain long-held cultural traditions through sheer ignorance. Living in the US for more than three years afforded me many an opportunity to be such a guest and to observe first-hand the fragility of cultural balance. I lived in a shared house in Washington, DC, with two Kenyans, one Argentinian/Israeli and three Americans. Suffice to say, we all had a chaotic influence on each other. The Africans couldn't understand the need to label sugar, milk, bread and butter with individual name tags. The idea that our non-African flatmates had four of everything separately compartmentalised boggled our minds. They would each rather have their milk turn sour than have to share it. Ants would routinely get into long-opened sugar containers, bread turned mouldy, leftover pizza became inedible, and so on. All this was done to avoid any instance in which someone would want to use something that had been consumed by a flatmate.

The Africans in the house had a completely contrasting cultural philosophy. We shared absolutely everything. Soap, sugar, milk, toilet paper was for all to use. There was an intuitive sense of who had used the most or the last supply of which product, so that they would feel a responsibility to top it up. Our 'system' was far from perfect. We very often ran out of things at precisely the wrong time. For things like milk and sugar, on the one hand, it is possible to make do when faced with sudden shortages; toilet paper, on the other hand, not so much! The point is that the three of us had an intuitive cultural approach to sharing that worked for us; the other four had a different approach. Neither approach was good or bad; it just was.

All hell would break loose when we had parties. Our African parties were always packed to the rafters with eclectic students from all over Washington, had fantastic music and were generally short on beer and food. We always clubbed together to put in more funds in order to keep the party going, but that didn't stop our guests from helping themselves to our flatmates' carefully labelled beer, milk, chips and other refreshments. This would lead to an 'all hands on deck' house meeting in which we would be berated for the behaviour of our guests. We would apologise profusely and explain that our guests acted independently of us. After about the fifth time, despite warnings not to disturb their supplies, things started to change.

Our flatmates adopted a strategy of 'if you can't beat them, join them'. Their whole system broke down and they began to live like us. No one had a meeting about it; our culture just sort of won the day. By the time we all left the house permanently, we were wearing each other's clothes and sharing beer, water and anything that was there. Who would have known that these four gentlemen's well-honed culture would be so fragile when faced with a completely different way of doing things? This is not to say we did everything the same. The Argentinian could still be found, tears flowing, wearing nothing but his underpants, re-watching the same Diego Maradona video every time he got drunk. The Kenyans insisted on listening to ndombolo music at full blast in the shower every morning. Our American friends never met a beer keg they didn't want to chug down.

The point is that as human beings we are highly susceptible to cultural influences. Small changes in one's life can lead to permanently altered ways of living. I understand culture to be the ways of thinking, ways of acting and material objects that together shape a people's way of life.[1] Culture consists of, among other things, symbols, beliefs, values, languages, norms, artefacts and social institutions. Culture manifests itself in material culture (symbols, artefacts and clothing) or non-material culture (beliefs, norms and social institutions). Both aspects are important and serve to reinforce one another. Tampering with any of these individual aspects can have a major impact on the growth and sustainability of a particular culture. In this sense, all cultures have a great deal of fragility.

The sources of Africa's cultural fragility can be uncovered by removing the dust that has settled, over time, on the effects of three worldwide social revolutions. These have combined to permanently change human social patterns, but have had perhaps their most profound effects on the way Africans conceive of themselves relative to the rest of the world. The effect has been the forced sacrifice of the ancient African mentality of abundance and its replacement by the modern capitalist mentality of scarcity. Understanding the breathtaking effect these social impulses have had on African culture is illuminating. It will allow us to understand why protecting one's culture while embracing modernity is so important. As always, the long lens of history has to be used appropriately to observe the contours of the change.

I showed in Chapter 1 that leisure time, defined as the permitted exercise of the individual's right to self-amusement, has been usurped by modern conceptions of work. I also posited that this threat was facilitated through the use of soft power, through the myth-creating machines of religion, law and media propaganda wielded by foreign imperialists. What I will describe more clearly in this chapter are the mechanisms used by Anglo-Saxon societies in possession of soft power to successfully usurp the African continent's shared reality of abundance and swap it for a mentality of scarcity. The adopted mentality of scarcity has manifested itself in a passive consumerism that continues to impoverish Africa to this day.

Three large social impulses have facilitated this shift in mindset:

1) the introduction of the alphabetic language structure, 2) the introduction of formal religion and 3) the creation of money. Although these impulses have produced many positive achievements worldwide, Africans at the cultural receiving end have suffered severe cultural disorientation. Without these social impulses, and the ensuing loss of the mentality of abundance, African history would probably have developed in a significantly different direction. These three impulses are intertwined and mutually reinforcing.

The adoption of alphabetic language

Consensus has formed regarding the location of where writing began. Archaeologists have unearthed remnants of hieroglyphics from the central Nile region in Egypt. These fragments have been carbon dated to between 3300 BCE and 3200 BCE. Tablets from Syria written in Sumerian script, also known as cuneiform or pictographic proto-script, have been carbon dated to roughly the same time. Western historians acknowledge how much Sumerian civilisation owes to Africa. Ancient Sumerians called themselves the 'black-headed' people.[2] This is not surprising given that Kushite Ethiopians (the term was used at the time to describe North East Africans in general) made up the governing class of Sumerian society. According to historian George Cox, Kush (modern-day Northern Sudan) colonised Mesopotamia around 2800 BCE.[3]

The next major development in writing came around 2000 BCE in a move by the Phoenicians and Canaanites (modern-day Palestinians) away from pictographic or syllabic forms to a phonetic form that represented the recording of spoken word.[4] The Phoenicians were a Mediterranean people, with a strong connection to East Africa and Tunisia, owing to their own African heritage (confirmed by both Herodotus and Cheikh Anta Diop). Their maritime society was based on a trading and merchant culture that demanded the use of highly detailed record-keeping. In the eighth century BCE the Greeks,[5] having colonised Egypt for over 300 years, modified this system, adding vowels and letters to create an alphabet.[6] The Romans further developed this new system to create letters that facilitated the writing of their language, Latin.[7] Rome's dominance in the Mediterranean world ensured that this alphabetic form of language spread far and wide.

The introduction of alphabetic language was a fundamental and, given its effect on our lives today, relatively unheralded transformation in the capacity of human beings to organise societies. It began a global trend that saw children being taught in a linear, sequential way that was bounded by both time and space. Gone was the oral tradition that required hours of storytelling time around the fire. Gone was the painstaking time spent drawing images that reflected day-to-day reality. In came the impetus for rationality, brevity and linear depictions of logic. Alphabetic language brought with it a more private, one-to-one, or one-to-many, form of communicating that could serve to advance the agenda of an individual who was fluent in the use of this new craft.

These changes started a journey that would last many centuries, leading to the promotion of left-brain-oriented work, that is, associated with logical, analytical reasoning, becoming the most rewarded in those societies that had an alphabetic language structure and associated culture. The creation of alphabetic languages changed how stories were told, how information was passed on and, more importantly, how young brains were trained to think. The design of stories and images around facts was now deemed to make information compelling.

The linear form of language presentation, and the construction of reasoning from the left side of the page to the right, had profound consequences for how the human brain processed and organised information. Though the brain works through information in unison, the left brain grasps details, logic, sequence and analysis while the right brain brings to life the big picture, emotional expression and context, and performs synthesis. Written versus pictorial depiction of knowledge forces the use of different parts of the brain. The development of the printing press in China dates back to the Tang dynasty, while metal movable type was first developed in Korea in the 13th century. It was only in the 14th century that Europe mastered a method of printing, pioneered by Johannes Gutenberg, who cast movable block letters and symbols out of various metals. He simultaneously developed his own type of ink, and found a way to mechanically transfer ink onto paper. These innovations improved upon early Chinese and Arab techniques by dramatically reducing the cost of printing. Using Gutenberg's precise moulds and oil-based-ink, producing 3 500 pages per day, mass printing of major manuscripts, including the Bible, became possible.[8] The use of the written word popularised both reading and writing and created a basis for many more people to join the literary revolution, finally breaking the stranglehold of the aristocracy on access to knowledge.

For many African societies, the wholesale adoption of alphabetic language was facilitated by changing belief systems. Many dropped their traditional belief structure in favour of formalised religions such as Christianity or Islam, both of whose teachings were encoded in alphabetic language (the Bible and the Qur'an). From Ethiopia to Sudan, northern African societies were infiltrated by foreign missionaries who worked with the local nobility to redefine how people worshipped, and how they documented information. Consequently, the way people thought about the world was forever transformed. These cultures now had to play catch-up to the Europeans in learning how to reason, write and articulate themselves in a linear fashion. The new constructs of heaven and hell separated, for the first time, the present and the future. Creating an intermediary between Africans and God severed a vital artery that had sustained a personal relationship to God. Disconnecting Africans from their ancestors changed their views of their purpose here on earth. Disconnecting the individual from the community required a new, individualistic set of survival skills.

These individualistic skills, requiring all Africans to read individually and write directly to each other, were in most cases underdeveloped. One can only imagine that this led to the development of anxieties about how people would fit into this new requirement by society. Social contingencies, which overcompensated for the lack of fluidity with the newly desired form of thinking, began to develop. (We will explore these contingencies in more detail in Chapter 7.) Suffice it to say at this point that the new construct changed the way Africans who adopted the alphabetic language judged intelligence. It changed their view of hierarchy in the community (those who could write in these new languages were held in high esteem). As a consequence of the new premium attached to contact with foreign cultures, which was the only way of learning the alphabetic languages at first, the balance between rural and urban Africans changed.

As Africans learned to adapt to the alphabetic literary age, the world continued to develop different appetites for skills, based on an evolving economic model adopted by the Anglo-Saxon and East Asian power axes. Having been successful in the agricultural era, Africans subsequently failed to prosper in the industrial or knowledge-worker eras. By this time, Africa had lost her autonomy and its people were still coming to terms with the prized left-brain-dominated skill sets.

We have reached another moment when a socio-economic revolution is at our doorstep. What is coming is the so-called fourth industrial revolution. This coming age of the creative connector, requiring right-brain-dominant skills, such as empathy, storytelling, symphony, play, design and meaning, may be the first culturally congruent epoch for Africans since the pastoral age.[9] The companies that will dominate this new epoch, such as Disney/Marvel, Facebook, Google and Amazon, are on the lookout for a completely different set of skills. According to Daniel Pink, author of several best-selling books on work and behaviour, this new conceptual age requires that people in the workplace create artistic and emotional beauty, that they detect patterns and opportunities, and that they craft satisfying narratives around them.[10] Such narratives will be all the more compelling when they combine, through sophisticated computer coding, seemingly unrelated pieces of information and are woven together, like a symphony, in a way that appeals emotionally to the recipient.

By the middle of this century, the African labour force will be the world's largest. How that labour force is allowed to express itself will depend on how its members have been educated. Education for this coming era will require drastically new techniques. A focus on the structure, form and quality of teaching of a modernised curriculum is imperative for Africa's future. One condition for success is the need for Africans to learn the hard skills of designing institutions around their own cultural impulses, as opposed to borrowing institutional designs from others. However, the best way to prepare for a new social revolution is by learning how older social revolutions affected us.

The adoption of Christianity

Before looking at how Africans have helped to form and adapt to Christianity, we must ask a few fundamental questions. What is the difference between myth and religion? Where do traditional African mythical beliefs go when they are displaced by new Christian or Islamic mythical beliefs? How has Christianity itself been shaped by African mythology?

There are three broadly accepted ways that myths have been deemed to have travelled around the globe. The first explanation of the appearance of similar mythology around the world is explained in the form of archetypes. According to proponents of this school of thought, exemplified by Carl Jung and Joseph Campbell, myths are a secondary elaboration of consciousness that is common to all human beings. Such so-called collective consciousness has in common certain stories, fables and scripture that have been passed down from generation to generation.[11]

The philologist Michael Witzel is a vociferous critic of this school of thought. In simple terms, Witzel asserts that, while we might all have the same ancestors, and as a result a shared heritage that binds humanity as a collective, this does not make us bound by one way of thinking and one collection of common myths.[12]

The second explanation is diffusion theory. This posits the idea that myths have spread around the world from one or more major civilisations. From a historical point of view, Christianity, Judaism and Islam are the best examples of the myth-diffusion hypothesis at work. It is well known that Joseph, Moses and later Jesus were all influenced by Egyptian knowledge systems. The Bible tells us that not only did Abraham have an Egyptian woman with whom he had a child, but also his wife Sarah married a Pharaoh and Abraham spent a significant amount of time in Egypt as the Pharaoh's guest. The anthropologist AL Kroeber puts it succinctly when he says, 'The direct origin of cultural traits are other cultural traits.'[13] Though some Christians would be reluctant to admit this, the mythologising of Jesus Christ and his time on earth was certainly influenced by the Ancient Egyptian myth of Horus, who was a son of Osiris and was also begotten by his mother, Isis, out of immaculate conception and was similarly born on 25 December.[14] Horus's uncle, Set (from whom the name Set-an gave us Satan), killed his father, Osiris, out of jealousy, prompting Horus to seek revenge when he grew up, leading to the resurrection of his father.[15]

Another example of myth diffusion is when two gods worshipped in the northern and southern regions of ancient Kemet (Egypt) were merged as Amun Ra, a god who was later widely worshipped in Greece (where he was identified with Zeus Ammon). His name was later more popularly spelt Amen-Re. It is no coincidence that modern Christians, as did millions of Egyptians before them, end their prayers with the word 'amen'. Even before the fall of Rome, some of the earliest Popes, for example Victor I, Miltiades and Gelasius I, were of African descent. One of the most famous theologians of the early Catholic Church, and a major contributor to the thinking of Calvin, Descartes and Luther, was an Algerian named St Augustine of Hippo.

The celebrations of both Easter and Christmas are strikingly similar to pagan celebrations occurring hundreds of years before the birth of Christ.[16] There is significant evidence from Roman temples, including one frequented by Emperor Constantine I (the Great) himself, that the Romans worshipped a god named Mithras. This sun god, thought to have originated in Persia, was the fusion of the Egyptian gods Horus and Osiris. In an attempt to solidify a fragile foreign-imposed dynasty in Egypt, Ptolemy I, one of Alexander the Great's most capable generals, invented a deity named Serapis (a fusion of Osiris and Apis, the sacred bull).[17] The worship of both Mithras and Serapis may be the critical link between these great civilisations and modern Christianity.[18] The existence of one myth neither negates nor invalidates the other; instead, current events are often recorded with an interpretation that is framed by the knowledge of older myths.

The third explanation is a comparative approach. In *The Origin of the World's Mythology*, Michael Witzel shows the value of such an approach to studying the occurrence of myths around the world. On the relationship between myths and religion, Witzel says, '… myths deal with questions of the origin, the nature and the ultimate destiny of the world and its human beings. Myths are part of the larger realm of religious thought that is characterised by symbolism.'[19]

There is no doubt that the ideas encapsulated in Christianity and Islam have great appeal among Africans. The power of Christian and Islamic symbolism, the beauty and simplicity of both the Qur'an and the Bible, the allure of Jesus as a saviour, dying on the cross to absolve all human sin, the structure of Islamic life and its centrality to a humanist conception of an all-powerful God (Allah) – these are all impossible to deny. Humans literally can't function without symbols, which reflect their current understanding of reality. Many of these symbols are benign. Some, like the race, sex and ethnology of the god we worship, have become fundamental to who we are. With this understanding, we can better take stock of the psychological influence that the depiction of Jesus as 'white' has had on the global psyche in general, and on the African psyche in particular.

According to Christian tradition, St Mark was the first missionary in Africa. The early Christian writers Clement and Eusebius both report that Mark preached in Alexandria, Egypt. Eusebius, an early ally of Constantine I, notes that Mark was martyred there. Ancient African Christianity was basically confined to northern Africa – Egypt, Algeria, Nubia and Ethiopia.[20] Following the division of the Roman Empire, churches in North Africa maintained close ties to Eastern Christendom and made many important contributions to how the Christian faith was shaped and ministered. In these early days (between the death of Christ and 325), African figures of authority dominated and shaped the Christian faith.

Christianity spread slowly westward from Alexandria and southeastward into Ethiopia. Throughout North Africa, Christianity was embraced as the religion of dissent against the Roman Empire. At the turn of the fourth century, the Ethiopian king Ezana made Christianity the kingdom's official religion. In a twist of irony, in 312 Constantine I made Christianity the official religion of the Roman Empire.[21] In 325 the First Council of Nicaea elaborated what is now known as the Nicaean Creed, resolving many differences between different Christian leaders and adopting a consistent message about the life and death of Jesus, which was to guide the propagation of the faith throughout the world through the printing of the Bible. In the seventh century, Christianity retreated in the face of the advance of Islam, but it remained the chosen religion of the Ethiopian Empire and persisted in pockets of North Africa. In the 15th century, Christianity came to sub-Saharan Africa with the arrival of the Portuguese. In the south of the continent, the Dutch brought the Protestant variety of Christianity in 1652. Georg Schmidt, founder of the first Protestant mission (Moravian Brethren) in southern Africa, arrived in Table Bay on 9 July 1737. In 1742, Schmidt baptised the local Khoi-khoi people.[22]

The missionaries set out into the interior of the continent to establish mission stations, with the aim of converting the local population to one or another variety of Christianity. The ability of missionaries to make and retain converts seems to have been somewhat in doubt. Historian Norman Etherington states that only 12 per cent of converts on mission settlements were there for 'spiritual' reasons.[23] The majority of converts sought either material advantage or psychological security. In addition, although some groups, such as the Basotho and the Batswana, openly welcomed missionaries, others, such as the Bapedi, the amaZulu and the amaMpondo, vehemently rejected their presence as a matter of national policy.[24]

Jacob Olupona, Professor of African Religious Traditions at Harvard Divinity School, explains the interface between African mythology and religion: 'For starters, the word "religion" is problematic for many Africans, because it suggests that religion is separate from the other aspects of one's culture, society or environment. But for many Africans, religion can never be separated from all these. It is a way of life, and it can never be separated from the public sphere. Religion informs everything in traditional African society, including political art, marriage, health, diet, dress, economics and death. This is not to say that indigenous African spirituality represents a form of theocracy or religious totalitarianism – not at all.'[25] This balanced approach to holistic spirituality has only recently been understood by Anglo-Saxons as essential to a healthy, happy life.

Today, there is no denying that there is a powerful attraction pulling Africans to the less ritualised, non-denominational evangelical churches, with their emphasis on music, praise and ecstatic worship. They are attracting record numbers of Christians. The World Values Survey (WVS), a global research project examining the values and beliefs of 86 000 people in 60 countries, indicates that Africans are enormously devout. According to WVS data, 90 per cent of Africans who call themselves Christian attend church regularly. Africans have made the great Abrahamic religions their own, bending some of the symbols and myths to fit into some of their ways of thinking.

In 2010, the Pew Research Center's Forum on Religion and Public

Life published a report entitled 'Tolerance and Tension: Islam and Christianity in sub-Saharan Africa'. The report examined the way Africans viewed themselves and their religious life, and surveyed more than 25 000 people in 19 countries throughout the continent. According to the executive summary of the report:

> In little more than a century, the religious landscape of sub-Saharan Africa has changed dramatically. As of 1900, both Muslims and Christians were relatively small minorities in the region. The vast majority of people practised traditional African religions, while adherents of Christianity and Islam *combined* made up less than a quarter of the population, according to historical estimates from the World Religion Database. Since then, however, the number of Muslims living between the Sahara Desert and the Cape of Good Hope has increased more than 20-fold, rising from an estimated 11 million in 1900 to approximately 234 million in 2010. The number of Christians has grown even faster, soaring almost 70-fold from about 7 million to 470 million. Sub-Saharan Africa now is home to about one in five of all the Christians in the world (21 per cent) and more than one in seven of the world's Muslims (15 percent).[26]

Christianity is increasingly becoming an African religion, not least because so much in Christianity is common to African mythology. Africa is already the largest Christian continent, with slightly more Christians than North America. But by 2050 the North American Christian population will be *less than half* the size, in relative terms, of Africa's Christian population (516 million vs 1.12 billion).[27] The task that Africans should undertake is to be firm about the basis upon which they adhere to Islam or worship Jesus Christ. It cannot be that such worship becomes part of a cultural displacement of African ancestral beliefs. It cannot be that Africans accept that Jesus was a blond-haired, blue-eyed Middle Eastern man at a time when it was obviously biologically unlikely to have been the case. The whitewashing of history has massive psychological implications that need to be fought and resisted. Despite attempts to erase the tracks of a black Christ, there are still more than 450 Black Madonnas venerated in Europe (depicting Mary, and often Jesus, as black).

Dr Yosef Ben-Jochannan said it best: 'Religion is the deification of a people's culture. Therefore religion empowers the people in whose culture the religion is expressed.'[28] Our personal identity is affected by the symbols we worship. If those symbols are racialised and the colour coding is reflected in our social hierarchy, the psychological effects are much worse. The consequence of a lack of rigorous resistance against the whitewashing of religious narratives is a major source of current cultural fragility.

The adoption of money

The concept of the merchant bank has been around for centuries. Ever since animal and plant husbandry became ways of life, humans have had problems matching their cash flow to their income.

Noble Hoggson traces the history of banking from 'the first prototype banks of merchants of the ancient world, which made grain loans to farmers and traders who carried goods between cities. This began around 2000 BCE in Assyria and Babylonia. Later, in Ancient Greece and during the Roman Empire, lenders based in temples made loans and added two important innovations: they accepted deposits and changed money.'[29]

It seems likely that the evolution of writing and the ability to document transactions made the concept of credit both possible and profitable. According to Egyptologist Toby Wilkinson, 'Writing certainly transformed the business of international trade. Many of the labels from the royal tombs at Abdju – whose miniature scenes of royal ritual serve as an important source for early pharaonic culture – were originally attached to jars of high-quality oil, imported from the Near East. An upsurge in such imports during the First Dynasty can be associated with the establishment of Egyptian outposts and trading stations throughout southern Palestine.'[30]

The principal form of money in Ethiopia, Egypt and other parts of Africa was salt. This salt had an abundant source in the Danakil Depression (northeastern Ethiopia and southern Eritrea) on the borders of Tigray and Angot. In exchange for this salt the Dankali people received tobacco, camels, bread and cloth. This form of money was transported by camel, mule or donkey around the continent. The value of the salt varied depending on supply and demand. In some instances, far enough away from the source of supply, salt was literally worth its weight in gold.[31]

In the areas dominated by Bantu-speakers, such as Kenya, Tanzania, Uganda and most of southern Africa, a cattle culture developed, which entrenched the conception of livestock as a proxy for wealth. Beads, sheep, goats and cloth served as small change. These cultures, whose conception of money has for thousands of years been based on cattle, had the hardest time conceptualising alternative forms of money. The physical representation of wealth they were used to was fundamentally different from money.

In other parts of the African continent, an array of currencies was used, ranging from cowrie shells in Sudan and Nigeria to gold dust in Ghana.[32] The logic was always consistent. Africans traded what they had in abundance for what they deemed to be in short supply. The principle of trading was by and large for personal subsistence, and for the tribe or community to build wealth as a buffer against future famine. The concept of individual capital accumulation was rare, and certainly never became widespread enough to be part of the cultural fabric.

The arrival of Europeans gradually served to change this. The major shift was in what value theory describes as the substitution of commodities that had both intrinsic value and intrinsic utility for a good, that is, money, whose primary feature was a derived notional value.[33] Even worse, money encouraged the individual to accumulate it privately without the community's participation.

Most of all, by adopting money Africans inherited another people's conception of value and its associated pathologies. These were different from the pathologies that would have been part of the cattle culture or that of the salt traders. Africans inherited alien pathologies that were not easy to identify at first.

In his classic work *The Psychology of Money*, sociologist Georg Simmel comments on the working of monetary pathology: 'Valuation as a real psychological occurrence is part of the natural world; but what we mean by valuation, its conceptual meaning, is something independent of this world; is not part of it, but is rather the whole world viewed from a particular vantage point ... Thus, value is in a sense the counterpart to being, and is comparable to being as a comprehensive form and category of worldview.'[34]

After thousands of years spent experiencing and judging value from a particular vantage point, Africans were forced to reconceptualise the value of everything. A necessary part of that process was a reconception of their own self-worth and the social standing of their fellow men and women in their communities. If one credits, as I do, Simmel's adage that 'value is a counterpart to being', then taking away a people's material value system is bound to lead to a dismantling of their moral one too. This new way of thinking about value has transformed the way we act and interact. The way we interact with the material world is now divorced from how we think about the spiritual world. Our actions are no longer largely moderated by traditional values and norms. Our values and norms have to be traded off, on a day-to-day basis, by the value we place on the creature comforts acquired by money.

Because of this background one is forced to ask: can Africans ever truly value money? Is it possible that they successfully transact from day to day with something that has historically had no natural basis of intrinsic value to them? Simmel again provides clarity on these questions by stating, 'Value exists in our consciousness as a fact that can no more be altered than can reality itself.'[35] If it cannot be altered, but reality requires that it must, our consciousness will find a proxy. That proxy needs to be suitably well rooted so as to allow the mind to rest easy with the new reality.

It is my contention that Africans have attached to money the symbol of modernity. For Africans, money is a proxy for progress. The material goods that money buys are flaunted to other members of our community as a sign that we have not been left behind. The proxy for progress was the closest available conception to individual monetary wealth that Africans could find. Together with the embedded African compulsion for relative gains, progress is a powerful social primer of action.

Value theory makes a distinction between moral goods and natural goods. At the general level, there is a difference between moral and natural goods. Moral goods, on the one hand, are those that have to do with people's conduct, and usually lead to approval or disapproval. Moral goods were at the apex of African society prior to the introduction of money. Natural goods, on the other hand, have to do with objects, not persons. These have become the apex of most of modern urban African society. My contention is that by moralising work, in the form of the Protestant work ethic, Westerners have elevated money to a product of a moral good. In the minds of many capitalists, money has as a consequence become a moral good in itself. Africans have historically seen wealth as part of an array of natural goods that have no moral value in and of themselves. Africa is experiencing a clash of values between rural areas, where moral goods are still at the apex of society, and cities, where natural goods rule supreme.

Plato explained this differently in *The Republic*, arguing that an instrumental value is worth having as a means of getting something else that is good.[36] This is very much in keeping with pre-colonial African attitudes to objects of value. An intrinsically valuable thing is worth having for itself, not as a means to something else. This is how Westerners approach the accumulation of money. These approaches to life are fundamentally different and bring with them diametrically opposed views on material value. Many of the social conflicts we see in African society have their root in these distinctions between what is most valuable in society.

What we choose to value (and why) may be different from one culture to another. What is not different is the way we react when we decide to make an object the centre of our desire, however temporary the pleasure it affords.

Simmel puts it this way: 'Human enjoyment of an object is a completely undivided act. At such moments we have an experience that does not include an awareness of an object confronting us or an awareness of the self as distinct from its present condition. Phenomena of the basest and the highest kind meet here. The crude impulse, particularly an impulse of an impersonal, general nature, wants to release itself towards an object and to be satisfied, no matter how; consciousness is exclusively concerned with satisfaction and pays no attention to its bearer on one side or its object on the other. On the other hand, intense aesthetic enjoyment displays the same form. Here too "we forget ourselves", but at the same time we no longer experience the work of art as something with which we are confronted, because our mind is completely submerged in it, has absorbed it by surrendering to it.'[37] The new shiny objects we purchase often consume us instead of our consuming them. Worse still, if my theory is correct, these objects say more to Africans about their social status than do most things in their lives.

The above quotation by Simmel aptly describes the intensity behind the new African obsession with material goods. As a consequence, Africans' passionate embrace of materialist consumption as a proxy for progress and modernity has generated many rudderless communities concerned only with keeping up with the material possessions of their friends, families and neighbours. This plays itself out in the consumption of clothes, cars, jewellery, social media and furniture. It also defines the competition to most grandly celebrate weddings and to out-mourn each other with lavish funerals. This obsession with material consumption is one of the major sources of African cultural fragility.

Conclusion

To successfully return Africa to prosperity, leaders on the continent need to explore how to return the mentality of abundance to African people. This requires the successful separation of individual material abundance from a shared conception of abundance that takes into account natural goods. In dealing with material abundance, Africans have to design their economic development policies in ways that moderate the effects of individual ownership and highlight the upside of collective resource ownership. (I will propose such an approach in Chapter 9.) Dealing with a conception of subjective poverty requires that Africans rebuild the psyche of a people made to feel worthless because of what they don't have. Moral goods have to resume their apex role in society. The final three chapters of this book will deal with these difficult topics.

The adoption of Christianity has changed many Africans' lives for the better. Sadly, the formal and rigid interpretations of the teachings of Christ by missionaries across Africa dislocated Africans from their traditional spiritual beliefs. An interconnected worldview became disconnected and sectarian. Africans put an image and a name to a unitary God who had, according to the teachings of the missionaries, a son born in the image of Europeans. This image was undoubtedly at odds with their conceptions of self. It facilitated Africa's ascription of a premium to white-skinned immigrants. If they were made more in God's image than us, so many Africans must have thought, it should stand to reason that they were more blessed and, as a consequence, closer to heaven's gate.

Christianity facilitated a move towards alphabetic languages in Africa because of the adoption of both systems by the Romans. This change to linear, left-brained reasoning led to an appreciation of skill sets that embraced a scarcity of time and space. With this came an ability to read and a willingness to embrace Roman (and later Dutch) law. This was further reinforced by Christianity's segregation of heaven and earth, which caused the loss of Africa's universality of thinking, as well as the introduction of discrete concepts of hell and sin.

Everything was no longer everything. Each of us, as Africans, now have our own place and label in a new form of social stratification that depends on material wealth. Everything now has a beginning and an end. The average African's actions are now structured around a productive purpose timed by a watch and centred on a limited utility or life span. The actions of the individual have become distanced from those of the community or tribe. The ancestors are no longer watching.

The introduction of money severed the individual's agenda from that of the community. Money made it possible to live for oneself and to see the results expressed in individual success. This was measured in the form of material wealth that was utterly divorced from the commune. Success could now be passed on to one's children, changing entire conceptions of endowment and lineage. Africans became defined by how much they had, as opposed to who they were. Their parents were defined by how wealthy they had been, as opposed to who they were. All Africans were therefore induced into labour to acquire status and power.

Abundance disappeared, and in its place came material poverty. Legions of miners, sharecroppers, slaves, gardeners and domestic workers can attest to the trauma caused by this new dispensation. They were forced to leave the countryside in search of jobs in the city. They were forced to split their families and live in separate places, dictated by the geographical availability of work. Mothers raised children without fathers. The moral authority of parents was eroded by their distance from their children, and by the children's proximity to messages advertising a new lifestyle. And so came the adoption of a mentality of scarcity, ending thousands of years of assumed abundance.

Ironically, modern philosophy has spawned innumerable self-help books designed to promote the power of the mentality of abundance. Some psychologists have made careers out of teaching this 'new' way of thinking. Spiritually, millions of Africans have learned of a book called *The Secret*, which emphasises the power of a mentality of abundance that emits an attractive force out into the universe. Yet again, Anglo-Saxons are repackaging an age-old African practice centred on forgotten belief systems. They espouse the freedom from materialism, the personal growth facilitated by nonlinear thinking. At the same time, business is increasingly looking for people with right-brained, creative skill sets capable of intense empathy and lateral thinking. According to Daniel Pink, a Fine Arts degree that teaches these skills is one of the most sought-after qualifications in America today.

One could almost say that the African way of thinking is back in vogue, except that Africans are still diligently working to acquire mastery over left-brain-oriented tasks. Being aware of what their norms, values and worldviews are, compared to what old wisdom has taught them, would enable Africans to recognise their strengths. These strengths are currently in high demand. Unless this recognition happens, Africans are at risk of losing out in another major economic revolution. Africa needs to reclaim abundant thinking to free itself from poverty. The following chapters explore how this can be done.

3

The evolution of African identity

AS A SEVEN-YEAR-OLD CHILD living in a township in Cape Town called Gugulethu, on a street called NY 108, I was confronted with a lesson in how philosophy can lead to shifting identities that in turn shape political action. The 'NY' in NY 108 stands for Native Yard.

Indigenous South Africans under British colonial rule were all referred to as 'natives'. As the policy of apartheid crystallised, 'Bantu' became the term specifically meant to refer to indigenous people and the term 'non-white' became the blanket classification for South Africans of colour. Black Consciousness blossomed in the 1970s largely in opposition to the indignities of the apartheid laws, the derogatory connotation of the non-white classification and its dehumanising intent. This set off a chain of events that led to the radicalisation of young indigenous people in South Africa. The mobilisation of like-minded anti-apartheid activists triggered an existential fear in the apartheid government that led to the killing of my father, the banning of my mother and her placement under house arrest far away from the eastern Cape Province (where she and some of the Black Consciousness leadership were operating from), and our family's eventual migration from the beautiful but unbearably hot Tzaneen to Cape Town eight years later.

From the vantage point of the pavement just in front of our home, I witnessed weekly displays of protest, sacrifice, brutality and death. The death was typically the instigator of it all. This was because, at the time, we lived about half a kilometre from a cemetery. Many African freedom fighters were buried there. Each week, hundreds or sometimes thousands of people would gather to mourn the death of a loved one, passing our house in a huge procession, which some of us children typically joined. This right to gather and mourn was contested by the South African Police. What the police feared most was the symbolic meaning of indigenous people's protest action and specifically the way the mourners glorified the death of the freedom fighter they were burying. Without fail, the tension in the air would be ignited by a rubber bullet fired, a stone thrown or a petrol bomb tossed. This pattern of protest, police brutality and killing, followed by funeral processions, which were themselves a protest action, was sparked in 1976.

From 1974 to 1976 a groundswell of resentment formed among African school learners against being forced to learn Afrikaans, which was regarded as the language of their oppressors. On 16 June 1976, learners in Soweto refused to go to school as part of their peaceful protest against the mandatory teaching of Afrikaans. This protest included the mobilisation of between 10 000 and 20 000 students, supported by the Black Consciousness Movement, to participate in a peaceful march to Orlando Stadium. The peace was broken when police sent a dog into the crowd to disperse the protestors, and the crowd responded by killing the dog. Police responded by opening fire with live ammunition, killing up to 700 children. That day, it was clear to all that the value of a so-called non-white life was deemed worthless. One dog's life equalled that of 700 children. This event changed the nature of protest action in South Africa forever.

In an interview a few months before his death, describing the change in philosophy from non-violent peaceful protest to confrontational protest, Steve Biko put it as follows: 'And of course, you see, the dramatic thing about the bravery of these youths is that they have now discovered, or accepted, what everybody knows, that the bond between life and death is absolute. You are either alive and proud or you are dead, and when you are dead, you don't care anyway. And your method of death can be a politicising thing.'[1] By putting into context the value of life, the importance of human dignity and the martyrdom of death, Steve Biko's philosophy, and later his actions, compelled millions of South Africans to risk all for freedom. This is how, more than nine years later, I learned the lesson from my father, indirectly, that philosophy is a powerful thing. Watching protesters both young and old die for a cause they felt to be sacrosanct was both sad and awe-inspiring. As a form of active resistance to tyranny, it was a validation of the internalisation of the philosophy of Black Consciousness.

It is unusual for philosophers to both have to and want to give up their life for a cause. Most philosophers have made their contribution to society purely in the arena of ideas, which were the result of accumulated wisdom turned into usable insights. Much of the world's knowledge has been put into context by great philosophers. The Ancient Greeks defined philosophy as the love of wisdom. For them, knowledge creation and accumulation was a deeply personal experience that liberated the student of philosophy from the tyranny of ignorance. It was also something to be shared among interested students. In Western culture, philosophy has been framed as an individual scholarly endeavour to contemplate, meditate upon and come up with original thinking that contributes to how humans approach particular problems. This was not always the case in ancient society.

The Ancient Egyptians, who invented philosophy, saw knowledge and the contemplation of wisdom as activities conducted by a small segment of the population assigned to understand the mysteries of the universe. According to historian George James: 'The Egyptian Mystery System had as its most important object the deification of man, and taught that the soul of man if liberated from its bodily fetters, could enable him to become godlike and see the Gods in this life and attain the beatific vision and hold communion with the Immortals.'[2] The Egyptians believed that man was different from a god because of ignorance. They were convinced that godliness was attainable through the mastery of old wisdom.

Ancient Egyptians saw the sharing of knowledge as an 'invitation-only' process whereby teachers, who were usually Egyptian priests, instructed students and imparted to them, through theories and heuristics, wisdom learned by the Egyptian intelligentsia. For them, the body of knowledge and its deciphering was a collective privilege of the privileged few. Egyptians viewed all things associated with knowledge creation, accumulation and dissemination as sacred work that fulfilled a divine destiny. They viewed wisdom as part of a journey towards immortality. This somewhat elitist concept of philosophy discouraged writing and encouraged learning in secret, both of which would prove to be the undoing of Egypt's natural legacy as the cradle of ancient philosophy. Historian Chancellor Williams explains this phenomenon: 'The most important fact to keep in mind, however, is that we are considering the early age when relatively only a few people could write – a small professional class, the scribes. All books, scrolls, inscriptions, letters, etc, were written by them. Therefore in any society where the scribes were either captured or disappeared from it for whatever reason, the art of writing in that society died.'[3]

The Egyptians restricted education to a select few within the society, and their approach to knowledge accumulation was characterised by secrecy. This sowed the seeds for the eventual destruction of their civilisation. It was because of this secrecy that the Greeks were able to appropriate Egyptian knowledge systems when Alexander the Great invaded Egypt in 332 BCE and took most of the works in Egypt's secret library. Many scholars to this day view much of Greek philosophy as a plagiarised body of Egyptian knowledge.

When the Greeks began teaching philosophy at the school that Aristotle and his followers established, the aims were somewhat different. The basis of Aristotle's peripatetic school (referred to as such because of his tendency to walk while lecturing), called the Lyceum, was twofold. First, like the Egyptians, the students came to learn philosophy and the wisdom that flowed from it. The second objective was the exploration of historical works with the aim of creating new philosophies and new schools of science using different forms of reasoning.[4] Out of this tradition of publicly celebrating wisdom came the idea of the public intellectual.

Plato described reason as the natural monarch that should rule over the other parts, such as spiritedness and passion.[5] Public intellectuals have, through the ages, used reason (which derives from the French word *raison*, meaning 'cause', and from the Latin *ratio*, meaning 'explanation') as a method of creating an ethical framework that governed how their societies framed their choices. It is my assertion that understanding the Western construct of reason and its application in philosophy is instructive. I believe that the emphasis on reason serves as a better proxy for the ethical framework condoning imperialism and its application to the African continent through race-based categorisation. In understanding the Western interpretation of the centrality of reason, we get a better grasp of the source of Western entitlement, which gave rise to imperial ambitions. Indeed, through this exploration we can understand what continues to fuel Western assumptions of superiority to this day.

Linked to the dominance of reason is the concept of whiteness, which is such a fundamental pillar of our world that we seldom question its legitimacy. The noted educationist Joe L Kincheloe describes the origins of this concept: '[W]e believe that a dominant impulse of whiteness took shape around the European Enlightenment notion of rationality with its privileged construction of a transcendental white, male, rational subject who operated at the recesses of power while concurrently giving every indication that he escaped the confines of time and space.'[6] Our exploration of how the world has come to be constructed, such that people who are not considered white have a hard time being both themselves and successful, has to start with an exposé of the myth of whiteness.

One cannot understand whiteness without understanding the Enlightenment period and its global manifestations. The Enlightenment was a period that saw a great flowering of scientific endeavour in many fields. These fields laid the foundation for the way Europeans saw the world. Two different European scholars can be said to have invented whiteness. First, in 1735, the Swedish botanist Carolus Linnaeus published a classification system for both flora and fauna. This new biological classification, or taxonomy, divided living organisms into orders, families, genera and species. Linneaus gave humans the same treatment as plants and animals, categorising them and giving them traits. Then, in 1775, the German naturalist Johann Friedrich Blumenbach published *On the Natural Varieties of Mankind*, and became the first scholar to categorise humans according to their so-called race. He created the concept of natural beauty, based on race, by collecting a variety of skulls that he classified as belonging variously to discrete peoples with shared physical traits. Blumenbach was obsessed with aesthetic beauty. Being a theorist of human variety (what would later be referred to as a social anthropologist), he felt the need to come up with a descriptive theory about the reasons for these observed and sometimes imagined differences.

Blumenbach also coined the term 'Caucasian' as a reference to an entire race, because he believed that the Caucasus region of Asia Minor produced 'the most beautiful race of men'.[7] Ironically, the people of the Caucasus region were very distinct from other Europeans because of their highly varied racial composition. What we know today as 'white' people came to be referred to as 'Caucasian' in the Americas, to give some basis to a new practice of racial discrimination that served to justify the treatment of slaves.[8] In his quest to construct a narrative around the size and shape of human skulls, Blumenbach began to develop a theory to account for the perceived superiority of certain humans over others. This theory was eventually developed into a white supremacy narrative that politicians and slave traders latched onto to justify actions that would otherwise have been morally indefensible. In fact, to show how quickly concepts travel, merge with others like them and become socially acceptable, Thomas Jefferson wrote in 1776, in *Notes on the State of Virginia*, that 'blacks were, whether originally a distinct race, or made distinct by time and circumstances, inferior to the whites in the endowment of body and mind'.[9]

Slavery, of course, was an age-old practice. The Enlightenment, on the other hand, was a period when many traditions were failing to live up to scrutiny. For people struggling to morally justify slavery, Blumenbach's system of classification was manna from heaven. In North America and in Europe, the proportion of white slaves significantly decreased and black slaves became the overwhelming majority. Blumenbach's European bias gave him a transparent incentive to create these false categories and ultimately forced him and others to create narratives to codify and attach stereotypes to the newly created racial categories. Blackness became a foil to the newly created category of whiteness, allowing those who felt they could to distinguish themselves from those who were, conveniently, newly perceived to lack the rational capacity to share their humanity.

The invention of whiteness and an intersubjective reality of supremacy

Looking at the evolution of both slavery and indentured labour from the late 15th century can give context to what Blumenbach and his ilk were trying to justify. As early as 1488, the Portuguese arriving in southern Africa for the first time used the term *negro* (literally, 'black') to describe the Bantu, Khoi and San people they encountered. Just like many literal descriptors before it – for instance, Ethiopia means 'land of burnt people' – this was a crude but relatively benign descriptor devoid of the prejudicial connotations it has today. Yet these interactions between the Portuguese and indigenous Africans were far from benign. The voyages of Diogo Cão (1483), Bartolomeu Dias (1488) and Vasco da Gama (1497) were part of an overall drive by the Portuguese to establish a global trading empire. Naturally this empire assumed that the superiority of Portuguese maritime technology translated into Portuguese superiority in all other aspects. In the 1490s, sugar plantations were established on the island of São Tomé, prompting the Portuguese to begin trading guns for slaves with their trading outpost in the Kongo. When Brazil became part of the Portuguese Empire in the 16th century, the demand for slaves increased significantly, leading to the establishment of large-scale slave trading. The increasing popularity of African slaves was the catalyst for changing European attitudes towards Africa and the need for racial distinctions that fit a socio-economic narrative of conquest.

Across the Atlantic Ocean, Christopher Columbus's first voyage to the Caribbean, in 1492, was the catalyst that led to the settlement of the New World by Europeans. The intentions from the start were the conquest and the exploitation of the local people to meet imperial ends. Columbus himself wrote in his journal that the Taino Indians, whom he first encountered on the island of Hispaniola, were uniquely suited to subjugation.[10] Even though imperialist attitudes to local people were inhumane, a systematic universal concept of a hierarchy of races had yet to be elaborated in writing.

As the scale of the commercial opportunity became clearer, 'worker shortage' in places like Virginia, the Carolinas and Georgia required abundant labour. According to Kristin Haltinner, to deal with these shortages, 'Virginia's powerful set up an increasingly harsh labour system, one that indentured white workers to their owners, the same as if they were tools or livestock'.[11] From 1641 to 1652 over 500 000 Irish people died during the Irish Confederate Wars, reducing the population of Ireland by close to 60 per cent. During this period of religious and ethnic conflict, between 30 000 and 80 000 Irish people were sold as indentured labourers, many to North America. This practice was reserved for not just Irish men and women. In the 1630s alone, almost 80 000 'whites' left England for the Chesapeake, New England and the Caribbean.[12] Indentured labour was an institution that was very similar to slavery. Labourers would have their labour sold, or sell their labour themselves, to settlers in the new lands in exchange for the prospect of a new life and, after working for between five and fifteen years, the allocation of a small tract of land.[13] Indentured labourers were whipped and abused by their masters indiscriminately. Many died during the period of indenture, and only a very small fraction of them ever received the promised land allocation.

From this example it is clear that before the racial categorisation of humans, the skin colour of slaves was not the overwhelming driver of the business of slavery. Slavery after all was very big business. To get a sense of how big, consider this example: in 1833 the British government paid £20 million to compensate 3 000 families that owned slaves for their 'loss of property' because of the abolition of slavery.[14] That figure represented a staggering 40 per cent of the Treasury's annual budget and equates to £16.5 billion today.[15]

As the risks to the slave industry became more apparent, negative racial attitudes soon came to be concretised in North America. One example of these risks was Bacon's Rebellion (1676) in the Virginia colony. This rebellion saw the first documented alignment of interests between 'black' and 'white' slaves.[16] The prospect of more riots and further unification of slaves against slave owners in America paved the way for the introduction of differentiated slave treatment. Bacon's Rebellion particularly disturbed the ruling class because of the potential instability they foresaw if European and non-European slaves could create an alliance to topple their masters. As a direct result of this rebellion, a caste-based slave system increasingly dependent on the importation of African slaves was instituted.

According to Kincheloe: 'Only after the racialisation of slavery around 1680 did whiteness and blackness come to represent racial categories. Only at this historical juncture did the concept of a discrete white race begin to take shape. Slowly in the eighteenth and nineteenth centuries the association with rationality and orderliness developed, and in this context whiteness came to signify an elite racial group.'[17] Though I agree with Kincheloe's point in general, there is a misleading lack of context to his commentary on race.

Race in the 17th century was very much a construct of the colonies. It was a necessary social construction to both divide and conquer, and to satisfy the guilty conscience of those committing the day-to-day atrocities needed to keep order under inhumane circumstances. The majority of Europeans were still shielded from these colonial and imperial realities. They would begin to catch up over the next two centuries. Provincial racism in the Americas was devoid of the scientific rationalisation that European scholars would later give it.

In 1735, Linnaeus published the *Systema Naturæ* (The System of Nature), the influential work that provided the intellectual tools for racial categorisation. His 'system' was based on four ethnic categories: Americanus (Native Americans), Asiaticus, Africanus and Europaeus. According to Linnaeus, each of these categories carried characteristics that defined them and their behaviour.[18] It was from these characteristics that a set of stereotypes was introduced into the minds of Europeans. These stereotypes were at once a rationale for why Europeans had the right to conquer and served as the explanatory variables that proved the new narrative of European whiteness and the savage otherness of all of those in the colonies. Africans, who were a common denominator across the colonies in the form of slave labour, occupied the lowest rung on a newly constructed racial ladder.

Though Linnaeus's categories were successfully used to discriminate against Asians, Africans and Indigenous Americans, he did not use the word 'race'. That distinction belongs to Blumenbach, who used the word to classify humans into five categories: Caucasian, Mongolian, Ethiopian, American and Malay. Blumenbach had a philosophical view of nature that made him search for the cause of things.[19] His work would ultimately birth the field of anthropology, and unfortunately seed that field with a racist undertone that seeks to justify the current socio-economic order by searching for difference and backwardness in Africans, Native Americans and Asians while promoting the narrative of the intellectual superiority of Europeans and Americans of European descent.

The modern theory of evolution begins with the publication in 1859 of Charles Darwin's *On the Origin of Species*. However, Darwin's idea of natural selection was soon taken up by so-called Social Darwinists, who propounded a 'survival of the fittest' narrative to explain why some genetic traits survive and others do not. This completed a trend of thinking called evolutionary racism, which assumes that humans have continually evolved and thus some races are more evolved than others. This was, of course, also used as a justification for colonialism and imperialism.

During the 19th century, the concept of race was still closely intertwined with classification and, as a result, immersed in scientific language to create distinctions between human characteristics. Race and the study of ethnography became an obsession across Europe. Between 1839 and 1863, societies of ethnology were founded in Paris, New York, London and Ireland.[20] Though this new-found interest in ethnology had a socio-political and philosophical basis, there was also a strong psychological influence.

The use of scientific theories to attempt to justify human hierarchy was driven by European imperialists in an effort to justify their role in the world as they saw it. One has to imagine that a continent of self-consciously enlightened citizens, whose public intellectuals vigorously championed their ascension to the highest possible levels of human consciousness and morality, must have had some psychological difficulty with the idea of slavery as an institution. In *The Moral Arc*, science writer Michael Shermer addresses this difficulty: 'Slavery is a case study on the power of self-deception as a work-around for a psychological phenomenon called cognitive dissonance, or the mental tension experienced when someone holds two or more conflicting thoughts simultaneously; in this case (1) slavery is acceptable and possibly good, and (2) slavery is unacceptable and possibly even evil. For most of human history people simply accepted the first idea, but as Enlightenment ideas about people being treated equally began to percolate throughout societies, sentiments began to change towards the second idea, which produced cognitive dissonance.'[21] Shermer here reveals the romanticising of the Enlightenment legacy that has been such a mainstay of the Western educational curriculum.

Although I agree that there was a moral move from the first position, which held slavery as a widely acceptable practice, to the second, which found slavery to be increasingly unacceptable, these moral positions only applied to other Europeans. The Enlightenment led to the end, or at least a significant reduction, of the practice of enslaving other Europeans and a concomitant increase in the enslavement of Africans. This increase was morally justified by the introduction of a racial categorisation framework that placed white Europeans at the apex of humanity, just below God. In this sense, paradoxically, the Enlightenment was the initiator of formal racism as it is practised today. Even after geneticist J Craig Venter proved that 99.99 per cent of all humans share the same genetic code,[22] and therefore that race is a social rather than a scientific construct, human beings continue to categorise each other in racial terms, and these racial categories are perpetuated in the form intended by imperial scientists such as Linnaeus and Blumenbach.

The chief reason for the rigidity of racial categories and their resilience to this day is that they preserve privilege and resolve a potential cognitive-dissonance problem posed by the legacy of slavery and imperialism. It was privilege preservation that turned a great man like Thomas Jefferson into a hypocrite who simultaneously espoused the universal virtues of humankind and justified the institution of slavery. It is in the resolution of the cognitive-dissonance problem that President Barack Obama couldn't, even as the first African American president, contemplate reparations to African Americans for slavery. For him to have done so would have required a painful (from the point of view of the establishment) acknowledgement that America was built on slave labour and that the founders were hypocrites who took the easy way out at the point of founding the country. The result of this failure to face reality, as Obama would no doubt acknowledge, is a nation that continues to suffer the nightmares (in the form of institutionalised racism and statistical discrimination) of a dream deferred for Americans whom the system deems to be black.[23]

According to Barbara J Flagg, an expert in US constitutional law: 'Whiteness is a social location of power, privilege, and prestige. It is "an invisible package of unearned assets." As an epistemological stance, it sometimes is an exercise in denial. Whiteness is an identity, a culture, and an often-colonising way of life that is largely invisible to Whites, though rarely to people of colour. Whiteness also carries the authority within the larger culture it dominates to set the terms on which every aspect of race is discussed and understood. Whiteness thus is many-faceted and pervasive. I believe it lies at the centre of the problem of race in this society. By [metaprivilege] I mean the ability of Whiteness to define the conceptual terrain on which race is constructed, deployed, and interrogated. Whiteness sets the terms on which racial identity is constructed.'[24] Ironically, whiteness is an enabled privilege. Those of us considered black, mulatto, coloured and mixed race keep whiteness alive by continuing to frame our own identities in racial terms. Whiteness does not exist. The sooner Africans realise that, the closer they will be to heeding Bob Marley's call to 'emancipate yourself from mental slavery'. Africans need to reimagine a future without racial categories.

Black mental boxes and the conceptual chain that holds them shut

Slavery has defined blackness ever since the words Negro, nigger, mulatto and black were used to describe Africans encountered by European imperialists. Based on these interactions in the 16th century and after, 'black' people have been commonly enslaved by the meta-institution of imperialism. It is widely known and documented that slavery was only successful because many Africans enthusiastically participated in the enslavement of other Africans. Slavery was incredibly profitable for some African merchants and rulers. The result of falling prey to that profitable temptation was that, between 1525 and 1866, 12.5 million Africans were shipped overseas into slavery. Ironically, those Africans left behind were slowly introduced into a psychological form of slavery that would last longer and arguably prove more debilitating than the type of physical bondage to which they subjected their brothers and sisters.

African people are still in bondage to this day. The four-link chain that binds them is conceptual rather than metallic. The four links can be articulated as follows:

1. The failure to democratise knowledge as a means of empowerment.
2. The acceptance of other societies' myths as gospel truths instead of recognising these myths for what they are.
3. The privileging of other people's social agendas above the preservation and development of our own culture.
4. The acceptance of the mentality of scarcity over that of abundance.

This mental bondage by a conceptual chain has nullified the need for the institutions of slavery, colonialism and even the prison system as mechanisms for control over those designated as being black in Africa. Using this framework to explore the mechanics of contemporary mental bondage is instructive to those who would like to understand how to make Africa prosper. Let's look at each link in turn.

1. The failure to democratise knowledge

The concept of knowledge generation and dissemination has, since antiquity, been regarded by Africans as the purview of a few. From the Ancient Egyptians to post-liberation leaders, informational elitism has been the enduring common practice. This informational elitism has created large gaps and fragmentation in the documentation of African history, making it incredibly difficult to teach young

Africans a holistic body of history from their own perspective. It has been left to European scholars to interpret and document African history, creating a litany of works with flawed premises, incorrect cultural contextualisation and false attribution of achievements, usually to the disservice of African historical figures. Because of this, unlike the people of other continents, Africans generally don't celebrate their historical achievements.

This failure to locate oneself positively in history books results in Africans' lacking an essential consciousness of self. Without consciousness, it becomes difficult to develop a healthy identity. They consequently interact in a rudderless fashion with the world on other people's terms. In his classic essay 'The Fact of Blackness', Frantz Fanon states, 'The Black Man among his own in the twentieth century does not know at what moment his inferiority comes into being through the other … The Negro, however sincere, is a slave of the past. None the less I am a man, and in this sense the Peloponnesian War is as much mine as the invention of the campus. Face to face with the white man, the Negro has a past to legitimate, a vengeance to exact; face to face with the Negro, the contemporary white man feels the need to recall the times of cannibalism.'[25] This extraordinary passage reminds us that, as humans, we have to be equipped with a thorough understanding of ourselves within the context of what we consider our legitimate history, in order to interact equally with each other.

Without this body of historical knowledge, Africans will continue to interact with the world on the back foot. Without prioritising the generation and dissemination of knowledge about African history and African culture, African leaders will continue to struggle to create societies capable of confidently participating as equals in the socio-economic global landscape. In other words, Africans will continue to live life as victims of memory loss, confused, disoriented and incapable of confidently walking through uncharted territories.

2. The acceptance of other societies' myths

We have already dealt with the fact that many of the things we hold on to dearly as 'permanent' institutions in modern society are myths whose legitimacy stems from their popularity. Religion, money, capitalism, law, citizenship, democracy and nation-states are all myths that we either choose to believe or are made to believe by figures of authority. The human mind is a myth-making machine. We cannot solve the problems of cooperating among large groups (anything over 150 people) without the use of such myths. Yet we have to choose our myths carefully. Any myth, once believed, exerts a powerful hold over our thought processes.

Writing on the importance of play in early childhood education, Olivia Saracho and Bernard Spodek comment: 'Play is a manifestation of the fundamental properties of myth-making, and cognitive, social and symbolic abilities are concomitant aspects of this process. The myths and fantasies of childhood are not eroded by the onset of reason; rather, they are replaced by more sophisticated adult myths about the importance of reason. Ironically, the mythical belief in reason by adults has led to the myth that adults have no myths.'[26] When Saracho and Spodek speak of myths, they are not referring to temporary beliefs but rather to what they call 'lived-in belief systems'. By that definition, one can see how many things can fall into the category of myth. Coming, as Africans do, from a holistic and mystical system of thought, it is easy to see why Africans are so quick to adopt new mythical systems that seem to explain worldly occurrences better.

Africans have accepted the false dichotomy that we either judge ourselves by Western standards of modernity or return to some form of pre-modern traditional state of being. In doing so, we tangle ourselves in a web of self-justification that constrains us from painting more authentic pictures of what social, political and economic freedom could look like if undertaken with a careful emphasis on the preservation and restoration of African cultural norms and values.

Reimagining history such that one sees Africans as a significant contributor to modern progress allows one to embrace modernity without the need to discard old wisdom.

3. *The privileging of other people's social agendas*

Many African countries have elected to take on the conventions of their coloniser by adopting their language. They have compounded this problem by accepting the coloniser's rule of law. They have also, by and large, made the death of their cultures a long-term certainty by retaining a schooling system based on the curriculum of one or another European country (or, in Liberia's case, America). By structuring our societies in this way, Africans have, to paraphrase investment guru Charlie Munger, become a one-legged man in an ass-kicking contest. They do not stand a competitive chance.

It is imperative that Africans, like other humans, look at the world from an African perspective. The 1970s and 1980s produced a strong Afrocentric movement espousing the need for just this perspective. Many different schools of thought, and their proponents, kept Afrocentricity alive for over three decades. The movement gradually fizzled out towards the end of the 1990s. The old wisdom of Afrocentricity, as espoused today by thinkers like Molefi Asante and Ama Mazama, has huge value in today's identity-crisis-stricken African countries.

What is powerful about this approach to the world is that it is a way of re-establishing an identity that need not be based on skin colour or artificially constructed borders, but rather on a commonly shared African heritage. It begs the believer and practitioner of Afrocentricity to start first with a question, to locate truths in an African context, and to seek to disprove and rewrite existing orthodoxies. It is a most effective springboard from which the empowered African can generate an alternative narrative, one that can form part of a reason for a new way of doing things.

Ama Mazama puts it this way: 'Afrocentricity contends that our main problem as African people is our usually unconscious adoption of the Western world view and perspective and their attendant conceptual frameworks. The list of those ideas and theories that have invaded our lives as normal, natural or, even worse, ideal is infinite. How many of us have really paused to seriously examine and challenge such ideas as development, planning, progress, the need for democracy and the nation-state as the best form of political and social organisation, to name a few?'[27] Mazama puts her finger on the central issue at play in African society – a lack of absolute intentionality in the way that our societies are constructed.[28]

If we reimagine Africa through an embrace of a modern sense of Afrocentricity that is without racial categories, we are then able to reconnect with our old mindset of abundance and unshackle ourselves from the fourth and final link to the conceptual chains that bind us. The mere acceptance of the descriptor 'black' is reductionist in that we are defined by one tiny genetic truth, the presence of melanin in our genes. The acceptance of the nation-state as the sole form of organising African society removes the myriad alternative ways of arranging the African continent that are yet to be explored, creating a scarcity of ideas to reorder the African political economy. This fixation immediately confines wealth to what is within the confines of arbitrarily created borders. It creates economic scarcity where Pan Africanism can create abundance at scale and optionality.

4. *The acceptance of a mentality of scarcity over one of abundance*

Scarcity in a continent as rich as Africa can only be self-imposed scarcity. African countries with more water than the continent needs (such as the Democratic Republic of Congo, or DRC) have a scarcity of infrastructure, which is a self-imposed scarcity because the financial markets do not trust the country's institutions enough to lend it capital to unlock its vast resources. Countries such as South Africa, Botswana and Mauritius, with great infrastructure and a high degree of institutional capital but a scarcity in both fast-growing companies and highly trained technical people in key industries such as engineering, teaching, medicine and information technology, could enjoy abundance within a Pan Africanist framework. They would get access to markets and skills that could lead to high growth and employment generation. Countries such as Kenya, Ghana and Nigeria, which have many fast-growing companies and abundant technical skills, but face shortages in private equity and venture capital (the likes of which are overflowing in South Africa), could benefit greatly from tighter regional economic integration. The failure to coordinate resources reflects a scarcity in leadership and imagination, both of which are self-imposed scarcities and can be overcome through shared appropriate goals and the inclusion of young leaders with new ideas.

The remainder of this book builds on the conceptual frameworks developed by Diop, Mazamba, Nkrumah and Asante, to name a few, as they pertain to the four links in the conceptual chain tying Africans down. The objective is to accelerate the process of creating an alternative shared reality that will go beyond putting Africa at the centre of our way of viewing the world, to equip the reader with the conceptual tools to practise Afrocentricity as they cope with the challenges of modern society.

4

Thinking differently about African institutions

In MANY WAYS, Africans are conceptually at the same cul-de-sac that forced Europeans to take an alternative path towards the Enlightenment in the early 1600s. As philosopher Charles Griswold suggests, 'The architects of the modern Enlightenment inferred that what has been made can be unmade, if only we gather the necessary courage. And they also suggested that once the chains are smashed there is no need to leave the cave, for the prison can be transformed into home.'[1] The call to reimagine Africa by overhauling the conception of what is possible, and by critically examining all that we hold dear as core beliefs, is long overdue.

Change is needed in the intra-African conceptual landscape that can jolt the continent from the status quo. It is no longer enough for Africans to look to their political leaders for revolutionary or even evolutionary attempts to frame Africa's essential problems or to supply the dynamic responses they require. African leaders need to be supported, prodded and directed by active citizens to achieve the goal of social reconstruction. To put the challenges in context, the average age of African leaders is 60. 'The average age of the ten oldest African leaders is 78.5 years, compared to 52 years for the world's ten most-developed economies. Compared to other continents, Africa has a very small proportion of younger leaders between the ages of 35 and 55. Paradoxically, the continent has the youngest population in the world, with a median age of 19.5 years according to the UN.'[2] This young population has to step up and assume a greater role in creating the societies they desire.

This chapter makes the argument for culturally reinforced moral, ethical and values-based institutional design as one of the keys to Africa's future. It seeks to tease out the essential questions Africans need to ask of themselves and their leadership. It seeks to fathom what type of institutions are required to create the necessary political stability as the foundation for long-term, sustainable economic growth.

The following key questions serve as guideposts for our discussion:

- What moral, ethical, ideological and philosophical pillars would shape modern Pan African institutions?
- How can Africans allow local cultures to breathe life and meaning into Pan African institutions?
- How do we strike a balance between a process of top-down rule construction and a bottom-up individual citizen's contribution and buy-in?
- How can African states balance the economic benefits of intra-African collaboration with the political compromises required to make coordination binding?

It is impossible, in the limited space available here, to provide comprehensive answers to any of these questions. At best, we can hope only to refine the questions and hint at where answers might be found. Just as the Enlightenment period was the beneficiary of a snowball effect, in which scholars built on the work of their predecessors, so will Africa's renaissance be the work of many minds.

Let us begin by distinguishing between different types of institutions. Institutions are key to how societies choose to both regulate the competition for goods and services and manage the social cooperation between citizens. To understand how society can be made to change for the better through the design of institutions, we must distinguish between *informal institutions* such as traditional customs or behaviour patterns, *formal institutions* such as a constitution or a central bank, and *meta-institutions*, which are broad enough to encompass other (both formal or informal) institutions such as the government or the family.[3]

The direction of inquiry we take is deliberately bottom-up. We analyse informal institutions first, searching them for signs of African conceptions of morality, ethics and norms. We then look at how these informal institutions are reflected in the construction of formal institutions and how their interactions affect meta-institutions. We should not be surprised to find that local culture is needed to reinforce laws; if this is not the case, families and governments will suffer multiple vulnerabilities as society implodes. Technically speaking, formal institutions that do not sufficiently reflect the moral and ethical norms of African informal institutions will have trouble sustaining themselves. To the extent that the interaction between informal institutions and formal institutions make the latter vulnerable, meta-institutions have very little chance of functioning optimally.

In the post-colonial period, local African cultures have been greatly eroded to make space for Anglo-Saxon assimilation, resulting in the removal of many crucial checks and balances. Gone or reduced are the natural accountability and built-in tolerance of pre-colonial chiefdoms and kingdoms across the continent. Gone is the right, using legitimised customs developed over thousands of years, to peacefully depose illegitimate or ineffective leadership. Gone or reduced are the reliance on trusted spiritual and political advisors, who served to temper the centralisation of power. Gone is the economic protection of the hereditary caste system. In came money and the need to be measured by a new yardstick of productivity. In came structural adjustment programmes run by left-brain-oriented bureaucrats. In came manipulated elections dominated by relatively new political parties and illegitimate governments disconnected from their constituencies. In came the material scarcity introduced by modern capitalism. In came the social contingencies that arose from being classified by skin colour and being on the receiving end of the crude false-isms that justified socio-economic categorisation.

These developments have excluded the vast majority of Africans from the fruits of modernisation that only a minority enjoy. A new way of thinking has to focus on making institutions capable of powering inclusive growth. Let's review some of the key questions that need to be answered.

Moral, ethical, ideological and philosophical pillars

Anthropologists, ethnographers and sociologists have argued for many years about the universality of cultural traits. Some scholars, such as anthropologist George Murdock, have made the argument that all societies possess certain common practices and beliefs. Indeed, in the mid-1930s Murdock made a list of those he found most universal, as part of a cross-cultural survey that became a key tool for those seeking to prove the cultural-universality thesis to be correct.[4] This list of shared cultural beliefs relate to athletics, sports, music, funeral ceremonies, sexual restrictions, cooking and medicine. Supporters of this school of thought tend to create a universal spectrum of social development along which different cultures can be measured, concluding that some cultures exhibit a superior state of development to others.

Cultural relativists, on the other hand, argue that culture has developed historically through the interactions of groups of people. These interactions have led to the sharing or diffusion of ideas, which makes it difficult to know where one group's culture starts and another stops. Therefore, cultural relativism holds that no one culture can be ranked ahead of another. The position of cultural relativism is most associated with the anthropologist Franz Boas, an early proponent of the idea that each culture should be judged according to its own standards.[5]

African philosopher Kwasi Wiredu compares these two approaches in *Cultural Universals and Particulars*. He makes the interesting observation that many modern Westerners tend to recoil from the purist version of the idea of cultural universality, opting instead to insist on the particularities of certain cultures.[6] Wiredu posits that, when objectively studied, the basis of humanity's common biology is not incompatible with our cultural particularities.

I will not attempt a complete reconstruction of African cultural particularism, nor will I continue to emphasise the fact that African cultures have had a major impact on other cultures around the world. I wholeheartedly acknowledge that African cultures have themselves been greatly impacted by cultures outside the continent. I believe, like Wiredu, that there are universal elements of culture as well as local particularities. This chapter is informed by Wiredu's view that while human beings around the world share a great deal from a genetic point of view, they have in the past shared cultural traits and ethical philosophies through diffusion. However, a space for cultural particularities needs to be carved out to aid our deeper understanding of human cultures.

I focus on those cultural particularities that are most obviously common across the African continent (which I call simply Pan African particularities). I have identified six such Pan African particularities:

1. collective leadership as a preferred form of accountability
2. the situational attribution of actions
3. the centrality of personhood or Ubuntu
4. a strong belief in servant leadership
5. a holistic conception of reality
6. a focus on relative rather than absolute gains

To begin to understand the moral and ethical foundations of pre-colonial African society, we must go back to the basis of the monarchical systems that Africans chose as a form of government all over the continent and study how these monarchical systems shaped African institutions until the advent of colonialism. In *Savage Constructions: The Myth of African Savagery*, Wendy Hamblet summarises the research of Cheikh Anta Diop by stating, 'The greater number of African societies, from early human time until the colonial era, prospered in relative peace and stability, without a break in their stable continuity, for most of those thousands of years … African political regimes, despite their mostly monarchical form, were exceedingly democratic in both structure and practical functioning. That is to say, early African peoples tended to be gathered into kingdoms, but the kings were not chosen according to family pedigree, but according to record as wise and beneficent leaders. The monarchies could not become tyrannous because of deeply ingrained practices of shared leadership; most of the important decisions the King faced required the agreement of a council of elders, which drew from and represented all the various villages of the territory and the many households of the kingship group.'[7] This brings us to the first Pan African cultural particularity – the widely practised collective leadership style.

In an interview conducted in 1993 President Nelson Mandela captured the essence of collective leadership by describing his own leadership within the African National Congress (ANC) collective in the following way: 'It was that leadership [the ANC collective leadership group] that decided to focus on a particular individual, not because he had qualities that placed him head and shoulders above others, but somebody who was part of a team, and who would never be able to play any important role if he had acted independently from that team. If you look at the matter like that then whatever was said by an individual [of] our organisation … must be looked at from the point of view that it was part of the efforts of a remarkable team of men and women that have led our organisation during the most difficult years of our struggle.'[8] President Nelson Mandela grew up at the tail end of a thriving, well-functioning Xhosa chieftaincy. Brought up as a member of Thembu royalty, he was groomed to lead within the ambit of traditional customary institutions that re-tained many years' worth of ancient African wisdom. It should have come as no surprise that men like him, Oliver Tambo and Chief Albert Luthuli endowed the ANC with this culture. This helps explain why the ANC, which has been around for over a century, is one of the oldest formal indigenous organisations in Africa.

Geneticists have pointed out that Africa has the greatest genetic diversity in the world. A top-down individually based leadership model wouldn't last very long in such an environment. It must have been necessary for Africans to adopt a leadership style that balanced the complex demands of differently oriented constituencies. Another clear reason for collective rather than individual leadership is to provide support for a leader within a societal context that is constantly assessing situational, rather than dispositional, explanations for actions. Such assessments would have proved too complex and laborious for one person to perform. This distinction between causal explanations for an individual's mistakes and moral explanations for them represents a sharp difference between the Western liberal tradition of leadership and Africa's collective leadership tradition.

The theologian Chibueze Udeani makes the following observations on the topic of moral versus causal attributions: 'Communal life in African communities has, at its root, the concept of equilibrium. All the different beings that exist in reality require harmony which the community enables. One always finds within the African world polarities and relational principles which should sustain or enable equilibrium … Within the African worldview, the quality of human action defines itself according to the two possible directions of inter-action. African traditional societies do not know or recognise objects or ideas as "good" and "evil".'[9] Udeani raises a fundamental point of difference between African and Western culture, namely, how each perceives intentionality, and how one assigns a moral character to the intentions of others. From a Western point of view, events that make up the course of one's mental life are given a discrete characteristic feature of being about something. The relation between two or three discrete characteristics creates a representation of something other than its original discrete characteristics. It is within this framework that Westerners form the foundations of intentionality.[10] In order to understand the word 'intentionality' as it is commonly used in the West, we have to delve into attribution theory.

Attribution theory is an attempt to understand why and how people explain events occurring in their lives as they do. In simple terms, it is what we all do every day when we judge the actions of others. We start by assessing whether what they did (both good and bad) should be assigned to their skill or lack thereof, or whether external factors are at play. We do the same when we assess the morality of people's actions. Attribution theory concerns itself with the crucial question of what cause and effect inferences people make about their behaviour and that of others. Fritz Heider, who developed the theory, identified two types of attributions, based on people's perceptions: *dispositional attribution*, which attributes behaviour to someone's personality, intelligence, temperament and morality; and *situational attribution*, which usually looks externally towards environmental, societal and spiritual explanations for someone's behaviour.[11] Heider clearly felt that people act on the basis of their beliefs, and therefore encouraged scholars to take beliefs into account when studying human actions. Relative to Europeans, Africans are on another spectrum when it comes to their reliance on situational factors, which they use to explain why certain events are occurring.

Thus, the second Pan African particularism is the fact that Africans tend to favour situational explanations for actions they deem both positive and negative. This is based on Africans' lack of willingness to attach negative or positive intentions to other people, unless those intentions cannot be explained by way of external influences. The act of exchanging perspectives on situational factors, to understand and learn from the way they impact actions, is part of the ritual of social interaction within African society. We have to understand someone's lived reality in order to accurately pass judgement on what contributed to their actions. These social rituals are just as demanding for interpersonal relationships, as it makes them rewarding. What would in the West be considered a tolerance for excuses in order to explain lack of performance is in Africa regarded as one of the defining characteristics of humanism, peoplehood or Ubuntu.

As we will see, providing situational explanations for things we consider part of our in-group is a universal human trait. Ask most children to explain the bad behaviour of their friends in class and they will look for external narratives. Ask them to explain why the same friend does well at school and they will point to an innate dispositional attribute such as intelligence, physical appearance or diligence as the answer. This is true for all age groups. Africans seem to be distinct from Anglo-Saxons in stretching this same tendency to explain the actions of strangers whom they have no reason to consider as part of their in-group.

This brings us to the third Pan African particularism, the notion of people-centricity. Polycarp Ikuenobe, a philosopher at Kent State University, places personhood as a concept within a moral context: 'Moral personhood involves responsibilities that the community prescribes for individuals in order to help them to lead meaningful lives and achieve their potential, self-realisation, or identity as a moral person. This moral view of personhood is distinguished from the descriptive or metaphysical sense of person. The moral view of a person, which is based on communal principles, indicates a complex set of relationships among people. The relationship between individuals and the community in African cultures seems to indicate that the notion of a person has a normative import.'[12] Indeed, it is not possible to understand African morality without unpacking the intertwined relationship between the person and the community. The duty placed on individual members of the community, both to 'show up' for each other in times of need and to cooperate with each other to achieve common objectives, is fundamental to who Africans are.

The famous phrase that 'a person is a person because of other people' is a universal African belief.[13] This core ethic of valuing people, the requirement to take everyone at face value, the compulsion to ask what your community needs of you before you act, has tremendous impact on how Africans choose to be led. It is perhaps because of such a delicate balance between individuals and the community that Africans have tended to rely heavily on the servant-leadership style to unlock difficult trade-offs and help communities make crucial decisions.

Servant leadership is the fourth Pan African cultural particularity. It is in contrast to the 'great man theory', a 19th-century European idea that championed the view that history can be understood or explained by unpacking the impact of 'great men', a dispositional explanation of history that has very little place on the African continent. To be sure, courageous leaders with strong diplomatic and military skills have been sought after and revered throughout history by Africans. Yet, in Africa, servant leadership was generally the more popular way for pharaohs, chiefs, queens and kings to lead. This approach reflects what was needed at the time – a form of extreme diplomatic dexterity precisely to enable leaders to walk the tightrope African communities have historically expected their leaders to tread.

The more charismatic the leader, the more allies this leader can garner. By constantly factoring in the views of these allies, and by a demonstrated empathy towards his or her people's plight, community constraints on a leader are ultimately loosened. Matsobane Manala expands on this understanding: 'In servant leadership, the vision is to see followers encouraged and empowered to take up the responsibilities that, in other leadership models, are the reserve of the leader … Through the trusting attitude of the servant leader towards the followers, the leader-member relationship, leader effectiveness and productivity are positively influenced.'[14]

The first four Pan African particularities explored above are greatly supported and/or facilitated by a fifth particularity – a holistic conception of reality. The African perception of reality is known to be a holistic one, in the sense that it combines both sensible (material) beings and non-sensible (immaterial) beings as elements of a single worldview. The material and immaterial have reciprocal influences on one another. An example of this is the explosion in the numbers of African Christians, which has mirrored the growth in the Pentecostal or so-called charismatic church movement. The success of these churches, led by ministers who are welcoming of Africans who want to worship God and honour their ancestors, is a sign of the yearning for a restoration of spiritual balance that is felt by young people in particular. This phenomenon may help to explain why, within a few decades, Africa will have more Christians than any other continent.

At its best, holism represents the belief that facilitates African peoples' face-value approach to all humans. It is the thing that made Steve Biko hope that Africans could one day bestow upon the world a more human face. It is what makes Africans more humane towards their neighbours than other cultures could conceive necessary. Holism moralises about the inhumanity of letting others suffer. From this view of human spiritual equality comes the general preference for economic parity within and between African communities.

This leads us to the sixth and final Pan African particularism – the bias towards a stronger concern for relative versus absolute gains. Historically, this difference is expressed primarily as an intertribal dynamic. Politicial scientist Gwyneth McClendon has analysed data gathered by Afrobarometer, which collated statistics from 18 sub-Saharan African countries. Her analysis shows that, when asked to prioritise policies, Africans are greatly influenced by the relative position of their ethnic group. Africans feel happiest when they are in the same relative position to members of their ethnic group than when they are above them.[15]

Taken in totality, the six Pan African particularities allow us to construct some generalisations about the factors that most influence informal institutions on the African continent. The importance of these informal institutions cannot be overemphasised. Economist

Svetozar Pejovich describes their value to society: 'Informal rules are often called the old ethos, the hand of the past or the carriers of history. They embody the community's prevailing perceptions about the world, the accumulated wisdom of the past, and a current set of values. Thus, informal institutions are the part of a community's heritage that we call culture.'[16]

African culture is dominated by its holistic conception of the universe. The centrality it places on the value of people, the way they attribute achievements or actions of those people to situational factors, and the social complexity generated by such a worldview demands a collective leadership style. From this collective leadership, whomever is picked as the chief, queen, king or president is expected to be a servant leader who represents the interests of the tribe or community towards the goal of keeping pace with other tribes' relative wealth. African politics is overwhelmingly local when compared to politics in the West. Conceptions of nationality and national interests will be hard pressed to supersede those of locality. This demands a distinctly different type of institutional architecture from the nation-state-centric model that dominates the African continent today.

How do local cultures breathe life and meaning into African institutions?

Scholars have developed two competing theories to explain how different societies function within an institutional framework. There are those who argue that institutions represent hard-and-fast rules that are chosen over time or through political contestation. The second school of thought is that societies, through a process of trial and error, produce a temporary social balance or equilibrium.[17] My research indicates that social balance or equilibrium is essential. An organic process of social construction through trial and error is inherently more sustainable.

The disservice done to Africa by colonialism was to dislodge or undermine indigenous culture and introduce foreign formal institutions (political parties, parliaments and judiciaries, to name a few) that had no cultural reference points within the country in question. The informal institutions (traditional authority structures, community decision-making bodies and traditional dispute-resolution mechanisms, to name a few) went underground and were prevented from legitimately taking their place alongside Africa's constitutions and laws. The incentive to comply with new foreign rules was removed. Society's equilibrium was undermined. The combination of these two circumstances has created a dead space between African culture, on the one hand, and formal institutions, on the other. This dead space has facilitated a subversive culture of rule-flouting.

This subversive culture has had its most obvious expression in the form of Africa's well-publicised corruption problems. As Pejovich writes: 'If changes in formal rules are in harmony with the prevailing informal rules, the interaction of their incentives will tend to reduce transaction costs in the community (that is, the cost of making an exchange and the cost of maintaining and protecting the institutional structure) and clear up resources to produce wealth. When new formal rules conflict with the prevailing informal rules, the interaction of the incentives will tend to raise transaction costs and reduce the production of wealth in the community.'[18] The cost of enforcing contracts in many African countries is very high because the expectations are that one or the other party, but more often a third party in the form of a government bureaucrat, will have to be financially 'induced' or incentivised to observe the terms of the contract. This has clearly been the case on the African continent, resulting in extraordinarily high transaction costs, high inequality and extremely low productivity in most countries.

The key decision that African leaders must make revolves around closing this dead space, elevating the core elements of their informal institutions (preferably the six Pan African cultural particularities discussed above) and formalising the moral, ethical and philosophical belief structures encoded in their culture by incorporating these elements into formal institutions. In doing so, African leaders will face the challenges of inertia, vested interests and the risk of opening old tribal wounds in national conversations.

It is necessary to promote conversations about which elements of their informal institutions deserve formal recognition. A good rule of thumb is for any African at the helm of a process of design (or redesign) of new or existing institutions to start with the assumption that there are informal institutions or cultural elements that can complement or impede the process that he or she is embarking on. By ceding seniority to the core values reflected in these informal institutions, and seeking to learn from them, this new institutional architect will have the pleasant prospect of being able to rely on thousands of years of accumulated wisdom.

What must drive this process is a singular belief in the abilities of ordinary African citizens to express themselves clearly and, ultimately, to reach a carefully constructed organic consensus on the core cultural elements that need to make their way into the formal institutional infrastructure. In 2016, Africa boasted a population of 1.2 billion people, who are generally overlooked in the debates about their future. Given the sheer numbers of people involved, and the ethnic nuances that permeate the continent, redesigning the architecture of Africa's formal institutions will be a complicated and demanding task. The key to seeing this task through is to focus on the opportunity to use historical African wisdom to make current African institutions antifragile.

The word 'antifragile' comes from the title of a book by Nassim Nicholas Taleb, author of *The Black Swan*. In *Antifragile*, Taleb draws on historical precedent: 'If one looks at history as a complex system similar to nature, then, like nature, it won't let a single empire dominate the planet forever – even if every superpower from the Babylonians to the Egyptians to the Persians to the Romans to modern America has believed in the permanence of its domination and managed to produce historians to theorise to that effect. Systems subjected to randomness – and unpredictability – build a mechanism beyond the robust to opportunistically reinvent themselves each generation with a continuous change of population and species.'[19] Given the universally acknowledged dysfunctionality of most of Africa's institutions, there is thus an opportunity to reinvent the African institutional ecosystem.

Unlike their recently engineered formal counterparts, African informal institutions are antifragile. Initiation through circumcision, for example, has survived among many African tribes around the African continent and has continued, despite the loss of political independence, to turn African boys into men. Other examples of informal institutions that have remained antifragile include dowry, traditional wedding ceremonies and funeral ceremonies. These have survived thousands of years of migration, invasion and colonialism. They travel in African fables, they are written on the walls of ancient structures, and they are sources of inspiration for art. This wealth of wisdom is there to be discovered by curious Africans the continent over. It is there to be harnessed and turned into new popular wisdom by means unimaginable to ancient philosophers. Through the use of cellphones, tablets and PCs, older Africans can share wisdom with young Africans eager for knowledge. A more deliberate approach to developing platforms to distribute this wisdom is central to the goal of bridging the gap between formal and informal institutions. African countries need to devote large portions of their national budgets towards capturing the imagination of their youth through the ideas, thoughts and creativity of their ancestors.

This circulation of the wisdom of the moral, ethical, spiritual and philosophical underpinnings of informal African institutions between older and younger Africans through modern mediums of telecommunication is the best ventilation mechanism possible to allow newly forming formal institutions to be positively impacted by African culture. This casual, informal process should be reinforced by a more formal adoption of historical African moral and ethical philosophies as the first point of teaching in school curricula. The future African child must be allowed to learn his or her history and cultural particularities first, then engage with those of the rest of the world, instead of the reverse order that seems to dominate many curricula around the continent today.

Balancing top-down rule and bottom-up citizens' contribution and buy-in

South African intellectual Joel Netshitenzhe seems to grasp the complexity involved in accommodating the voice of African people in policy-making and institutional design. In a conference paper, he says, 'Who are these "people"! They are the peasants, workers, entrepreneurs, intellectuals, artists, traditional healers, professionals, religious leaders and others. They are made up of various nationalities within and across boundaries. In my opinion, there is no abstract African, imbued with a mythical virtue called "Ubuntu". We are made up of classes and strata, nationalities, religious affiliations that have absorbed virtually everything from the globe, races, gender and age and other differences.'[19]

In the face of these contradictions, how do Africans talk intelligently about themselves as a people? At first glance, the answer is that they can't. The sheer diversity of people, living in varied topographies with vastly different climates, is bound to produce divergent characteristics and desired ways of life. In a recent study of genetic diversity in Africa, Michael C Campbell and Sarah A Tishkoff observe that there are more than 2000 ethno-linguistic groups on the continent.[20]

On top of these patterns of 'organic internal' diversity, migration has had a major impact on the genetic variation of Africans. For example, the migration of agricultural Bantu-speakers from West Africa throughout sub-Saharan Africa over the past 4000 years, and their subsequent admixture with indigenous populations, has had a major impact on patterns of variation in modern African populations. Nonetheless, there are some amazing consistencies, in the form of language, belief systems, farming practices and community organisation, across much of sub-Saharan Africa that point to shared cultural bonds.

Bantu-speaking communities live south of a line stretching from Nigeria in the west across the Central African Republic (CAR), the DRC, Uganda and Kenya to southern Somalia in the east. Most language communities between that line and the southern tip of Africa are Bantu. The exceptions are the small and sadly fast-dwindling pockets of Khoi and San in the south and the larger Cushitic-speaking communities in the northeast. Along the northern margins of the Bantu area are many communities speaking Nilo-Saharan languages and Adamawa-Ubangian (Niger-Congo but non-Bantu) languages.

As important as it is to celebrate African ethnic diversity, we need to recognise the ties that bind. In *Population in the Human Sciences*, an interdisciplinary examination of world population trends, the following statistics are laid out: 'The Bantu branch of the Niger-Kordofanian family includes some 500 languages spoken by more than 400 million people throughout sub-Saharan Africa.'[21] In all, Bantu-speaking communities are indigenous to 27 African countries. This makes up over 400 million of Africa's 1.2-billion population. There are close to 180 million Nigerians, most of whom are not considered Bantu. Despite Nigerians' significant diversity, they have managed, however uneasily, to live together for the last 50 years. There are close to over 200 million Nubians (some of whose ancestors are also Bantu) living in the Sudan, Ethiopia and Egypt, and they share more similarities in culture, language and belief systems than is generally acknowledged. These three large blocks of Africans – Bantu, Nigerians and Nubians – represent by far the majority of the continent's population, up to 65 percent, or 780 million people. This compares favourably with some of the large ethnic blocks in Europe. By comparison, eight groups account for about 65 per cent (465 million people) of the European population:

- Russians (±95 million residing in Europe)
- Germans (±82 million)
- French (±60 million)
- British (±60 million)
- Italians (±55 million)
- Spanish (±50 million)
- Ukrainians (38–55 million)
- Poles (±38 million)

Ethnic diversity has not stopped Europeans from focusing on what they have in common. As varied as these nations' histories are, their concept of being part of a broader European heritage, and the concomitant need to submit themselves to the rules emanating from the institutional infrastructure of the European Union (EU), has come a long way over the last 50 years.

In *The Nordic Secret*, which examines the economic and social transformation of Denmark, Norway and Sweden since the late 19th century, authors Lene Andersen and Tomas Björkman successfully demystify the aggregation of European socio-economic interests: 'What we need to understand is the radically different way that Europeans felt towards each other and society 300 years ago. First of all, Christianity was a culture and a set of norms that one internalised, one way or another. It was not a personal faith the way that Christian faith is a conscious and personal belief today where our culture is individualistic and there are several alternatives. The structures of society, Christianity and the church were so intertwined that everybody was embedded in the same mode of being.'[22] The powerful takeaway from this is that the sharing of informal institutions that bind norms, values and culture should precede the creation of formal pan-continental (whether European or African) institutions. By focusing on the shared values, moral frameworks and philosophical guideposts contained in the Bible, formal institutions could be put in place that aggregated European interests. Of course, global events such as the two world wars helped to define Europe. These experiences of war led to the development of formal institutions (League of Nations, UN, NATO and the Bretton Woods system) that found traction because the rooted informal institutions had created fertile ground.

Africans have to overcome the complexities tearing them apart in order to focus on the cultural particularities that can bind them. They have to popularise the excavated historical documents that show, without a shadow of a doubt, that the Nubians, Nigerians and Bantu have a rich shared historical and cultural heritage. This heritage needs to be mined, philosophised and entrenched in learning systems from the Cape to Cairo. This process could spread quickly by means of modern technology, thereby becoming more widely distributed than European efforts of 300 years ago.

Complexity in any organisational structural design is introduced by considering too many variables. Fifty-five variables (the number of African countries) are a lot to manage before considering legitimate ethnic, religious and linguistic claims for further fragmentation. Given that the Berlin Conference generated the current realities of socio-political and economic fragmentation on the African continent, African people must reconstitute the benefits of scale and abundance and protect themselves from the complexity of fragmentation. Such reconstitution cannot be carried out without the benefit of institutions.

It is time for Africans to concede publicly that the borders and nationalities they have become accustomed to were arbitrarily conceived. What is much more meaningful are the local communities to which African people have historical, emotional and psychological ties. A Pan African continent centred less on the nation-state than on the local community can thrive by focusing on diffusing authority to local government. For this to happen, local governments have to be reimagined, such that a service-oriented, transparent and responsive collective leadership, directly elected outside of political party lists, can emerge as a more sustainable long-term model. This cultural and institutional change should be the precursor to power being transferred to local governments at the expense of national governments.

We have seen that there are six cultural pillars (what I have called Pan African particularities) that Africans can use as guideposts towards reconstructing their societies: collective leadership as a preferred form of accountability, the situational attribution of actions, the centrality of personhood or Ubuntu, a strong belief in servant leadership, a holistic conception of reality, and a focus on relative rather than absolute gains. By ceasing to be constrained by arbitrary borders, Africans can enjoy the significant economic benefits of scale while continuing to enjoy the protection and services of their local governments. To have a sound footing, African leaders need to find a balance between being led by the voice of their voting public and leading their people through what will no doubt be decades of dynamic, disruptive change.

Balancing the economic benefits of intra-African collaboration with political compromises

Africans will not need to start from scratch in their constitution of a governing body that can run the United States of Africa. Thanks to the foresight of what may one day be considered Africa's founding fathers, an organisation is available to pick up this Pan Africanist mantle. The Union of African States was founded in 1961, through the signature of a charter by Ghana, Guinea and Mali. These countries were later joined by Ethiopia, Liberia, Tunisia, Egypt, Sudan and Libya. The Union's aims, as expressed in its charter, were to strengthen ties between member states, pool their resources to consolidate independence, safeguard territorial integrity and harmonise domestic and foreign policy.

Today's African Union (AU) has its origins in the inspiration provided by Kwame Nkrumah of Ghana and Emperor Haile Selassie of Ethiopia. The AU's predecessor, the Organization of African Unity (OAU), was formally established in May 1963. Independence leaders such as Julius Nyerere, Sékou Touré and Kenneth Kaunda joined prominent intellectuals in the cause of advancing African unity. The OAU's early years brought remarkable success as a peacekeeping and conflict-resolution mechanism, mediating conflicts between Morocco and Algeria (1964–1965), and between Somalia and its neighbours (1965–1967). It also halted civil wars in Nigeria (1968–1970) and Chad (1966–1990).[23]

Almost from the outset, the OAU faced problems of disunity and infighting. This disunity can be simplified by appreciating the two cliques that formed around ideological differences: the so-called Casablanca group, which had a staunch anti-imperial posture, and the Monrovia-Brazzaville group, which was anti-socialist and anti-communist in its orientation. The OAU would eventually grow to a 51-country membership, which proved an unwieldy structure for decision-making. The ethnic identity of these members served as a lightning rod that would further weaken the OAU, with the so-called Arab states (Egypt, Libya, Tunisia, Algeria and Morocco) viewing themselves as distinct from the so-called black states.

Over time, the Arab states accepted and formed a new intersubjective reality called the Maghreb, which served to further divide and weaken Africa. Though the OAU talked about economic integration, this never went beyond aligning tariff regimes and making intercontinental visa applications easier. The gradual institutional decay of the OAU was punctuated by complete dysfunctionality in the 1980s as many African states, facing economic crises, turned against their commitment to a Pan African agenda, opting for structural adjustment packages administered by the International Monetary Fund and donor loans from the World Bank.

The AU was established in 2001 to distance itself from its predecessor. Its establishment would not have been possible without the enormous financial and political support of Libyan president Muammar al-Gaddafi. The organisation has developed into a credible and increasingly consistently positive force at the heart of the African integration agenda. Despite an uneven record in peace-keeping and institutional development, the AU has pushed forward with a more inclusive agenda. For example, it established the African Union Youth Programme, which in 2015 started a Youth Volunteer Training Programme. Its voluntary peer-review mechanism is another positive move towards accountable Pan African leadership. In the field of formal institutional development, the set of political and economic institutions (the Pan African Parliament, the continued growth of the African Development Bank and the recent signing of a Pan African Free Trade Zone) supported by the AU have set the platform for accelerated integration and a drastic improvement in the overall Pan African political economy. Laudable as these efforts are, the significant majority of Africans have very little idea about the mandate of the AU, and what they as citizens can do to help achieve its goals. It serves as a meta-institution hampered at the national level by dysfunctional formal institutions, which are also hampered by their lack of alignment to informal institutions across the continent.

The Nobel Prize-winning economist Douglass North reminds us of five propositions that define the essential characteristics of institutional change:

1. The continuous interaction of institutions and organisations in the economic setting of scarcity and hence competition is the key to institutional change.
2. Competition forces organisations to continually invest in skills and knowledge to survive. The kinds of skills and knowledge individuals and their organisations acquire will shape evolving perceptions about opportunities and hence choices that will incrementally alter institutions.
3. The institutional framework dictates the kinds of skills and knowledge perceived to have the maximum pay-off.
4. Perceptions are derived from the mental constructs of the players.
5. The economies of scope, complementariness and network externalities of an institutional matrix make institutional change overwhelmingly incremental and path dependent.[24]

We can clearly see that an organisation such as the AU fails dismally when judged against these five points. First, for the last 55 years the AU and the OAU have served as the sole bodies furthering Pan Africanist integration. Second, based on the lack of competition or support by an independent Pan African business body or a Pan African traditional council, the AU and the OAU have been the playgrounds of African ministers and presidents. This elite, ageing constituency has been grossly out of touch with ordinary Africans and the informal institutions that they are part of. Third, the kinds of skills necessary to win positions in the AU are those associated with lobbying, which leaves subsequent leaders indebted to their supporters and thus captured by their agendas. These leaders (with the notable exceptions of presidents Julius Nyerere, Thomas Sankara, Patrice Lumumba, Robert Mugabe, Samora Machel and Paul Kagame) have fallen into the conceptual trap of accepting orthodoxies about how society should be organised, without attempting to create new socio-economic systems more in tune with their countries' informal institutions.

Young Africans have so far failed to build on the original ideas of great men such as Haile Selassie, Kwame Nkrumah and Jomo Kenyatta, to name a few. Young leaders have failed to understand what is at stake if they let institutions such as the AU decay. The next generation of leaders cannot afford to perpetuate the status quo. They have everything to gain from the entrenchment of this nascent Pan African institutional system. Subsequent generations have decided to prioritise their own national post-liberation challenges, not realising that the mechanism for unlocking sustainable growth has been handed to them by the AU's founders.

As fragmented as Africa is today, there are signs that point to its economic potential. In 2013, Africa was the world's fastest-growing continent (5.6 per cent growth in Gross Domestic Product, or GDP).[25] The continent achieved an average real annual GDP growth of 5.4 per cent between 2000 and 2010. Its economy is forecast to grow at 6 per cent between 2018 and 2023.

Yet only 10–12 per cent of total African trade is intra-African. Africa ships 80 per cent of its primary commodities overseas, mainly to the EU, China and the US. According to the World Bank, in Africa a truck servicing supermarkets across a border may need to carry up to 1 600 documents based on permits and other licence requirements.[26] This economically crippling legal regime must be taken apart.

The economic stakes are enormous. Africa has 38 per cent of the world's manganese, 60 per cent of its cobalt, 56 per cent of its diamonds and 38 per cent of its chromite, not to mention the solar and hydroelectic potential to power both the African continent and potential customers to the north. Many of the continent's mineral-rich countries, such as the DRC, have the worst infrastructure. Wealthy countries such as Botswana, South Africa and Mauritius need places to invest. What is currently unavailable is an institutional regime that would facilitate the flow of money from where it is concentrated to where it is most needed (and where returns would be highest).

It should be anticipated that many will call for a slow and gradual approach to African integration, a response very much at odds with the approach that is needed. African leaders should look to the example of the EU as a warning of the perils of partial integration without a total submission to the dictates of powerful institutions.

It is time for Africa to undertake an institutional revolution predicated on a cultural revolution that re-establishes African norms, values, ethics and virtues, and that can, once and for all, break its economic shackles. This has to be preceded by a new way of thinking about Africa and its place in the world. Africans have to be dogmatic about connecting their cultural past to their future.

5

African social capital's triple threats

AFRICAN SOCIETIES ARE TRANSFORMING at a dizzying pace, driven by local and international trends that require rapid response times. Understanding the importance of African informal political institutions, allows us to more accurately analyse the most pertinent sources of modern dynamism and friction within the African political economy. This will give us a good idea of the threats and opportunities to which African institutions must respond. Understanding how to build economies that reflect the best interests of indigenous people is essential for Africa's long-term stability.

Africa's political economy is threatened by the triple challenges posed by urbanisation, migration and unemployment. These three dynamic and interactive forces create urgency for leaders to ensure that African economies have both the institutional flexibility and political stability necessary for accelerated growth. The leadership of the AU is currently championing Agenda 2063, a strategic framework to eradicate poverty and produce a people-centred culture driven by a fast-growing Pan African economy by the year 2063 (100 years after the establishment of the OAU).[1] Reading this plan, one feels a sense of comfort that many of the future pillars of African economic growth are being put in place. Though institutions are an area of focus, the AU leadership should beware of the perils of attempting Pan African political and economic development without an intense focus on the role that institutions play in distributing economic outcomes more evenly within society. Given how closely relative gains will be monitored by African communities, inclusive growth should be the mantra adopted by African policy-makers.

Historically, many economists have been intellectually captured by the efficient-market hypothesis, according to which all asset prices fully reflect all available information, and have made only passing references to the role that institutions play in securing peace and facilitating economic growth. In reality, history has shown that information asymmetries exist all the time between different market actors, leading to severe mispricing of assets, skills and services. In other words, we as economic actors do not have all the information necessary to help us understand the motives, ethics and intentions of other actors in the economy. Recent history has proven over and over again that nations with superior institutions, which can compensate for the differentiated information available to people within the economy, will outperform those with inferior institutions.

In *Why Nations Fail*, Daron Acemoglu and James Robinson show that it is 'man-made political and economic institutions that underlie economic success (or the lack of it)'.[2] The good news is that many commentators have begun to espouse an increasingly popular consensus about the importance of both institutional strength and political stability in creating conditions for economic growth. Economists Claudia Williamson and Rachel Mathers, for example, describe this linkage: 'Our economic culture variable is constructed by identifying four distinct categories of culture that should constrain behavior related to social and economic interactions and, thus, economic development. These four components are trust, respect, individual self-determination and obedience that serve as rules governing interaction between individuals, including market production and entrepreneurship.'[3] We continue to learn the lesson that rules governing social interactions are made possible by culture. National (or continental) cultures either support or hold back the development of trust, respect, self-determination and obedience. With this ability to hold back or support these most critical social commodities, cultures have a pivotal impact on developmental outcomes.

Williamson and Mathers' four cultural measures are critical to understanding how informal institutions shape society.[4] First, *trust* has a direct impact on development outcomes. Societies develop high transaction costs to compensate for low trust, and those that have successfully created high levels of trust have the benefit of transacting with fellow members of society off a low transaction cost base. Second, *self-determination* measures the level of control individuals have in determining their own actions. This impacts on the ability of individuals to feel that they have autonomy over the selection of choices in their lives. Third, *respect* strongly correlates with the tolerance of others and how individuals feel themselves to be valued. Finally, *obedience* reflects the natural tendency within all societies to observe the constraints that come from customs and rules of thumb passed on by elders. There is a natural tension between obedience and entrepreneurship, which requires actors to think outside the box in order to change how things are done.

When institutions work, they create predictability, which allows individuals or groups to act intentionally, comforted by the understanding that certain norms or values bind their fellow members to react within certain parameters. Anyone who has travelled around the African continent will tell you that the one thing they did not experience was predictability. Whether one is trying to get a passport stamped at the airport, trying to choose the best taxi service, exchanging currency or finding a working bathroom facility, African institutions are visibly challenged by the task of providing predictable, efficient environments for the sale of goods and services. We would gain some comfort if this lack of predictability could be explained away by the fact that the institutions work for locals but don't work for foreigners. The truth is that predictability in Africa (knowing, for example, what is going to happen when using our passports in transit, how to exchange money at a decent rate, or how to find an adequate taxi or working bathroom) is usually created by paying someone to break the rules. This clearly indicates a failure to have the current rules accepted and therefore made enforceable.

The fact that these institutions continue to be tolerated means that they benefit someone. The key question is, who? Immigrants take advantage of the gap between formal and informal institutional rules by using their high intra-community trust base, as well as lower transaction cost base, to outperform indigenous people. Immigrants within pockets of Africa's urban centres have a distinct advantage over locals because they bring with them strong informal institutions that facilitate trust, self-determination, respect and obedience.

Even though these cultural character traits may not be dominant in the sending countries, immigrants often represent an exceptional minority capable of forming networks that mimic or genuinely create these four socio-economic advantages (trust, self-determination, respect and obedience). This allows them to establish fast-growing, cash-flow-generating enterprises that serve as the nerve centres for the employment and patronage of fellow immigrants. From this comparative advantage base, such immigrant networks can often become daunting competitors to local actors.

The colonial legacy of most African states includes immigrant-friendly sets of legislation that can be leveraged through lobbying by immigrants to ensure their retention. Incumbency of tenancy or licence holding, for example, means that if someone has a licence to operate a shop, liquor store, abattoir, mortuary or butchery (historically dominated by immigrants of a higher 'caste' than indigenous Africans in almost all formal and informal settings), then these rights can be passed down from generation to generation. The widening of these rights and their advantages enables immigrants to successfully establish prosperous commercial and political footholds in host countries. Successful immigrants therefore expose the failure of local institutions to provide economic opportunities for local population groups, creating a level of animosity towards foreigners that eventually threatens national stability. Tackling the unintended consequences of this colonial legacy head-on is an essential condition for successful Pan African integration. Africans can do this only by understanding how to harness social capital and make it work towards creating opportunities for indigenous people to thrive.

This chapter is divided into four sections. First, I give a short introduction to social capital theory and how it applies to the problem I have outlined above. This is critical to enable us to build a shared, fact-based hypothesis on how to deal with some of these intractable problems. Then, I attempt to analyse in turn the role that each one of the three challenges (urbanisation, immigration and unemployment) plays in taking advantage of, and in some instances undermining, the generation of sufficient levels of local social capital to build and support the sustainable creation of formal institutions.

Understanding African social capital

Without a thorough understanding of the work of Karl Marx, neither capitalism nor communism can be properly grasped. Today, it has become fashionable to talk about 'social capital', but to grapple with what this concept actually means, one has to go back to the original meaning of capital, which is material wealth available for investment. Marx was the first philosopher to popularise a theory of capital, in his monumental book *Capital* (1867). He developed his theory using the ideas of the liberal economists Adam Smith and David Ricardo. Marx broke capital down into two discrete types of value – use value and exchange value. He argued that any commodity needs to satisfy a basic level of usefulness to society. Importantly, Marx underscored the fact that no commodity can be produced without labour power, so in this way labour is most fundamental to underpinning capital.[5]

This expression of the difference between use value and exchange value, on the one hand, and the acknowledgement and appreciation of the value of labour in the production process, on the other, reflects Marx's keen understanding of social relationships. This dynamic, illuminated by Marx, is the biggest challenge facing African leaders. The blatant exploitation of cheap African labour to produce products with both high use value and high international exchange value has been systemic throughout the African continent. Few of these products are value-added before they leave the African continent; thus, they are extracted without the significant participation of indigenous African people. This compels both the electorate and African leaders to question the legitimacy and relevance of market forces on the African continent. As a result, capitalism as a system of organising African economies has not been accepted widely by ordinary people.

After Marx came various forms of neo-capital theories, which contested the principle of which class of economic actors is able to capture surplus value, and how this surplus value is to be used to invest in higher returns that would ultimately result in improved standards of living for citizens. Surplus value is a translation of the German word *Mehrwert*, which simply means 'value added' (sales revenue less the cost of materials used).[6] Marx was concerned with the ruthless pursuit of operating profit created on the backs of labourers, and his theory foretold how this would lead to a pursuit of capital for its own sake without consideration of the individual commodities made, bought and sold.[7]

One of the first neo-capitalist theoreticians was Max Weber, who also propounded the idea of the Protestant work ethic. Weber focused his attention on the ability of status to provide a leg up to a different stratum of society. Weber believed in the enduring importance of status groups as a source of identity and privilege. In his view, status groups are seen as competing with class as the bases of solidarity and collective action. Both Weber and Marx agreed that, over time, markets tend to erode the importance of status groups in society.[8]

Africa has been an unwitting experimental ground for Weber's theory. In many African countries, some immigrants use their status as 'whites', or some other ethnic group regarded as superior to the local ethnic groups, to create an alternative basis for identity and class formation. Even before formal colonialism began, Africans began the practice of delineating between *umutu* (person) and *umlungu* (white), which over time took on the meaning that these 'white' individuals were revered above an ordinary person. This has literally coloured class formation in Africa in ways that are discriminatory to locals. This is largely because of social contingencies and stereotypes that formed over time to typecast what roles indigenous people could play in the economy, relative to the privileged roles that were mostly reserved for foreign elites. The voracity of stereotyping that came with these status groups has ensured that, in many African countries, Marx and Weber's shared prediction that capitalist markets will tend to erode status groups has been proven false. Nonetheless, Weber laid the foundations upon which fellow theoreticians came to develop theories such as human capital (coined by Theodore Schultz), cultural capital (developed by Pierre Bourdieu) and social capital (first espoused by Alexis de Tocqueville).[9]

According to a major survey of social capital theory, 'capital represents two related but distinct elements. On the one hand, it is part of the surplus value generated by capitalists (and their misers, presumably the traders and sellers). On the other hand, it represents an investment (in the production and circulation of commodities) for capitalists, with expected returns in the marketplace ... It is the dominant class that makes the investment and captures the surplus value. Thus, it is a theory based on the exploitative nature of social relations between two classes.'[10]

The key challenge for most African countries is that those in control of the production process (and the assets required to produce) are usually not indigenous Africans. As such, they have alternative social networks within which the criteria for productivity, credit risk and effectiveness are different from those internalised by Africans, who make up the majority of the workforce. This undermines what human capital theory would regard as the logical outcome of a functional meritocracy. In a functional meritocracy, a prospective worker's increased investment in their own high-quality education has a direct link to an increased expected return in the form of higher wages.

The majority of citizens in countries such as South Africa have not had this experience. In South Africa, out of the 31.2 per cent of unemployed young people, 7 per cent have graduated with some sort of higher education qualification.[11] Graduates who are able to keep a job for longer than a year are 90 per cent more likely to avoid unemployment.[12] So, the most important determinant of future success is the social network required to secure employment straight from school and the relevant social and hard skills to keep that job for longer than a year. The good news is that tertiary enrolment in Africa is increasing at breakneck speeds. In fact, according to Unesco, annual tertiary enrolment in Africa has doubled from 6 million (a very low base for over a billion people) to 12 million over the last 15 years. The downside of this increased appetite for higher learning and upward mobility is that 12 million young people will be joining the job market every year for the next decade.

African economies are currently struggling to come up with enough economic opportunities to keep up with the growth in the labour force. Instead, what is more common on the African continent is for highly educated indigenous workers and managers either not to be allowed into the workforce or to find a 'glass ceiling' preventing their penetration into the privileged class. The privileged class is usually exclusively occupied by governing-party loyalists and non-indigenous people. These governing-party loyalists and upper-class immigrants possess social capital (within their respective social clusters), in the form of high trust, high respect and high discipline, that is unavailable to the majority of the population. As a testimony to this economic reality, over one-third of all public protests in Africa between 2014 and 2016 focused on salaries, working conditions and unemployment.

This is the critical challenge that policy-makers must address. Growth will not be inclusive without an adjustment to the reality that there are pockets of productivity supported by high-trust networks that create more economic growth for select members of the population while locking others out. Without structural reform, human capital in Africa will not be rewarded for improved skills and additional education.

Current patterns are that Anglo-Saxon immigrants dictate to indigenous Africans the criteria for being hired and retained. The imposition of Eurocentric notions of personal presentation, social networking and productivity will persist and strengthen if there is not a conscious effort to root out this subtle but effective form of discrimination. This has forced urban Africans to erect and take advantage of patronage networks with alternative criteria for job opportunities and commercial success. This issue is most disadvantageous for rural Africans coming to the city looking for economic opportunities. They find themselves caught between patronage networks and ethnic enclaves.

We must ask ourselves why it has been so easy for non-African immigrants to succeed in Africa. As predicted by Pierre Bourdieu, African leaders have made the classic mistake of attributing cultural capital to the emulation of Western culture.[13] Educated as most of them were in the West, many African leaders have internalised the symbols and meanings of colonial power and prestige as their own. They have cloaked themselves in these Western symbols: Western business suits, private European education and expert command of French, English or Portuguese. These symbols signal to their fellow citizens that modernity, development and sophistication can only be derived from the imitation of colonial leaders.

This has resulted in a weakening of the bond between Africans living in rural areas, who have been less exposed to Western symbols of modernity, and those in the cities, who are, as a strategy for prestige-building and wealth-generation, typically tripping over themselves to be more Western than others. It is against this backdrop that, since 1950, Africans have flooded into African cities in search of economic opportunities, generating ever-increasing urbanisation. Having been misled by Western-centric African leaders, modern urbanised Africans find themselves in the difficult situation of trying to regenerate the social capital necessary to create high-trust interactions in order to facilitate low-cost transactions in the cities where they live.

Social capital can be defined as those resources inherent in social relations that facilitate collective action.[14] These resources include trust, norms and networks of association, representing any group that gathers consistently for a common purpose. In urban Africa, trust, norms and social networks of association have not been consciously built in ways that can lead to consistency of transactions between large groups of strangers. The spatial design of most African cities reflects the extractive mindsets of past colonial leaders. Since liberation, African leaders have not thought deeply enough about how to import informal institutions from rural Africa into the urban setting to promote family-centric urban development strategies, governed by community-centric local administrators.

Fortunately, some African leaders have abandoned the idea of modernising existing city centres and have chosen to develop new nodes that have a better balance between communitarian African values and modern architecture. Ghana is building two mega-developments in the form of King City and Appolonia. Kenya is following suit with Tatu City. Nigeria has led the way with the Eko Atlantic development just outside Victoria Island. The most ambitious of these new developments is Egypt's New Cairo development, established in 2000. This is a £30-billion investment designed to house five million people on a 30 000-hectare site. Intentional city planning, design and architecture of these social spaces will prove key to their ability to support high social capital.

These developments are attempts to move away from the typical colonial-model cities that have become congested and overrun by urban slums. Within these old African cities, a survival-of-the-fittest mentality has been the dominant mode of social interaction. This has led to increased crime, high childhood mortality and chronic social anxieties about everything from welfare to safety and security. The durability of social capital within these urban environments has been weak, making it difficult for urban development to replicate the stability of trust, norms and social networks in rural Africa.

Colonial infrastructure was built to maximise an urban-focused extractive economy, reliant on the export of raw unfinished products to manufacturing centres abroad. This is slowly changing as mega-infrastructure projects, increasingly financed by the Chinese, are giving African economies the opportunity to develop capacity to engage in value-added manufacturing. Unfortunately, given Africa's demographics, it is hard to generate sufficient jobs on current manufacturing capacity alone. Individual African countries' economies are simply too small, and thus local businesses cannot export competitively enough to sustain the massive job creation needed.

Social capital, migration and ethnic enclaves

Exploring how migration, urbanisation and unemployment threaten Africa allows us to reimagine a different way of organising economies in Africa to shape a different future.

Africa is not new to voluntary or forced migration. According to the World Bank, the African diaspora amounts to over 170 million people. This consists of close to 40 million people in North America, 113 million in Latin America and just under 14 million in the Caribbean. Europe has absorbed just 3.5 million people from the African continent.[15]

This huge African diaspora is a tremendous source of remittances. As large as the remittances are today, coordinated effort can better channel these resources and reduce the financial costs of receiving them. In addition, the opportunity to shift the focus from subsistence towards investment in micro-enterprises run by the recipients would multiply the amounts received. According to the World Bank, 'In 2012, an estimated 30 million African migrants sent an estimated

$60 billion in remittances to support more than 120 million family members back home.'[16] This form of foreign direct investment (FDI) can be expanded if Africans can design and operate institutions that give predictability to members of the diaspora.

Patterns of migration have changed over time. In general, Central Africa is one of the principal centres of refugee movement, with most refugees in the region located in Chad, Cameroon and the DRC. Gabon hosts the largest number of migrant workers in Central Africa (due to opportunities created by the oil industry). In West Africa, labour mobility has increased significantly since the creation of the Economic Community of West African States (ECOWAS). In southern Africa, intra-regional migration and circulation are estimated to involve seven million economically active persons and an unspecified number of undocumented migrants, of whom 44 per cent are female and 20 per cent are under 19 years of age.[17]

While immigration is a disruptive factor in many African economies, new immigrants have a far smaller effect on African economies than those immigrants who are already well entrenched over several generations, and thus are able to take advantage of their high social capital relative to their indigenous counterparts in urban Africa. Most African countries have the common feature of superior urban infrastructure and inferior urban social capital. Over time, pre-colonial and post-colonial migration has facilitated the creation of what sociologists Alejandro Portes and Richard Manning call 'ethnic enclaves', which have three common features: 'first, the presence of a substantial number of immigrants, with business experience acquired in the sending country; second, the availability of sources of capital; and third, the availability of labour'.[18] Pakistani, Chinese, Indian and European immigrants in Africa have taken advantage of their access to these three factors, combined with their possession of superior social capital, in comparison to indigenous people, to create successful ethnic enclaves. Over the last three decades, Somalis, Ethiopians and Nigerians have followed suit. Any detailed research into Africa's post-liberation socio-economic development shows how debilitating these enclaves can be for local competitors. They conspire to make indigenous Africans outsiders in their own economies. Though there are many structural reasons to blame for high unemployment in African countries, the example of South Africa provides some proof that ethnic enclaves shelter immigrants from unemployment. With just under two million immigrants, who constitute about five per cent of ages 20–64 (working-age population), unemployment among all foreign migrants in South Africa is just 14.6 per cent, or under half the rate for South African nationals.[19]

Poverty is the most obvious consequence of unemployment. According to a 2012 report, 'On average 72 per cent of the youth population in Africa live [on] less than \$2 per day. The incidence of poverty among young people in Nigeria, Ethiopia, Uganda and Burundi is over 80 per cent (World Bank 2009). The highest rates of poverty can be observed among young women and young people living in rural areas.'[20] It is time for African leaders to actively unlock rural social capital assets (high trust and lower transaction costs). Rural development strategies need to begin with a thorough understanding of this asset base, such that it can inform key interventions.

Legislation has to be drafted to force open urban ethnic enclaves to create the type of continent described in the AU's Agenda 2063. To do so, African leaders will need to have a deliberate framework guiding their execution of a rural and urban development strategy. Understanding the collective cooperation challenges unique to rural and urban Africa is critical. The sooner policy-makers grasp these nuances, the faster the triple threat of urbanisation, unemployment and immigration can be neutralised.

From the above analysis, it seems to follow that there is currently a misallocation of resources leading to overinvestment (on a relative basis) in urban African economies. More resources are allocated to low-trust, high-transaction-cost urban centres; in contrast, fewer resources are being allocated to high-trust, lower-transaction-cost rural areas. This has accelerated a brain drain out of rural Africa. The chief reason for this misallocation is that at the heart of the decision-making process governing capital allocation in African economies is a bias towards Western-centric cultural capital, leading to an attribution bias in favour of the urban centre's trappings of modernity.

The ultimate beneficiaries of this misallocation of capital are foreign immigrants, many of whose families came to Africa as part of colonialism. They are able to operate in the relatively over-capitalised, consumer-centric, urban environment within ethnic enclaves. They are well equipped to compete with Africans, who have low intra-African trust and weak social capital, resulting in deficient social networks invariably characterised by high transaction costs. Understanding this framework makes it easier to identify the socio-economic impact that the challenges of urbanisation and unemployment are having on African economies.

To illustrate the importance of high trust in economic growth, consider the following quotation from 'Trust and Growth', a paper by economists Paul Zak and Stephen Knack: 'Trust is generated by informal institutions such as social sanction, or by formal institutions such as courts ... (According to data collected by the World Values Surveys): The percentage of respondents in each country who agree that "most people can be trusted" varies from about 5.5 per cent in Peru to 61.2 per cent in Norway. Trust is to be positively associated with investment rates and growth in per capita income controlling for other standard determinants of economic performance. Investment as a share of GDP rises by about one percentage point for every seven-percentage-point increase in trust. Average annual income growth rises by about one percentage point for every 15-point increment in trust.'[21] These are truly staggering numbers that should demand our attention as we reimagine Africa's political economy.

It is no coincidence that Norway ranks number one in social trust. Beginning around 1800, men and women from Nordic civil society joined politicians to reimagine their country. After 50 years of constructive debate, research, formal institution-building and soul-searching, they began (in 1850) to develop a deliberate agenda.[22] They focused on the large-scale development of the inner self within the average Nordic citizen. They called this *Bildung*. Their specific aim was to narrow the gap between the farmers living in the countryside and the educated elites. *Bildung* became the basis of a social compact for a lifelong learning journey by the citizen in exchange for the state's commitment to find economic development opportunities for them. This citizens' empowerment model promoted the emergence of citizens with an ownership mentality, a sense of civic duty and a deep sense of trust in both their fellow citizens and the institutions that define their cooperation with them. African countries need to find a way to popularise the 'discovery' of this Nordic secret. If truth be told, a knowledge of their own history, and of how closely old African societies resembled the principles espoused in *Bildung*, will place their own cultural fingerprint on *Bildung* and point the way towards embracing it as a modern update of old African wisdom.

Urbanisation

Communities faced with the failure to solve collective cooperation challenges, due to their inability to gather and compute key information about each other, tend to reduce the scale and scope of the cooperation challenge in question. They do this by opting to decrease the number of people with whom they have to transact. This is done in the hope of reducing trust deficits, and of elevating the chances of transacting within a high-trust, mutually respectful, and individually empowering environment. The triple challenges of urbanisation, migration and unemployment, against the backdrop of weak or misaligned formal and informal institutions, have denied indigenous Africans the luxury of such selective transacting. All three challenges actually increase the number of people locals have to transact with, thereby compounding the problem of creating a supportive environment for transactions.

Let us look at the most dominant of the three challenges – urban-isation. According to the Brookings Institution, in 1950 Africa had just two cities (Lagos and Cairo) with a population of more than one million. By 1975, that number had risen to eight cities, rising further to 35 in 2000 and reaching 63 in 2016. The total number of Afri-cans living in urban areas rose from 33 million in 1950 to 295 million in 2000. This number is set to jump to 748 million by 2030. In the coming decades, the report continues, 'many sub-Saharan and North African cities – for example, Johannesburg, Nairobi, Dar-es-Salaam, Khartoum, Casablanca and others – will reach [the] 10 million person threshold. Unsurprisingly, then, the total number of individuals living in Africa's urban areas is expected to rise from 400 million in 2010 to 1.26 billion in 2050.'[23] Urbanisation is currently most advanced in South Africa, where, according to the South African Institute for Race Relations, close to two-thirds of the country's population now live in urban and peri-urban areas.

These figures present a daunting challenge for Africa and her leadership, involving an unenviable series of socio-economic trade-offs. How does one facilitate trust within economies where trust has not been organically established? How do leaders discern when to proactively manage intra-national migration to the cities and inter-national immigration? How can African businesspeople be asked to make capital investments towards the generation of jobs, given that most economic activity takes place within city centres around the African continent, where informal institutions are most fragile and degrees of trust-based social capital at their lowest?

Many African countries have historically mismanaged these trade-offs, resulting in high youth unemployment. This leads to pent-up frustration in some instances and to visible anger within a young population with a high propensity for volatility. Depending on each country's set of socio-economic institutions, those with poor social safety nets can suffer when this youth unemployment becomes a cat-alyst for emigration or more intense urbanisation. It can also become a hotbed for criminal activity and or a recruiting ground for terrorists.

Africa is a rapidly urbanising continent, but this is by no means a completely Pan African trend: Côte d'Ivoire, Mali and Zambia have actually seen a reduction in the number of citizens living in urban centres.[24] A report by the African Development Bank (ADB) groups countries into five categories based on three indicators: their current level of urbanisation, their stage of transitioning to lower fertility ratios, and their degree of structural transformation from low-productivity economic activities such as traditional farming to higher-productivity ones such as manufacturing.

According to the ADB report:

1. **Diversifiers** (such as Egypt, South Africa and Tunisia) are at the most advanced stage of each process.
2. **Agrarians** (Chad, Niger and Malawi) are at an early stage in each.
3. **Early urbanisers** (Côte d'Ivoire, Ghana and Senegal), while not showing a lot of progress in their structural transformation, are generally more urbanised and have lower fertility ratios.
4. **Late urbanisers** (Ethiopia, Kenya and Tanzania) have begun urbanising but are still predominantly rural, with high fertility ratios and generally low income levels.
5. **Natural-resource-based countries** (DRC, Nigeria and Zimbabwe) are generally more urbanised, particularly around a single prime city. Fertility rates remain generally high, and income levels vary widely depending on what natural resources they produce.[25]

At a conference convened by the World Bank in 2016, economist Edward Glaeser, a leading Harvard University expert on urbanisation, remarked, 'Cities are the best path we know out of poverty. They are the best transformers of civilisations. But there are also demons that come with density.'[26] There is no doubt that the countries listed above as either early urbanisers or late urbanisers are the ones doing the best economically (across a range of measures). What is not clear is whether urbanisation is driving economic growth or economic growth is driving urbanisation. To understand why Glaeser is so sure-footed in his belief in the positive economic value of urbanisation, we have to probe a little deeper into orthodox economic theory.

A 2011 study exploring the relationship between density of human capital and productivity (what the authors call 'agglomeration')[27] argues that close proximity in cities offers opportunities for companies and people to share in a common flow of knowledge. The study further suggests that the higher level of knowledge and skills acquired by urban individuals enhances the quality of relationships in urban areas.

Classic textbook-framed theories do not play out this way in reality on the African continent. There are three reasons for this. First, in many African metropolises, close physical proximity does not often lead to a sharing of ideas, because of the basic lack of trust, obedience, self-determination and mutual respect – all key factors in building social capital. Second, such cross-pollination leads to productivity gains only when there is close to perfect information. Outside of ethnic enclaves and patronage networks, information is highly imperfect. Lastly, the glass ceiling on indigenous Africans (because of ethnic discrimination or bias in the workplace) places a constraint on their ability to use their human capital for their personal advantage. These factors together produce an anti-meritocratic environment, diminishing the appetite of the very best to compete for opportunities. The result is often international emigration by those with underutilised expertise. Anti-meritocracy also succeeds in deterring those who remain in their home countries from striving for the highest possible qualifications, and contributes to Africa's youth unemployment problem.

Unemployment

The past 50 years have seen a stagnation and relative neglect of Africa's agricultural sector. Agriculture's share of total output has been practically the same over this period, while the industry as a whole has suffered from chronic underinvestment compared to other sectors (such as mining, services and tourism). According to a report from the Brookings Institution's Africa Growth Initiative, 'Africa urgently needs massive increases in investment for energy and transport. Employers need reliable energy to produce goods and services, and reliable roads to compete in product markets. The region's infrastructure gap is currently estimated in the order of $65 billion to $70 billion per year, roughly 2.5 times current spending.'[28] I have suggested that this may be due to an inherent bias on the part of African leaders in favour of urban development. The numbers certainly seem to bear this out. Agriculture contributes about a fifth of Africa's GDP. This has been relatively consistent over several decades. With agriculture stagnating and the formal economy not generating job growth, the informal sector has had to pick up the slack.

Turning to the informal economy, a report from the International Labour Organization states: 'Further, the informal economy in the region contributes 50–80 percent of GDP; 60–80 per cent of employment; and 90 per cent of new jobs. What is more, 9/10 workers in both rural and urban areas are estimated to hold only informal jobs. The share of informality varies across the region: informal employment is lower in southern Africa, where it ranges from 32.7 per cent in South Africa to 43.9 per cent in Namibia. In other sub-Saharan African countries, the percentage exceeds 50 per cent and reaches as high as 76.2 per cent in the United Republic of Tanzania, 89.2 per cent in Madagascar and 93.5 per cent in Uganda. After leaving school, a striking majority of young people enter the informal economy, while many migrate, looking for opportunities elsewhere.'[29] Classic economic theory does not neatly explain what is happening in African labour markets. Moreover, what is often not acknowledged is how inefficient this informal economy is (compared to the formal one) in trapping the profit pools that its scale generates for the benefit of its entrepreneurs. (In Chapter 9, I explore this as a potential key to unlocking hidden growth.)

The informal economy is where indigenous African people have been able to use their close cultural proximity and trust networks to share resources, provide each other with capital support and overcome their lack of access to the formal economic centres. They do this by controlling both the type and number of people that they deal with. This helps them manage the challenge of trust deficits. The informal sector has continued to be the largest new generator of jobs over the last 20 years. African leaders need to consider what they can replicate from successes in the informal sector. To date, the sector has been lauded without sufficient attention being paid to the factors driving its disproportionally large contribution to the economy.

According to classic economic theory, perfectly competitive markets work to ensure that all workers are paid according to their marginal productivity. Involuntary unemployment would not exist because of the flexibility of wage structures. Marginal workers would be indifferent to losing their jobs since wages would equal the amount they could earn pursuing alternative opportunities.[30] Unfortunately, nowhere in the world do labour markets operate as predicted. Issues of trust, corruption, bias, social distance and in-group versus out-group solidarity, among others, facilitate differentiated socio-economic outcomes.

In Africa, status stemming from place of education, political party affiliation, accent, style of dress and ethnic group identity may all affect an individual's employment status and wage level much more than his or her actual or potential productivity as an employee. Neoclassical economists recognising this reality have had to come up with alternative explanations, citing the presence of dual labour economies.

What sometimes goes unseen is that many Africans, both skilled and unskilled, find themselves stuck in the informal economy and unable to capitalise on their track records. They are unable to build up a credit record, a 'sufficiently respectable' curriculum vitae or an in-depth set of relationships that would allow them to break into the formal economy. These factors may be the biggest blockages to broader labour market participation.

Ethnic enclaves are not protected from the general economic underperformance that comes from an inefficient labour market. They are just efficient enough to eat into the market share of indigenous competitors. They do not need extremely fast growth in order to generate sufficient profits to sustain themselves. A good example of this is the South African economy. Despite anaemic growth, hovering between one and four per cent for the last 14 years, it still manages to consistently deliver double-digit stock-market returns for the majority European-immigrant investors. Most white South African families are richer, by orders of magnitude, than they were ten years ago.

The existence of ethnic enclaves makes discrimination in the workplace a certainty. If we accept the presence of discrimination in the workforce as a factual starting place, we have to anticipate that markets are distorted by social factors that influence who gets which job opportunities and how they are remunerated. This has a negative overall effect on the ability of economies with a discriminatory culture to efficiently allocate and aggregate talent towards the positive end of sustainable economic growth. The presence of ethnic enclaves may solve a localised cooperative problem, but it creates national headwinds to growth. South Africa shows how this works in practice. The nature of the problem may vary within each African country but its character is similarly hierarchical. Those European immigrants currently in positions of relative social privilege (in-groups) have no problem working with an out-group member, but they will not work under the leadership of indigenous Africans.[31]

Similarly, in many African countries new entrants are kept out of labour markets, because they are 'over-skilled' and incumbents won't work under them. Those clinging to patronage networks, having attained jobs for themselves in fields such as teaching, nursing, the civil service, etc, often use seniority to frustrate new, better-qualified employees in the workforce, or to ensure that they do not get jobs at all. Finally, those in various ethnic enclaves, recognising that a new employee may threaten their position, refuse to give them a chance to enter the workforce.

These factors are all at play in making it difficult for many African countries to generate enough new jobs to keep up with the numbers of new entrants. According to the CEO of Coca-Cola for South and East Africa, Kelvin Balogun, half of the 10 million (12 million as of 2017) graduates churned out each year by the more than 668 universities in Africa do not get jobs.[32]

The failure of African economies to generate jobs has one positive feature, though. Young Africans in particular are taking matters into their own hands by turning to entrepreneurship as a way of realising their dreams while generating an income. A recent study, conducted by an African communications consultancy, surveyed some 4 000 young people (between the ages of 16 and 40) from Angola, Ghana, Mozambique and Nigeria and came to the following conclusions:

- Job creation is the most important issue for the future of the sub-Saharan region, with the largest percentage (48 per cent) of survey respondents citing it. Job creation takes precedence over other important issues, such as eradicating corruption, health and sanitation, or political stability.
- Entrepreneurs are among the top drivers of job creation for young people (36 per cent), but technology and education are equally important for job creation. When asked about how entrepreneurs can help develop the economy, the majority of survey respondents (59 per cent) said that they look to entrepreneurs to advance the economy by creating jobs.
- Corruption and lack of business transparency are the top barriers to entrepreneurship, according to 45 per cent of survey respondents, followed by lack of access to capital and financing (35 per cent).
- Agriculture and natural resources are the sectors that will, over the next five years, create the most jobs, according to 43 per cent and

35 per cent of survey respondents, respectively. The survey considered extractive natural resources separately from agriculture due to the two sectors' different dynamics and issues.

- Sub-Saharan societies have largely positive views about entrepreneurs, with a majority (56 per cent) counting on them to create jobs, and believing that they worked hard for what they achieved (56 per cent). A significant majority of those surveyed (72 per cent) would prefer to start a business than to work for an existing organisation.[33]

Young Africans desperately want economic opportunities that don't come with corrupt or nepotistic strings attached. They are willing to invest in themselves through education and the development of their entrepreneurial ideas. Enormous effort should be expended to support the most successful of these entrepreneurs to ignite large job-creating companies that can inject dynamism into local economies.

Conclusion

It should be clear by now that the triple threats of urbanisation, unemployment and migration and are both real and significant. It is also fair to say that they are compounding structural economic problems. They decrease the intake of workers into the formal sector, decrease investment into the rural economy, and entrench or create ethnic enclaves. The result is the failure to increase levels of social capital among indigenous urban Africans.

I have divided social capital into four critical components as they pertain to the economy: trust, respect, individual self-determination and obedience. These serve as rules governing interaction between individuals and are tools we use to resolve collective cooperation problems. Immigrants who thrive do so because they are able to take advantage of sufficient levels of critical components of social capital. The unemployed youth often remain unemployed because they don't possess enough of each of these factors.

I have identified three positive outcomes that need more urgent policy consideration by those in leadership positions. First, there is a significant investment opportunity in many parts of rural Africa, with the potential to unlock the high-labour-absorption capacity of African agriculture. A Pan African marketplace for agriculture, twinned with sufficient investment capital and intelligent trade protections, could be a boon for sustainable economic growth. I have made the argument that such investment is one of the safest bets, due to the fact that rural Africa possesses far more solid informal institutions and higher social capital than urban Africa.

Second, African governments need to embrace the entrepreneurial spirit of its youthful population. This new inclination towards self-determination should be nurtured. Everything should be done to reduce red tape, increase venture capital and re-tailor tertiary educational curricula to support entrepreneurs. A focus on lowering the cost of capital for entrepreneurs, bringing down the cost of access to international markets and amplifying their inclination to employ other local citizens is critical.

Third, in trying to support African economies, leaders need to start with the informal sector. They need to promote social capital development within this oasis of growth. Capital needs to be unlocked by these informal enterprises to reward the genuine businesspeople who operate such firms and facilitate their growth as a job-creation strategy.

Fourth, African leaders should be actively promoting bespoke ecosystems, with embedded social capital in the form of universities, faith-based organisations and concentrated communities with strong cultural linkages. These ecosystems would replicate the advantages that allow immigrants to thrive. In so doing, leaders can work with the grain to build scalable job-creating nodes that will absorb newly trained young people and reduce youth unemployment, or, in the worst case, keep it from getting worse.

These nodes should be consciously and strategically placed or identified in underdeveloped parts of African countries, most obviously in rural areas. Governments should restrict themselves to the design and delivery of enabling infrastructure and enabling legislation in this regard. Local development initiatives have to be guided by those most affected. Social capital is Africa's most cherished asset. Let us protect and nurture it to the best of our ability so as to see off these triple threats.

6

Modern African state institutions

ONE OF THE MOST EMBARRASSING MOMENTS for many South African citizens occurred in November 2017, when we heard the country's Minister of Water and Sanitation speaking about an anticipated rapid depreciation of our currency with both ignorance and disdain for the very people for whom her ministry is charged with providing vital services: 'The rand [South Africa's currency] falls. It fell in apartheid and we will pick it up again now.'[1] To put the statement in context, S&P Global, a major international credit-rating agency, had just downgraded South Africa's credit rating. The currency and the institutions that served to protect its value were being trivialised as part of a justification for why the then president, Jacob Zuma, should stay in power despite evidence that he had overseen the systematic corruption of the entire South African state. International and local investors were voting with their feet by externalising and repatriating capital, leading to a sell-off of the South African currency. That billions of rands were transferred from poor people to a wealthy Indian family, the Guptas, bothered our minister not one bit.

Her stance was consistent with the attitude of many government ministers on the African continent, who are happy to let the state fall prey to kleptocracy if the governing party and the elites who control it get to benefit. The state and its institutions are, to such ministers, new avenues of wealth creation for a few. Under such leadership, the security apparatus that is typically set up to guard national interests is turned against the people, to protect a handful of members of powerful elites. All state institutions are dismantled bit by bit to prevent them from providing checks and balances against the ruling elite. This playbook has been repeated so many times that Africans look at each other knowingly when they read news reports exposing corrupt schemes.

Elites in these positions need to be restrained from rigging elections, flouting constitutions and destabilising whole regions to entrench themselves in power. Presidents Jacob Zuma, Robert Mugabe and José dos Santos were all leaders in this mode of governing, and Africa has done well to see them off, particularly given the tremendous efforts each made to cling to power. What is easy to understand is the temptation for formerly beloved leaders to stay in power long after they have lost the trust of the electorate. What is harder to understand is why, despite laws preventing them from so doing, these individual Africans get to impose their will on the masses. To understand this phenomenon, we have to get to grips with modern African state institutions.

It is impossible to analyse Africa's past, present and future without understanding the role the state has played in shaping events on the continent. Thus far, I have focused on the failure of African societies to ensure that their cultures remain the supreme reference points governing Africa's political economy. This is reflected in the inability of formal institutions to take root. It is important to understand how, in practice, the four key informal institutional measures of trust, respect, individual expression and obedience relate to state institutions. As we saw in Chapter 5, these four measures are the foundation of social capital. However, social capital development in post-liberation African countries has failed to keep pace with formal institutional development.

There is a poor relationship between formal state institutions and informal institutions in Africa. Politicians seem to operate above the law. They are frequently embroiled in corruption scandals, and evidence of vote-rigging is exposed on a regular basis. Yet corruption and vote-rigging rarely receive the public condemnation one would expect. Even when they do, those committing these crimes seem to routinely escape legal consequences. Are we to conclude that the formal legal rules do not closely reflect what Africans feel is fair? What is it about the rule structures responsible for organising politics that leads both citizens and politicians not to deem them sacrosanct?

Based on Transparency International's Corruption Perceptions Index for 2017, African countries are among the most corrupt in the world. Out of 180 countries, Africa's best performer is Botswana, which is just below Israel as the 34th least corrupt nation. Only the Seychelles (36th), Cape Verde and Rwanda (tied for 48th) join Botswana in the top 50. Africa has 20 of the 50 most corrupt countries in the world.[2] Transparency International has been able to show that there is a linkage between societies with lower corruption and the presence in these same societies of a free press, a larger space occupied by civil society and the strength of both formal institutions and the rule of law.

My view is that, since liberation, African societies have not spent enough time embedding their norms, cultures and values into their written laws. African politics is weakened by the resulting societal imbalance that condones political agents' flouting the rules associated with the offices they hold. The performance of modern African state institutions is further impeded by the fact that those in power view themselves as above the social group that elects them. Thus, there is enormous social distance between the electorate and those who govern. Much of this situation can be blamed on the emulation of colonial systems of governance.

The concentration of power in the hands of political parties indicates that there are not sufficient informal institutions to support and counterbalance the formal institutions needed for thriving multiparty democracy to take root. National social capital is often insufficient to promote the holding of all members of society accountable to its written laws. The absence of socio-political checks and balances triggers a chain of events that manifests as a race to the bottom in the quality of the accountability relationships between politicians and citizens.

The very concept of a state is relatively new in African politics. Most Africans don't have a statist reference point to compare what they see today with what modern civic participatory democracy in a multiparty state should look like. In the pre-colonial period, traditional organisational structures were more fluid, propped up by a system combining social stratification and hereditary castes, and were often less ambitious in their make-up and locus of control.

I described this sophisticated system of governance in the previous chapters, and made the claim that, historically, African tribes coexisted without burdening themselves with understanding or changing the way their neighbours organised their lives. (This of course excludes the times when African tribes went to war with each other.) Each society created independent leadership development processes. The Oromo people of Ethiopia offer a good example.

The Oromo have an ancient form of democracy called Gadaa, dating back to the early 16th century. Gadaa was a widely practised, structured, generational, rotating system of government featuring a strong emphasis on the training of future leaders in core governance-related matters. It was supported by informal institutions in the form of deep-rooted belief systems.[3] The Oromo cornerstone institution, *qaallu*, reflected a commitment to social justice, the laws of their god, the rule of law and the belief in fair and transparent deliberation on critical societal issues.[4] Any leader elected under the Gadaa system was restricted to a term of eight years, with an election held at the end of each term. The philosophy was to publicly select and prepare leaders across generations for future leadership roles as a method of professionalising political institutions. This system lasted for close to 400 years before imperialism destroyed it.

It is astonishing that this documented democratic model of

governance, which flourished centuries before the West adopted what we know as liberal democracy, has been largely ignored across the continent. This has not happened by accident, of course. The Abyssinian people of Ethiopia (the Amhara and Tigrean tribes), who were early adopters of Christianity, aligned themselves with Italy, which gave Ethiopia protectorate status while supporting the marginalisation, murder and fragmentation of the Oromo people.[5]

African states unfortunate enough to have endured direct colonialism did not have the opportunity to continue the development of their own leadership and organisational models. Their social capital was ripped apart by the deliberate actions of oppressive regimes. Unfortunately, as many Ethiopians would attest, even under indirect control Africans managed to oppress each other and to willingly eradicate indigenous customs at the behest of their colonial or imperial masters. This has left a void in the historical depth of experience in statecraft and the management of national agendas.

The distinction of individual leaders from their political office, the accountability of individuals through performance management, the use by voters of their power as taxpayers as leverage over the governing party, the leveraging of the power of voters to separate ethnicity from economic interests – none of these sit comfortably with the stunted development of core Pan African cultural particularities discussed in Chapter 4. Informal institutions have not been able to grow fast and strong enough to keep those in power in check.

For example, though African societies are learning to recreate collective leadership models within the modern democratic context, some modern African politics function differently. Instead of voters driving the process of electing who is to lead them, leaders club together to present a collective that uses the electoral process as a rubber stamp for their legitimacy to occupy public office. In order to retain political power, this collective leadership often chooses to divide and rule the population by promoting ethnic and tribal competition for resources. In all but a handful of African countries, resources are distributed through patronage networks that distort incentives to hold leaders to account.

By way of illustration, the democracy in Somalia includes a strong participation of elders in local and national government structures. Yet, not only is Somalia, according to Transparency International, the most corrupt nation in the world, but a full 34 per cent of elders interviewed in 2016 admitted to taking bribes during the election process. In 2016, civil servants, the police and the state intelligence force went unpaid for seven months. The elections that year were deemed illegitimate as a result of widespread vote-rigging. Votes were being bought by officials for as much as $30 000 per vote. Unsurprisingly, 76 per cent of the winning candidates won by a margin of victory of between 84 and 100 per cent![6]

The process of perverting traditional governance structures lowers the expectations of citizens and of those governing them. An extractive attitude to state assets and national resources is facilitated by this political culture. Once in place, this new culture builds an insatiable appetite for corruption to maintain power through patronage networks. As the public becomes more aware of this systematic patronage, they are themselves acculturated to cut corners and participate in low-level corruption in order to survive. This systematically lowers trust levels and facilitates an increase in crime and corruption, which in turn lowers levels of mutual respect within society. The ability of individuals to express themselves is undermined in such an environment, ultimately leading both leaders and followers to break the social compact that formal institutions are supposed to enforce.

Political parties have made this problem much worse by creating an alternative allegiance, away from citizens' normal allegiance to their countries. An increasingly pervasive set of patronage networks surrounding Africa's governing parties has become the dominant focus of allegiance. According to political scientist Kwame Boafo-Arthur, 'A political party is an institution that (a) seeks influence in a state, often by attempting to occupy positions in government, and

(b) usually consists of more than a single interest in the society and so to some degree attempts to "aggregate interests".[7]

In my view, the second objective of African political parties is undermined by the first. In attempting to influence and ultimately control the direction and allocation of state resources, political parties in Africa have disaggregated national interests. By playing up class, ethnic, religious and racial divisions, political parties have fragmented African societies in order to retain power. This has led to the dismal failure of African multiparty politics to create responsive states with cohesive national agendas.

For these reasons, liberal democracy has not done a great deal to increase trust in society. Nor has democracy done a good job of facilitating respect among citizens. This lack of trust by citizens is reinforced by high unemployment, rampant corruption and poor educational and healthcare outcomes generated by underperforming public-sector institutions. State institutions across Africa are preoccupied with their obligations to service patronage networks and to run campaigns for the re-election of governing parties. This analysis leaves us with a feeling of unease about the sustainability of modern African states.

As with any element of change management on the African continent, there is strong evidence that the primary African development challenge is cultural readjustment. As Ali A Mazrui and Francis Wiafe-Amoako have shown, African cultural codes of conduct are not reflected in the institutions that set the broader rules of the game for modern African society: 'The problem has always been how to carry out cultural readjustment. The readjustment would not be a demotion of African culture. The readjustment that is needed in culture is a better balance between the continuities of African culture and Africa's borrowing from Western culture. Until now Africa has borrowed Western tastes without Western skills, Western consumption patterns without Western production techniques, urbanisation without industrialisation, secularisation (erosion of religion) without scientification.'[8]

The failure to include these core cultural codes of conduct undermines the legitimacy essential for adherence to the rules governing modern African states. We need to focus on understanding where the bond between our cultures and the rules we follow has been broken, and what the breaking point has done to our attitudes to these rules and attempt to self-correct. The self-correction has to start by redrawing existing rules to better fit our current set of values, ethics and understanding of fairness. Continuing on a path set by rules we do not believe in is pointless. African citizens are victims of haphazard decision-making by African leaders who are not focused on how their actions weaken or strengthen local institutions.

The loss of freedom through colonisation forced African leaders down a defined development path that was not of their choosing. The need to send Africa's brightest leaders into exile was created by circumstances beyond the control of liberation movements. Many leaders were banned from studying at local higher-learning institutions, or there was none available for them. The decision to study in foreign institutions, exposing African leaders to foreign value systems, in foreign languages, was neither consciously made nor recognised at the time as being a turning point.

Many of these leaders developed a reflexive foreign bias or preference, through the process known as social reproduction. As previously mentioned, these leaders have popularised a dominative Western mode of thought, conduct, dress and forms of entertainment within their societies. This has been accelerated by the media content of public broadcasters and the educational curriculum.[9] This social reproduction affected Africans' tastes, consumption patterns, preference for urban lifestyles, partiality to the secular state. Ultimately, this facilitated African leaders' general capitulation to demands for the adoption of Anglo-Saxon multiparty electoral systems and associated institutions.

The majority of intellectually astute, committed and brave African leaders who remained in their countries during the colonial period, and thus retained their connectedness to African informal institutions, values and cultural beliefs, were either killed or side-lined in the establishment of post-colonial governance systems. The assistance of former colonial intelligence agencies ensured that these home-grown leaders were kept out of power. The net result was a type of Western-centric institutional design carried out by foreign-trained leaders, which produced the asymmetric institutional realities I have outlined above. This was, in many ways, colonialism's parting kiss of death to Africa. The resulting disorientation has remained at the heart of African peoples' Western dependency syndrome for more than six decades.

The elites in African society have been co-opted, and have in turn co-opted government's agenda through their use of political parties. Consequently, these countries have failed to produce the radical economic transformation necessary to make African economies more equal and inclusive. A few examples can illustrate this point. Twenty-four years after South Africa won its liberation, just 1.2 per cent of total rural land and just 7 per cent of formally registered properties in the cities are owned by indigenous people.[10] Close to 30 years after independence, indigenous Namibians own just 10 per cent of all land in Namibia, while the European immigrants to Namibia (who make up just 6 per cent of the population) have the balance. The richest 5 per cent of the population (mostly Namibians of European descent) enjoy 71 per cent of the country's GDP. Equatorial Guinea ranks 138 out of 188 countries in the UN's Human Development Index for socio-economic development, despite a per capita gross national income of $21 056. In 2017, oil-rich Angola had only one doctor per 10 000 people, a symptom of the condition of a country whose public-sector spending on healthcare is just 3.3 per cent of GDP (among the lowest such percentages in the world).

Against this backdrop, it is all the more alarming to read *Forbes* magazine's estimate that Isabel dos Santos, the daughter of former Angolan president José Eduardo dos Santos, amassed a fortune of $2.6 billion during her father's long term in office.[11] It is equally unsettling that the president of Equatorial Guinea, Teodoro Obiang, is estimated by *Forbes* to be worth over $600 million.[12] The Gupta family, the architects of state capture in South Africa, were in 2016 worth $773 million. The list goes on and on.

There has been large-scale failure to activate citizens in service of participatory democracy across the continent. As a direct consequence of the low participation of African citizens, African economies are not sufficiently transparent. The African social order is currently far from just. In addition to the above, the blind emulation of the Anglo-Saxon convention that completely separates church and state has had the effect of accelerating the moral decline in society. Without strong faith-based leadership, expediency has inserted itself as the chief decision-making protocol of leaders.

The corruption of politics and democracy by political parties is a global phenomenon. Countries like the US, France and the UK have been dealing with these structurally flawed institutions for hundreds of years and have succeeded to some degree in checking their most insidious tendencies while keeping their members loyal to the broader patriotic mission of state-building and economic development. This success has come after hundreds of years of building social capital and establishing checks and balances that both the elites and the electorate are invested in. Africa has had only a few decades to rebalance their societies and reorganise how these societies are led. The insidious tendency of strong political parties to dominate weak societies has yet to be stopped in its tracks.

The predicted democratic dividend from the adoption of multi-party democracy has not paid off. The reality is that, culturally, Africans have not found multiparty democracy to be a natural way of managing their societies. It is for this reason that Africans have to reimagine their political system and bring to life a political model that is more responsive to citizens and restrictive of those who govern them. We are duty-bound as Africans to test whether multiparty democracy is indeed the chosen form of political organisation by and for African people, or whether what we are seeing is a mere historical pit-stop on the road to an alternative long-term political system. After counting the costs of Anglo-Saxon democratic systems in Africa, we will attempt to contextualise multiparty democracy in Africa and then to explore alternative systems.

Counting the costs of multiparty democracy

As has been well documented, multiparty democracy was not the natural choice of post-liberation Africa. Before the era of colonial conquest, African countries had a wide variety of traditional political systems. As was the case in the rest of the world, these models varied from authoritarian chiefdoms and kingdoms to communitarian state-less populations, and included democracy of the type practised by the Oromo people during the 1600s. The Anglo-Saxon version of liberal democracy came to Africa in waves. The 1950s and 1960s brought independence for close to 30 African countries, leading to ideological battles waged in writing and sometimes in blood. Communists, despots, democrats and realists sat side by side, sometimes in the same political parties, ushering in an extended period of political conflict.

Political scientist Samuel P Huntington describes the worldwide process of so-called democratisation as having occurred in three waves.[13] The first wave, triggered by the granting of suffrage to white males in the US, led to the democratisation of 29 countries, starting in the early 19th century and continuing until 1922. The second wave lasted for roughly twenty years between the end of the Second World War and 1962. The third wave began with the 1974 revolution in Portugal, which triggered the democratisation of large parts of South America, followed by Asia-Pacific countries such as South Korea, Taiwan and the Philippines. The momentum of the third phase was sustained by the collapse of the Soviet Union, which began in 1989, precipitating the democratisation of Eastern Europe and large parts of Africa.

Huntington describes the spread of the third wave of democ-ratisation to Africa as 'the most significant political change on the continent since the independence period three decades before': 'Throughout the continent, significant political liberalisation result-ed in the emergence of a free press, opposition parties, independent unions and a multitude of civic organisations autonomous from the state. In 29 out of 47 states in the region, the first multiparty elec-tions in over a generation were convened between 1990 and 1994. In a smaller set of countries, elections were fully free and fair and resulted in the defeat and exit from power of the erstwhile authori-tarian heads of state. By the end of the decade, only a small minority of states were not officially multiparty electoral democracies, even if the practice of democratic politics was often far from exemplary.'[14]

From the early 20th century, during the struggle for liberation in Africa, party politics has dominated liberation movements. The organisations had the legitimacy, political experience, social net-works and discipline to become the dominant political forces in their respective countries, and they provided bonding social capital among elite groups in the modern African polity. Given that libera-tion movements were, by definition, the custodians of the aspirations of oppressed and marginalised peoples, they were the perfect post-liberation vehicles to bridge ethnic, racial and class barriers.

Over time, the build-up of bonding social capital within the membership group creates a state of bounded solidarity that be-comes the basis for efficient, low-cost transacting between these elites. This builds deep, trust-based relationships that are very resilient in nature. According to political scientist Robert Putnam: 'Bonding can be valuable for oppressed and marginalised members of the society to band together in groups and networks and support their collective needs.'[15] This solidarity factor, combined with patronage networks, makes these political insiders formidable competitors in the quest for economic resources. Political parties have built wider and wider con-centric circles of influence, support, patronage and solidarity.[16] Any factor threatening these concentric circles is dealt with severely, using the full arsenal of the state. It is small wonder, then, that the political outcomes, measured by the goals of inclusiveness, transparency, trust and accountability, have been shockingly undermined.

The legacy of colonialism has been effectively harnessed as a galvanising force for liberation movements turned political parties. Given Africa's collection of unequal economies dominated by what we described earlier as ethnic enclaves, indigenous people are pre-vented from successfully participating in the job or entrepreneurship markets without political party membership as a protection against exclusion. The dominant ownership of land by members of these ethnic enclaves is often the trigger for conflict between locals and immigrants. In almost all instances, political war is waged against these internal economic forces. Much-needed redistribution of land and economic opportunity galvanises support for the political par-ty in question and fractures society even further. This comes to a boiling point, as it did in Kenya (under Daniel Arap Moi), Zimba-bwe (under Robert Mugabe's Zanu-PF), South Africa (under Jacob Zuma's ANC) and Namibia (under Hage Geingob's Swapo). These developments often lead to the withdrawal of foreign and local capital investments, triggered by fear of a weakening of guarantees of property rights.

The above dynamics provide context to explain why African countries have struggled to make sense of modern liberal demo-cracy. Africa has been bedevilled by political instability, wars, poverty, famine and underdevelopment, despite the outward signs of democratisation.[17] A handful of elites in charge of the state – and, by extension, the economy – without significant capacity for oversight and sanction has predictably failed to secure the rights of African citizens. Instead, African citizens have ceded their historic agency to a corrupt institutional network of political parties.

African scholar Mahmoud Mamdani argues that uneven political development in Africa is a product of the colonial administrative sys-tem, which Mamdani dubs the 'bifurcated state'.[18] This means that there are two different forms of governance in the society. The rural populace is still under the leadership of the traditional authority, while the people in the urban areas are under a different government. According to Mamdani, the colonial state excluded a large number of the public from the affairs of the state on the basis of race.[19] The colonial authorities found existing institutions in almost all the colonies they conquered in Africa and they were faced with the dilemma of what Mamdani calls 'the native question', which they answered with 'direct and indirect rule'.[20] In his words, direct rule for the colonial authorities meant 'there would be a single legal order, defined by the "civilised" laws of Europe. No "native" institutions would be recognised.'[21]

Post-colonial corruption started with simple instances of abuse of power, but, over time, greater skill was acquired to exercise complete control over all aspects of the state and its resources, effectively institutionalising corruption. As a trade-off for this transfer of power, citizens as principals have been reduced to recipients of limited social welfare and basic infrastructure benefits by those meant to be their agents. Those living in rural areas, away from the centres of power and off the priority list of governing parties, have received even less.[22]

The result, in most instances, has been the dismantling of traditional African institutions that had the capability, legitimacy and authority to stand up to political parties. Sadly, traditional authorities were often coerced into joining the patronage networks, and, in so doing, compromised themselves in the eyes of ordinary people. Additionally, the need to generate personal income drew strong community leaders into patronage networks and thus compromised their moral authority to speak out in the community in support of old African values.

The introduction of a hyper-efficient, flexible and often ruthless institution (the political party) at the beginning of the phase that introduced liberal democracy had dramatic results. Inadequate knowledge and understanding of the rules of the game on the part of ordinary citizens simply exacerbated the situation. Political parties quickly learned how to game the system, fix elections, use infrastructure spending for patronage, starve non-politically supportive parts of the country of resources, and, most damningly, retard the roll-out of education to create a larger more malleable pool of voters they could continue to manipulate. This cycle of manipulation lowers the credibility of political parties as change agents and often leads to disillusioned voters seeing all political actions as disguised attempts at further corruption. African states have consequently become highly mistrusted by their citizens.

According to an Afrobarometer/Transparency International survey in 2015 across 36 (out of 55) African countries, Africans ranked the following as their top five major issues of concern: 1) unemployment, 2) healthcare, 3) education, 4) infrastructure/transport and 5) water supply. In large measure, it is the responsibility of state institutions to deliver on these issues (though unemployment obviously includes a great deal of private-sector influence).[23] The same report concludes that 74 per cent of respondents lived in poverty. Given how disappointed African citizens must be in their politicians, it is perhaps not surprising that many have become disengaged from politics. Only 53 per cent of youths aged between 18 and 35 are engaged in civic affairs. Only 33 per cent of youths have attended campaign rallies, while just 11 per cent of youths participate in protests.[24] Given that young people are the majority of the African population, this is a damning statement about the state of democracy in Africa.

The liberal democratic wave in Africa is delivering optically pleasing democracy – regularly held elections, free (but not fair) voting, semi-peaceful protests and the (diluted) participation of media – without actually reflecting the will of African peoples to force their leaders to deliver on their top priorities. To make matters worse, some of these parties have taken traditional authority structures and bent them to their will. It is interesting to reflect on how different political parties in Botswana, South Africa and Namibia have treated the institution of traditional leadership, and what this has done to strengthen or weaken democracy in their respective countries. Of the three, Botswana has been by far the most forceful and successful at integrating traditional governance with democratic practices. The Batswana have achieved equilibrium between their traditional African institutions and the modern democratic ones. As a result, the country has remained stable and voters are invested in the democratic process. Botswana has achieved the desired goal of making leaders accountable to the electorate, who feel a deep sense of ownership of their democracy.

Botswana has kept its social capital intact because it successfully resisted direct colonial rule, and its indigenous governments retain the supremacy of traditional systems of thinking. At the time the country achieved independence, in 1966, many of its customs, norms and values were largely intact. Botswana performed the rare feat of intertwining formal institutions, such as the constitution, parliament and executive branch, with traditional leadership institutions, including all the indigenous informal institutions. This created a measure of authenticity and harmony between its culture and its formal institutions, one that has led to not only stability but also sustained economic growth, underpinned by a strong sense of national accountability.

Ghana presents an interesting example of how the co-option of traditional leadership at independence could turn into a poisoned chalice. It has taken the country many decades to heal from the betrayal of traditional authority in the 1980s and 1990s. Under the astute leadership of President Nana Akufo-Addo, Ghana is acutely aware of the need to strengthen national social capital through a more tightly knit relationship between traditional leaders and democratic leaders. In Akufo-Addo's government, the Ashanti king, the Asantehene, occupies a prominent leadership role in society. King Osei Tutu II is himself accountable to the Kwasafomanhyiamu, or governing council, and thus is diligent in his duty to represent the best interests of the clan. More than most African states, Ghana has sought to promote harmony between informal and formal institutions. Ghanaians seem to have found that if traditional authority can find its voice to check the excesses of politicians, public confidence in the overall political system will strengthen, and subsequent generations will benefit from increased state legitimacy.

Throughout Africa, political parties have turned to traditional political structures for help in consolidating their rural power bases. In return, traditional leaders are often awarded large amounts from state budgets and granted local autonomy. In most cases, these transactions have left rural Africans worse off. Their ability to hold these leaders to account is undermined, and their entitlement to a fair share of national investment in basic needs and services often shows diminishing returns. In a reimagined African future, constitutions should restrain the president from tampering with the budgets and assets dedicated to traditional leaders, who should feel secure to play their rightful role as custodians of people's interests. If these traditional leaders find their voice and become the due north that politicians and the electorate can look to in moments of doubt, turmoil and indecision, then society will be the richer for it.

Exploring alternative systems

Africa has choices. None of the choices I present here are clear-cut. Aspects of what works in some countries have to be retrofitted to local cultural realities. Evaluating choices made by other societies can, however, be instructive for Africa's future. China has concluded that the one-party-state model is the way to go. The United Arab Emirates (UAE) is a federal kingdom organised around a monarchy. The United States has chosen to structure its system such that only two parties can effectively exist. In this section, I look at what can be learned at a high level from these three different systems. I then present a fourth, more appropriate example for Africa to emulate.

One-party states are states in which only one political party is allowed to form a government. The rationale for setting up or instituting a one-party-state system is unity. Politicians identify and rail against the divisiveness created by multiparty competition. All other parties are usually outlawed or face significant challenges to their existence and functionality. The enforcement of this single-party hegemony usually leads to a paranoid, authoritarian state that seeks out and suppresses perceived opposition. China is the shining example of a successful one-party state. The one-party model has allowed China the benefit of long-term strategic planning and execution, and its single-minded pursuit of social stability has been strengthened by having a homogeneous society. The Chinese Communist Party has, since 1978, followed an economic model characterised as a state-directed market economy.

Since taking office in 2013 President Xi Jinping has further consolidated the power of the Chinese Communist Party. In foreign policy, he has appealed to nationalist sentiment by seeking to assert China's superpower status. He has consolidated legitimacy by publicly fighting corruption and arresting party insiders. He has grown national social security and supported the broadening of the Chinese middle class. But there are signs of an increasing concentration of power, and President Xi's supporters have successfully lobbied to do away with presidential term limits. These are warning signs to those who might want to copy the Chinese system. The perilous proximity between one-party state and despotic rule should set off alarm bells. One-party states demand even more checks and balances and stronger alternative institutions than does liberal democracy.

A successful one-party state requires a combination of cultural homogeneity (sameness), national ideological alignment, flawless service delivery, skilled bureaucracy, outstanding intelligence agencies and ruthless discipline. China has, by and large, demonstrated its capacity to successfully achieve the above preconditions. For many African countries, the combination of these factors is not remotely attainable. They simply do not have the experience and depth of skill in the management of state affairs for this to be a valid option.

It has taken the Chinese Communist Party almost seven decades to gain the legitimacy that allows it total control over China. Yet the state bureaucracy that runs China has been in place for thousands of years. Given the legitimacy issues that force African political parties onto the back foot based on their track record of governance, more appropriate models need to be found.

A second model is the UAE's federal monarchy. After the seven sheikdoms ceased to be a British protectorate in 1971, Emirati leaders voluntarily formed a political union called the United Arab Emirates. One would be hard pressed to find a more significant political initiative in the history of the Middle East region. The political stability created by the UAE has facilitated enormous socio-economic achievements. The form of government of each of the seven emirates (Abu Dhabi, Ajman, Fujairah, Sharjah, Dubai, Ras Al-Khaimah and Umm Al-Qaiwain) is absolute hereditary monarchy. A wise choice was made from the outset of the UAE's existence to retain the independence of each emirate while simultaneously creating a federal-like government.[25]

At first united by a long-standing ancient culture and a mono-religion in the form of Islam, these seven states developed independently as kingdoms. The growth of the oil industry gave rise to border disputes that heightened the need for cooperation and unity. The UAE's cultural homogeneity and shared devout religiosity, together with a common feudal history, allowed seamless integration of the seven states. Informal institutions were allowed to do their job of reinforcing the new laws created to promote the country's economic development.

Were it not for colonialism, Africa might have followed the UAE's development path by consolidating its kingdoms and chiefdoms in similar fashion. Whether the leaders of that period would have had the skill and farsightedness to seek and use aspects of cultural homogeneity as the glue for a unified state is anyone's guess. What we can safely say is that the last 3 000 years of cultural interference and sabotage of traditional authority structures, first by Asians and Persians, more recently by the West, and later by indigenous political parties, makes this option difficult to execute. Any federal model adopted by Africa in the modern world would have to entrench the democratic rights to which Africans have become accustomed.

The US two-party-state model is one that, by default, currently exists in many African countries. This system is usually the product of institutional arrangements made by elites at independence to discourage multiparty pluralism and allow the state to settle on a dualistic structure. Over time, the competition between parties either hyper-accentuates or obliterates differences in policies and ideologies. Limiting voters' options to two bad choices is the same as giving them none at all. The choices converge into bad ones because of the system's tendency to promote patronage, not to punish institutionalised corruption and to centralise power. The lack of campaign finance restrictions and transparency relative to internal party elections worsens the political climate. Even institutionally sophisticated and politically experienced states find that this system promotes inertia and policy paralysis.

Charles Wheelan, author of *The Centrist Manifesto*, spells out how this problem manifests itself in America: 'The current two-party system gives too much power to the extremists in each party. Much of that is actually institutional in nature. So, for example, the primary system means that in a lot of states, independent voters are essentially unrepresented in choosing the two candidates who are going to appear on the general election ballot. So each party spits out more extreme candidates than would be elected if all of us chose our top two preferences. Problem number 2 is that, on the House side at least, we're gerrymandering [moving electoral boundaries to suit certain candidates] electoral districts. Once you do that, you're more likely to get challenged by someone who's even more liberal [or conservative] than you are. So, therefore, as a member of Congress you're always protecting your more conservative or more liberal flank.'[26]

We have seen this dynamic happen all around the world when two dominant parties exist. Given the economic inequalities in Africa, and the ethnic and/or racial characteristics of African societies, a movement to the extremes can have very dangerous long-term consequences. The other reason the two-party model will not bring long-term stability to Africa is its tendency to generate factions, which periodically break away from parties, creating short-term instability as the dominant party's power base is threatened. These breakaways often have deadly consequences for the breakaway leader and their followers. Countries like the US and the UK have legitimised two-party dominance over hundreds of years. This has built societies that are fully vested in supporting this dual-party hegemony. Africans are far from vested in a dual-party structure.

Africans will have to be more creative in conceiving of a new political accountability mechanism. We have to break the cycle of blindly adopting institutions from the West and then complaining about their relevance when they fail to produce the desired out-comes. Most of Africa's problems come from the failure, at the time of liberation from colonialism, to intentionally conceive of, or intentionally retrofit and implement, locally relevant solutions without fear of what contradicting Western orthodoxy would have brought. African flags were new and, as such, were meaningless to the citizens of the new countries. Their borders were arbitrary and therefore meaningless to their citizens. The foreignness of the new rules that made up their constitutions and laws made them immaterial to citizens, because the logic that informed them did not resonate with their own recognised organic knowledge base.

Political parties have stepped into this stateless vacuum to mould society as they see fit. Imagining life without political parties, and the unending multiparty political dance, is therefore difficult. It is this current challenge of conception that Africans need to overcome in order to climb the development ladder fast enough to deal with the triple onslaughts of urbanisation, unemployment and migration.

Reviving the ability of communities to directly elect local heroes to political office, based on the singular criterion of trust, is critical for Africa's successful future. African politics has always been local, and the political system it chooses going forward needs to reflect that reality. What should matter once again is who a community's counsellors are, who the mayor is, and what type of revenue system allows local structures to deliver services to their people. A first step in creating accountable democracy is a localisation of political budgets. The way government taxes and expenditures are allocated has to be re-evaluated. A public conversation has to rekindle the link between elected officials and their constituencies, taxpayers and the neighbourhoods they live in. The outcome of these conversations should be the realignment of the needs and demands of local voters and competent, accountable local government officials.

Perhaps counterintuitively, one of the smallest European countries might provide answers on how to constitute modern African states. Faced with the challenge of integrating two religious groups (Protestants and Roman Catholics) and four language groups (German, French, Italian and Rhaeto-Romansh), Switzerland has developed a hybrid political structure that has allowed it to prosper. The Swiss federal model has the following core tenets: localised democratic participation, which allows for bottom-up nation-building; strong political participation by the cantons (the more autonomous equivalent of US states); and a blend of both direct and proportional representation that seeks to amplify individual voices in national affairs.

The Swiss federal system consists of the Confederation (national government), 26 cantons and roughly 2 500 communes. Each level has a separation of powers, with its own executive, judiciary and legislature. The cantons have their own constitutions (which cannot contradict the principles of democracy, human rights and rule of law guaranteed by the federal constitution). They are allowed their own political organisations, and their own taxation and financial policies. The communes also have constitutionally protected rights to political organisation, and to the production and distribution of public goods. They finance these through the independent collection of local taxes.

This extremely decentralised version of federalism relies on the active participation of citizens, the use of referendums and a healthy dose of court participation in the formation of improved legislation: 'According to the basic constitutional rule, every transfer of power to the federation requires a constitutional amendment which is ... subject to a popular vote.'[27] This fosters autonomous policy design and implementation in the cantons and effective execution in the communes. In this way, the Swiss have produced a balance between top-down and bottom-up power that Africa could do well to learn from.

Africa has five geographical regions (North, Southern, East, Central and West Africa), each with between six and eight countries. To date, regional integration efforts have focused on economic integration. At a Pan African level, a Pan African Parliament has been in place since 2004. This parliament has ten subcommittees, a president and four vice presidents. The parliamentary president works together with the chairperson of the Assembly of Heads of States and Government and the chairperson of the African Union Commission to run the AU. This unwieldy structure is put in place to limit the ability of any president of a member country to lead the Assembly of Heads of States for an extended period of time, and thus become more powerful than their peers. The presidency is currently a ceremonial job held for one year. The Pan African Parliament has no ability to enforce decisions made during its parliamentary sittings, and instead has merely consultative and advisory powers. Africa must be bolder than this.

The Swiss model offers a way out of the current morass. It can deal with the elephant in the room, which is how nation states and the presidents they elect retain enough autonomy in a Pan African federal government structure. There are several critical steps to take towards this objective. Number one is that all countries hold a referendum to join the AU as states bound by a new federal system, with the federal government having ultimate authority on military budgets, monetary policy, foreign policy, social security, national infrastructure, telecommunications, commercial law, civil law and penal law. The expectation should not be that all countries vote yes, just that those countries that choose to join get the lion's share of the economies of scale generated by the emboldened AU.

Member countries that choose not to join the federalised AU can have limited benefits and observer status in its processes. African countries that join the new federal structure need to be redesignated as states that keep their own constitutions but make the necessary amendments, such that they do not contradict the major pillars of a new supreme constitution of the AU. The states should have governors (instead of presidents or prime ministers) who are elected by direct state-wide election (not subject to party lists). These governors should elect five regional peers (for Southern, East, West, North and Central Africa) who would form a six-person standing committee to collectively lead the federal government, which runs the new AU. The sixth member should be the president of the AU, and she or he should be elected on the same ballot paper as the governors are elected (also directly, without party lists) by citizens of each African state. The president should have a tie-breaking vote in the standing committee (in the event of a 3–3 tie on any vote, the president's vote should count as two votes).

The new African states, led by the governors, would retain many of their current functions and features. They would be culturally, linguistically and religiously autonomous. They would retain control over education, healthcare, policing, local infrastructure, land use and planning, and natural resource management. Their parliaments, whose members should be elected by proportional representation without party lists, would retain the right to make laws within this delegation of authority, and, where necessary, to call referendums challenging the implementation of federal laws.

In parallel to this, the Pan African Parliament should be given teeth. It currently has five representatives from each member country. In the Parliament's new form, each state would keep intact its legislature, but with certain modifications to allow them to operate within the new delegation of authorities flowing from the AU constitution. They should continue to elect five members from their peers as members of the Pan African Parliament. The major change would be to give the Parliament legally enforceable legislative power. African states need to collapse the intermediary structure between local and national government. What are called provinces in some countries, or states in others, need to devolve their authority to municipalities or local government structures, which would operate like communes do in Switzerland. These local structures should have the right to collect local taxes and the right to build, distribute and maintain local public goods.

Better-empowered voters can encourage complementary relationships between traditional African leadership and modern democratic structures in the way Botswana has done. Africans need to heed Mazrui's advice – to be discerning about which Western habits, practices and traits to emulate – by allowing informal institutions to accommodate proven modern formal institutional models that are both productive and progressive. A good way of enforcing this discerning modernisation would be to establish a Pan African council of traditional leaders, consisting of five traditional leaders from each state (each country would select a top five traditional leaders' list based on the number of people living under their traditional leadership). The new body would have the opportunity to comment on and shape legislation prior to its being voted on.

A continent as rich in human and natural resources as Africa cannot be poor unless that poverty is artificially generated. Unchecked political party structures and the illegitimate borders that they have upheld have served to perpetuate poverty in Africa. This continent will remain poor unless it decides to drastically change how leaders are elected and what rules they have to follow while in power. Putting power back into the hands of African citizens through direct political representation in non-political-party-oriented states that fall under a decentralised federal government would help ensure that this continent has an opportunity to rebuild its state institutions to reflect the wishes of its people.

7

Case study: how identity affirmation works against Pan Africanism

As someone who has been married twice, I have had occasion to experience the pain caused when individual identity fails to succumb to the fledgling joint identity of a married couple. Good marriages are acts of submission of one's individual identity to that of a new one. That act of submission has to be done freely and joyously in order to be sustainable. As men, we often have to let go of a free-spirited adolescent identity. Fatefully for my first marriage, I clung on to my independent identity even in my late twenties. This identity recoiled at the idea of accountability to the institution of marriage. In my second marriage, the shoe was on the other foot.

Through marriage, humans have occasion to learn to find joy in the submission of personal identity to a frightening and beautiful new joint identity, to learn patience with one another and to accept the other's imperfections. As in any good marriage, one of you has to fight hard when the other wants to give up. Usually it is one person who does most of the fighting to save the marriage. I believe that a big reason for this is revealed by understanding which party has the most invested in the identity of being in a stable, loving marriage. That emotional investment is hard to give up on. This allows us to understand why, even when faced with a threat to their personal economic and emotional well-being, people choose to stay married to keep this social identity alive.

These experiences have made me more sympathetic to the seemingly irrational moves made by people who cling to their public identities at the cost of their long-term self-preservation. In African politics, for example, we see leaders who choose to stay in power, proclaim their innocence and fail to strike an amnesty deal with the incoming leadership. This is driven by a need to keep alive their imagined identity (as a powerful, all-knowing, benevolent strongman/woman). Former president Jacob Zuma is the latest example of such an African leader. Despite being warned, President Zuma displayed a response that was against his long-term interests. He opted to protect the image he has projected of a man who was innocent of any and all charges against him. He saw no need to resign from office, or to cut a deal, until it was too late. His midnight capitulation on 14 February 2018 was made under major duress from his own political party, who promised to begin impeachment proceedings against him the next day should he fail to resign.

When faced with a potential threat to group identity, groups of people (such as ethnic or religious groups) often show the same reaction as individuals. They seem to 'irrationally' cling to earned and unearned social privileges attached to their preferred identities. European ethnic minorities in Zimbabwe have clung to their preferred identity as 'whites', which to them meant being better than indigenous Zimbabweans, steadfastly refusing even commercially advantageous land resettlement arrangements for two decades prior to the land invasions that saw their dispossession.

The question this chapter engages with is this: what is it about our identity that is so precious as to get in the way of our long-term social, political or economic goals? I use South Africa as a case study to delve into this socially complex issue. Such an exploration of the role of what is called 'identity affirmation' paves the way for useful generalisations later in the book that are key to the mission of reimagining Africa.

Many people on the African continent continue to look to South Africa for ideas relating to the promotion of economic development. Some of them might also think that South Africa has lessons to share on how to manage the transition from colonialism to liberal democracy. Many South Africans talk about their country as one that is an exception to the African rule. This of course presumes that African countries are united in their mediocrity relative to the rest of the developing world. South Africa has done some of the big things right. The work embarked on to limit the negative effects of tribalism, to create stable and robust formal institutions, to build an all-encompassing social security system and to invest heavily in infrastructure development has been outstanding. Despite all this, social formation in South Africa leaves much to be desired.

For reasons I will make clear, South Africa has many lessons to share with the rest of Africa about what *not* to do in trying to create social harmony in a country. These lessons are a cautionary tale for future Pan African leaders. At their root is a basic failure by almost all South Africans to ground themselves in a broader Pan African identity. This has created psychosocial imbalances that have given rise to crippling alternative identities. As a result, South Africa is in a state of identity crisis that threatens its socio-economic progress.

This case study explores what is at the heart of this identity crisis and how to understand its threat to the future of Africa's development. My research reveals the presence of deep unconscious bias and ethnic-privilege preservation that drives South Africa's approach to talent aggregation. This approach is alienating to indigenous talent and is holding back indigenous institutional formation. I use a field of study known as identity economics to explain what is happening in South Africa. The theory behind identity economics predicts that, because people's identities define who they are, and because their identities within social categories define their belief about what norms ought to be, individual gains and losses in identity affirmation trump other economic considerations in determining how they act.[1]

Identity economics in South Africa continues to be influenced by the aggregation and consolidation of the economic interests of minority European ethnic groups. These ethnic minorities enjoy privileged access to capital and economic opportunities over the majority of the population. European ethnic groups in South Africa have benefited from becoming the standard by which all local South African talent is judged and benchmarked. This creates an anchoring bias that distorts views about the capability of indigenous professionals.

Social categorisation is a function of human beings' survival instincts. Norms are formed when people develop ideals about how they and others in their society should act. These norms, over time, begin to create hard-coded views of exemplary social characteristics. Transgressions of these norms are often a source of gossip that in itself is a social tool to discipline behaviour through exclusion or inclusion. All societies exhibit such behaviour in one way or another. Human beings are happiest when they, as individuals, can do things in a way that reflects their own interpretation of their society's norms and ideals.[2]

In the South African context, societal norms and ideals are evaluated with a very strong anchoring bias towards Anglo-Saxon norms and ideals. Anglo-Saxon values, mannerisms and character traits are embraced, localised and cultivated within ethnic enclaves. Enclave members interact with other South Africans outside their ethnic enclaves by using their understanding of norms and ideals as a yardstick to assess the presence of a cultural, relational and values fit. Because these ethnic-enclave members control the economy, by owning and operating the vast majority of South Africa's businesses, what they say matters. Whoever they regard as trustworthy are invited into economic opportunities, while those not trusted are excluded.

The above process serves as a prerequisite to talent being properly assessed, friendships being kindled and trust being conferred on individuals. This happens both consciously and unconsciously by using cultural homogeneity as a proxy for bestowing trust only on individuals in an in-group worthy of opportunities for upward progression in the corporate world. Creditworthiness, fundability and risk assessments are routinely done through a cultural lens that is biased in favour of minority ethnic groups based on social cues that trigger automatic preferences. This is most acute in the form of an automatic preference for those most like ourselves. Such automatic preferences override objective judgement. Subconsciously, these citizens attribute competence to people they meet based on familiar characteristics. This form of positive value attribution to members of a dominant ethnic group facilitates a gravitational pull towards sameness that works against the national transformation agenda. It also makes establishing a credible Pan African agenda in South Africa impossible.

Biases, sometimes of an unconscious nature, make a mockery of government efforts to put policies and regulations in place to enhance efforts towards changing the composition of enterprises and the profiles of their shareholders. Indigenous professionals who make it in the corporate world do so largely through mimicking their ethnic-minority counterparts to pass a 'benchmark', which they may or may not be consciously aware of. This mimicking process is a way of compensating for an anchoring bias driven largely by superficial first impressions. Indigenous professionals internalise the risk-reward frameworks of those in power through this process. In order to thrive economically, indigenous people have to look at the world through the lens of the minority ethnic groups. This allows them to understand what these minorities think makes a particular team or individual in the corporate environment more or less risky to invest capital or time on.

These internalised frameworks are inherently biased against the majority of indigenous professionals, whose response is to exhibit behaviour referred to as 'stereotype threat'[3] – the fear of failure due to anticipated bias, which further perpetuates discrimination. These ingroup psychosocial traits actively and passively serve to undermine a successful meritocracy. At the core of the idea of a meritocracy is the belief that all individual talent, regardless of skin colour, culture, gender, ethnicity, accent or place of birth, is randomly distributed in society. Psychosocial traits underpinning stereotypical systems programme individuals along a journey through which the need to affirm existing in-groups and out-groups is sustained by automatic preferences.[4] These automatic preferences are cued by stereotypes that have facilitated the reintroduction of a form of 'social apartheid', exhibited through a bias towards sameness. In the quest to affirm the in-group identity of 'white South Africa', norms, stereotypes and values are marshalled to justify the supremacy of 'whiteness' and the deficiency of otherness.

South Africa's European ethnic minorities have been highly successful at using banks and other financial institutions as catalysts for entrepreneurship and the promotion of the growth of large companies led by leaders of the same ethnicity. I contend that this success has been promoted through the institutionalised use of the Pygmalion effect.[5] This term describes the effect of high expectations on ethnic minorities' performance. When these high expectations are held by members of society who are already visibly more privileged than others, the result is the ultimate self-fulfilling prophecy.

Decades of concerted efforts to homogenise previously disparate European immigrant ethnic groups' views on family values, productivity, politics and risk assessment have helped build and consolidate social capital within minority ethnic enclaves. While the building of this social capital has been long in the making, the post-apartheid South African obsession with racial categorisation, born out of the expressed intent to discriminate positively in favour of 'blacks', has led to a heightened sense of 'bounded solidarity' – comprised of selfless acts that promote a group's agenda – among South Africans of European descent. As a result, for most 'white' South Africans today, their 'whiteness' has become their primary form of identity.

Four conclusions flow from using identity economics as a framework to evaluate present-day South Africa. First, corporate South Africa cannot successfully balance all its stakeholders' expectations until companies deal with the issue of identity. Corporates in South Africa have to embrace the theory that firms will only maximise their output per employee when employees identify with the company's norms, values and mission. Second, how much education (as opposed to schooling) learners get is largely determined by whom they think they are (their identity), whether they feel it is their right to be educated, and if they are confident that it is their right to reap the concomitant opportunities that this education affords them. Third, norms can create limitations (through embedded stereotypes that create chilly environments and culturally based glass ceilings) that foster underperformance. Fourth, but most importantly, the choice of identity may be the most important economic decision a person ever makes.

Lessons from this case study suggest four key recommendations. First, the removal of racial classification altogether is essential to rebalance the loaded dice that is 'white' skin privilege. Second, it is critical to overhaul South Africa's education curriculum to make it more Afrocentric, particularly in the teaching of history, language studies and geography. Third, the removal of privileges of admission to private and Model C schools based on previous family members' attendance at the school or on the proximity of students' residence to the school is critical to redistributing educational opportunities and changing the texture of learning environments. Fourth, reconstituting the ethnic composition of the teaching profession, at both secondary and tertiary level, is critical to positively transform learning environments and create positive role models.

These four measures would go a long way towards dismantling anti-meritocratic 'white' skin privilege. If this 'white' skin privilege is allowed to continue much longer, South Africa will implode. A national agenda split along racial lines will lead to decaying institutions and a failed state. In the rush to blame Jacob Zuma for South Africa's current ills, South Africans have failed to look to their identity crisis as the underlying cause of long-term instability. For the country to be stable in the long term, indigenous South Africans have to be socially encouraged to be both themselves and successful in their chosen fields of work or study. Doing so will strengthen their sense of ownership of, and commitment to, the success of the country in the future. South Africans in general have to let go of their divisive primary identities, and choose instead to root themselves in an African identity that will provide the basis for national bounded solidarity.

Socio-economic background

There is a maxim, often used in modern business, that culture eats strategy for breakfast. This is illuminating in the context of South Africa, where, despite the country's well-thought-out economic development strategy, the National Development Plan (NDP), a culture of fear and mistrust has perpetuated and reinforced conscious bigotry and unconscious bias in both the corporate and public sector.

Conscious bigotry in the form of racism has been thoroughly explored by researchers in South Africa and around the world, and does not warrant further exploration here. However, its equally insidious twin, unconscious bias, is rarely explored by commentators looking at South Africa's economic performance. Unconscious bias works in ways that are both socially destructive and reinforcing of conscious bigotry. According to Dr Renee Navarro, vice chancellor in charge of diversity and outreach at the University of California at San Francisco, 'Unconscious biases are social stereotypes about certain groups of people that individuals form outside of their own awareness.[6] Because ethnic minorities and indigenous South Africans have been forced to develop apart at two very different speeds, first by colonialism and then by apartheid, both types of bias have become hard-wired through widely held racial and ethnic stereotypes. In many ways, discrimination has become part of South Africa's cultural and institutional fabric.

Automatic race preferences have tainted the talent-selection process. Assessing competence has taken a back seat to many other impulses that shape South Africans' views on merit. The period of racial integration since 1994 has birthed different forms of talent selection and risk-reward frameworks, most of which are anti-meritocratic. These frameworks undermine the core requirement for executing the NDP, namely, public- and private-sector coordination. The country is fractured in its ability to assess talent and attribute trust to professionals. This fracture has hardened over time as stereotypes and caricatures reinforce old bigotry. Increased suspicion about motives and the genuine versus perceived capability between ethnic groups has led to mistrust of talent-selection processes.

In corporate South Africa, European ethnic minorities see talent expressed as the reinforcement of their long-held views about how one expresses oneself, how diligent people present themselves (their physical appearance) and how one quantifies and assesses risk. This seems logical if one has been indoctrinated to reinforce a way of doing things through institutionally replicating one's ethnic group as a means of protecting ethnic privilege. These long-held beliefs create self-fulfilling biases toward talent and performance that are expressed in Anglo-Saxon-centric terms. It would seem that, after many years of forming a consolidated view of how a 'white' in-group looks, acts and thinks, all other out-groups are defined as the antithesis to these positive attributes.

The most common organisational trick performed by the human mind is that of categorisation. The mind requires the aid of categories in order to think. Once formed, categories are the basis for normal prejudgement, upon which orderly living depends. Since the introduction of formal apartheid legislation in the early 1950s, indigenous South Africans have been formally categorised by all other ethnic groups as the lowest in the pecking order. In fact, prior to 1950 there was some discussion among colonialists about whether or not indigenous people belonged to the human race at all. This has created a way of thinking about fellow South Africans that has become embedded in language, thought processes and in the interpretation of each other's actions.

The modern South African fixation with race-based categorisation arose out of a genuine effort by the ANC-led government to enable restorative justice by positively discriminating in favour of 'black' South Africans. Positive discrimination is hard to implement without baseline statistics and hard-and-fast categories according to which policy-makers can construct discriminating laws. The statistics tell a terrible socio-economic story of inequality and poverty that has been repeatedly told to the South African public as a means of justifying the need for positive discrimination. Over time, the political imperative of winning elections has seen more and more pronouncements on the ills prevalent in the indigenous community, painting a picture of helplessness and of the need for government intervention to help alleviate the tragic effects of socio-economic inequality. The results of positive discrimination, and the continued categorisation it necessitates, is the hardening of in-groups and out-groups and the accompanying narratives that justify these groups in the form of social stigmas and stereotypes.

Race-based categorisation did not happen in a vacuum. It is a result of close to 50 years of legal justification for the superiority of Afrikaners as an ethnic group, and of hundreds of years of imperial justification for the superiority of Anglo-Saxons. To say that post-1994 race-based categorisation was laid on a toxic foundation would be a gross understatement. During the apartheid years, deliberately fashioned stereotypes were cultivated: black equals non-believer (the origin of the word 'kaffir'); black equals immoral (heavily propagated by the Dutch Reformed Church); black equals incompetent (the justification for Bantu education); and, finally, black equals childlike stupidity (a paternalistic view shared by liberals and conservatives alike).

These stereotypes receded for the first eight years following the formal end of apartheid, covering the Mandela presidency and Thabo Mbeki's first term, as people began to accept and embrace the primacy of their South African identity. However, during its second term the Mbeki presidency effectively waged a war on 'white' skin privilege in the form of black economic empowerment (BEE) legislation, which actively sought socio-economic rebalancing. The term 'usual suspects', to denote a select few who benefited from the first wave of empowerment, caught the public's imagination. This began a steady process of the delegitimation of BEE. The BEE project did not enable the jettisoning of the poor-equals-black stereotype. Instead, that stereotype sat side by side with the new stereotype of rich-black-equals-corrupt.

These two stereotypes have birthed or, in some instances, re-birthed other, more damaging stereotypes, such as black equals helpless, clever blacks equals troublesome blacks, black equals lazy, black equals unproductive. This ultimately has led South Africans back to an old apartheid favourite − that black equals cognitively inferior. The formation of these stereotypes has been made easier by the preceding decades of similar stereotypes as a justification mechanism for apartheid. Whereas so-called whites were previously somewhat divided in their interpretation of apartheid stereotypes and in the need to propagate them, two decades of positive discrimination in favour of 'blacks', and persistently high interracial income inequalities, have made the post-apartheid stereotypes more widely and uniformly accepted.

Just as European minority ethnic groups have been rallied to solidarity by the justified discrimination against them, indigenous South Africans have had to react to this consolidation of European ethnic minorities. Other ethnic groups have also reacted by forming their own cabals (the Chinese and Indian ethnic enclaves, for example) geared to counteract this consolidation of economic interests. The indigenous majority in particular has coalesced around the only form of institutional power that it currently wields, namely, the ability to use the patronage network of the ANC government to further its own economic interests. The consolidation of power, authority and wisdom in the hands of a few decision-makers has created incentives to use loyalty, seniority and tenure as alternative means of judging performance. This has completed South Africa's journey towards an anti-meritocracy. Those who are neither considered 'white' nor politically connected have been sadly left behind in the race for economic prosperity. This has created a polarised, unequal society that is unsustainable as currently structured.

Economist Thomas Piketty, speaking on the topic of inequality in South Africa at the 2015 Mandela Annual Lecture, cited the jarring statistic that 60–65 per cent of South Africa's wealth is concentrated in the hands of just 10 per cent of the population (compared to 50–55 per cent in Brazil, and 40–45 per cent in the US): 'Of course, this group historically has been predominantly, almost exclusively, white. Even today if you look at the data, especially within the top 1–5 per cent, it will be up to 80 per cent white …'[7] The most important cause of this persistent and extreme inequality is the high transaction costs that set higher barriers to entry into the wealthy class. These are the consequences of an economic model that sought to integrate all of South Africa's ethnic groups (indigenous and immigrants) into a liberal capitalist democracy after 1994. Introducing different ethnicities to the 'perils' of transacting with perfect strangers has had the effect of increasing transaction costs. Given that European ethnic minorities had been transacting with each other commercially for many decades prior to 1994, they could simply opt out of those transactions they deemed too risky or too costly. Indigenous people, on the other hand, could generally only opt out if they had access to government funding that backed the completion of the desired transaction. The unintended consequence of restorative justice in South Africa has been a closing of ranks within the European ethnic community. This has led to persistent widening of inequalities in wealth distribution, which are currently at world-record levels.

Piketty's celebrated book, *Capital in the Twenty-first Century*, argues that, as a general rule, wealth grows faster than economic output, a concept he captures in the expression $r > g$ (where r is the rate of return on wealth and g is the economic growth rate).[8] All things being equal, faster economic growth will diminish the importance of wealth in a society, whereas slower growth will increase it. This is of great importance when we appreciate that South Africa has hugely unequal economic wealth distribution and has experienced over ten years of anaemic growth in GDP. The importance of wealth has been amplified as the economy's growth rate has stagnated.

Many economists argue that South Africa's slow growth is a result of a lack of sufficient policy certainty, labour market inflexibility and an unfriendly regulatory environment for business (exchange controls and progressive taxes are most often mentioned). Depending on which economists you believe, these policies are created out of administrative naiveté or an inept attempt to pander to South Africa's majority of poor voters or minority of rich taxpayers.

These are simplistic explanations for a very complex set of factors at play. If you believe the proposition that 'in a perfect world of perfect information and low transaction costs, (different) parties will bargain for a wealth-maximising result',[9] then you can easily understand the reverse, that imperfect information, based on years of interracial mistrust, leads to higher transaction costs. These high transaction costs in turn necessitate constant and often disruptive bargaining between government, business and trade unions. Unions, largely representing poor indigenous people's interests, and big business, largely representing rich European ethnic-minority interests, often fail to see eye to eye when it comes to sharing economic upside and downside. This situation leads to wealth-minimising results for the majority of the population. Those who can wield undue influence over government policy, for example through tax policy or financial services regulations, tend to do exponentially better than other citizens.

To make matters worse, the culture and values of the dominant economic class in South Africa are 'misrecognised' in our education system as the culture and values of the entire society. As a result, the indigenous majority population has begun to normalise the undesirable gap between its culture and values and those of the dominant minority class. This has entrenched interracial trust deficits and the need for alternative institutions to regulate newly empowered political and commercial participants.

A thorough dissection of the effects of racial categorisation in South Africa today is crucial to understanding which direction South Africa's political-economic overhaul should take. The goal of such an inquiry will be to enhance the understanding of future policy-makers on how and why racial categorisation has produced such a wide gulf between winners and losers. I hope that a deeper investigation into South Africa's segregation into psychosocial ethnic enclaves will convince change agents in both the public and private sector to create alternative forms of remedial action. It is critical to abandon policies that reinforce old racial categories and further create hardened stereotypes that perpetuate racism in South Africa.

According to the *Oxford Dictionary*, racism is 'the belief that all members of each race possess characteristics, abilities or qualities specific to that race, especially to distinguish it as inferior or superior to another race or races'. There is a fine line between believing that each race possesses certain qualities and characteristics, which are usually stereotypes, and assigning connotations of inferiority or superiority to such characteristics. The nature of the 'inter-race' experience in South Africa has been inextricably shaped by imperialism and an extended period of colonialism. All citizens of South Africa are bombarded by stereotypes that support a 'white racial superiority' myth, and many adult South Africans meet the above definition of a racist. More importantly, South Africans are largely united in their internalisation of negative stereotypes about the performance of 'black' academics, managers and professionals.

There is a consensus among biologists that race-based categorisation is an imprecise way to assign differences between human beings. The philosopher Anthony Appiah states: 'The statistical facts about the distribution of variant characteristics in human populations and sub-populations are the same, whichever way the matter is expressed. Apart from the visible morphological characteristics of skin, hair and bone, by which we are inclined to assign people to the broadest racial categories – black, white, yellow – there are few genetic characteristics to be found in the population of England that are not found in similar proportions in [the DRC] or in China; and few too (though more) which are found in [the DRC] but not in similar proportions in China or in England. A more familiar part of the consensus is that the differences between peoples are in language, moral affections, aesthetic attitudes or political ideology.'[10]

Despite this consensus, South Africans have continued to act in support of a belief in the superiority of so-called white South Africans over South Africans who are considered black. Today's racism in South Africa is characterised by what psychologists John Dovidio and Samuel Gaertner call 'aversive racism'. One of the critical aspects of aversive racism is 'white people's denial of personal prejudice and underlying unconscious feelings towards and belief about blacks. Because of current cultural values, most whites have strong convictions concerning fairness, justice and racial equality. However, because of a range of normal cognitive and sociocultural processes that promote intergroup biases, most whites also develop some negative feelings towards or beliefs about blacks of which they are unaware, or try to dissociate from the non-prejudice self-images.'[11]

Coming as they do from a dominant in-group, most members of European ethnic minorities are unconscious of their privilege. This racism without leaving the fingerprints of prejudice is self-empowering in that you get the benefits of discrimination without the negative baggage of acknowledging that deep down you exhibit bigotry. A universal truth is that the prerogative of privilege is the ability and need to replicate itself. Those in possession of wealth and the ability to be gatekeepers of wealth-generating opportunities tend to exhibit a preference for members of their own group.

Racism on the part of indigenous people is reactive and driven largely by the development, throughout both colonialism and apartheid, of an inferiority complex that seeks to define itself as better than a stereotype generated hundreds of years ago. Indigenous South Africans expect to be treated unfairly by members of other races and resent those who confirm this expectation. This represents a form of internalised bias, commonly known as a victim mentality. Indigenous South Africans who are self-aware catch themselves feeling grateful to those members of European ethnic minorities who do not treat them unfairly, and ultimately become resentful of this automatic gratitude, serving to sabotage their relationships with ethnic-minority contemporaries.

Indigenous people's views on race are facilitated by a constant fear of stereotype threat. The fact that many indigenous people have not had as much access to formal education and training as their European ethnic-minority counterparts results in their feeling under-prepared in the workplace. This only serves to entrench the inferiority complex they harbour, and creates social and professional unease in interactions with ethnic minorities. Further cementing European ethnic superiority complexes is the reality that many uneducated indigenous people tend to shy away from evaluation and measurement, resigned to the fact that the system is rigged against them.

Despite the hundreds of thousands of qualified indigenous middle managers in the economy, real transformation has not yet taken place. Notwithstanding the fact that there has been a dramatic rise in the number of indigenous people in senior management, we must remember that this rise has come off an extremely low base. For indigenous South Africans to make up only 30 per cent of all managers, when the indigenous population is 79 per cent of all South Africans, indicates the presence of what is called statistical discrimination.[12] New indigenous managers, perhaps in part because of the embedded stereotype that indigenous people in general lack sufficient skills, have not been institutionally trusted to be genuinely ready for senior leadership roles with full institutional authority. Those individuals who have been overpromoted for reasons other than competence have only served to justify a hardening of these stereotypes.

It is against this backdrop that the country is entering the post-BEE era. The days when so-called whites had to empower those considered black as a precondition for participation in corporate shareholding are effectively over. The research presented below shows that describing the impediment to economic transformation in South Africa as a phenomenon driven purely by racism is not helpful in understanding the dynamics and the motivation that drives the actors behind it.

Locating theory in practice

Social context moderates what people conceive to be fair. The norms governing how people behave depend on their places in society and their different social identities. Economists use the catch-all language of tastes in an attempt to aggregate identity into decision-making.[13] The fast-growing field of behavioural economics has introduced the idea of cognitive bias and how these biases affect economic decision-making. Identity economics presents a much richer, more socially framed way of assessing decision-making. Identity economics argues that individual actors make economic decisions based on monetary/financial incentives, as well as on factors that advance their conception of their identity. Holding monetary incentives constant, actions that conflict with the individual's core identity are generally avoided.

Many people have forgotten that before whiteness was their primary identity, European immigrants to South Africa were highly fractured. They have consolidated themselves as 'whites' at the expense of the rest of the country. Some European ethnic enclaves have existed side by side in South Africa for close to 400 years. There are at least eight different lineages of European immigrants that are today classified as white South Africans. They comprise 9.1 per cent of the nearly 55 million people in the country. Dutch, French, British, German and Irish immigrants began settling in the Cape from the late 17th century. The first group of permanent immigrants was a group of 90 Dutch Calvinist settlers in 1652. Between the 1680s and 1717, the colony's European population rose from 289 Europeans to just under 3 000.[14] After Britain took control of the Cape in

1806, British citizens began to trickle into the country. In 1820, more than 5 000 middle-class British immigrants (from Ireland, England and Scotland) came to settle around Grahamstown (now Makhanda) and Port Elizabeth.[15] The discovery of diamonds in 1867, near what is now Kimberley, lured many thousands of foreign-born fortune-hunters, while the discovery of gold on the Witwatersrand in 1886 increased the European population of the Transvaal eightfold, including thousands of Jewish immigrants (many were attracted to this region at this time because of their expertise in diamond trading). Between 1876 and 1976 approximately 460 000 Italians immigrated to Africa.[16] By the mid-1990s, the Italian population in South Africa was estimated at approximately 120 000 people.

Portuguese immigrants arrived in South Africa in three waves. The first and longest wave brought impoverished people from the island of Madeira in the 1920s. The second wave of more skilled mainlanders arrived between 1940 and 1980. The final wave of Portuguese immigrants consisted of ex-colonists from Angola and Mozambique, who chose to migrate to South Africa after Portugal granted independence to its colonies in 1975.[17] Today, Portuguese South Africans constitute between 10 and 15 per cent of the ethnic minority population.

The story that has not been told well enough is how disparate many of these European immigrants were, living completely isolated in hundreds of small enclaves that formed nuclei around which social capital slowly grew. Instead of seeing commonalities within their European ancestries, many of these ethnic enclaves were actively hostile to each other. Discrimination was based on religion, the perceived inferiority or superiority of their respective country or region of origin, historical family names and associated social status and lineage.

Alejandro Portes and Julia Sensenbrenner believe 'social capital' to be a three-dimensional form of capital. First, it comprises 'value introjection', which demands that members of a particular group act in a values-based manner above petty self-interest or greed. Second, it comprises 'reciprocity transactions', which are an accumulation of social credits for good deeds done in the past. The third dimension is bounded solidarity, which is often instigated by exogenous circumstances that can unify a group into synchronous action.[18] Together, these three dimensions of social capital can be very powerful in moderating behaviour within a tight-knit group, leading to a set of values and codes of conduct that can lower transaction costs and increase productivity in that enclave.

This analysis goes some way to describe why some mono-ethnic pockets of South Africa have a high degree of social cohesiveness and exhibit low transaction costs. An example is the ecosystem in Stellenbosch, in the Western Cape, which has seen some of the most successful models of venture capital, igniting start-up companies and expanding them into corporate giants over short periods of time. Any careful exploration of the business culture in Stellenbosch would show all three dimensions of social capital at work, which serves to reinforce the business community's two inherent advantages – access to financial capital and the presence of social capital within their business networks. As a result, of South Africa's top 40 companies, ten have their roots in Stellenbosch.

Portes and Sensenbrenner describe how the physical or geographical manifestations of ethnic enclaves operate. But what makes the insulation within ethnic enclaves so powerful, and so effective as a means of economic progress, is captured in the identity economics concept of identity utility, or the affirmation of self that comes from operating within an environment that reflects one's values and beliefs. Such an environment achieves a healthy equilibrium between formal and informal institutions. In many ways, corporate South Africa offers this sense of comfort for European ethnic minorities. Everything that is held dear in terms of norms and ideals has European roots that affirm the European identities of so-called white South Africans. This allows them to use social tools such as gossip, social categorisation and stereotyping to ostracise those who exhibit beliefs and values opposed to those of the in-group. This ostracising is in itself affirming and contributes further to a feeling of belonging for those who stay in the in-group. Those ostracised in this manner lose identity utility by being forced to come to terms with the gap between who they are and who they need to be in order to share a sense of belonging with work colleagues or fellow students.

Pockets of South Africa, where inhabitants have had the benefit of this type of bounded solidarity for many decades, are incredibly stable subsets of society. They have strong family values that serve as the foundation from which individuals can make themselves competitive in the professional careers they choose. This socially privileged background is a major differentiation factor between the fortunes of 'white' and 'black' urban South Africans. It is worth noting that some rural indigenous South Africans have exhibited many of the same tenets of social cohesiveness described above for many generations, even predating colonial conquest. What these rural areas have not enjoyed is the confluence of high social capital, the abundance of investment capital and overt government support.

The consolidation of white ethnic enclaves in South Africa

South Africa's first truly democratic election in 1994 represented the convergence of the interests of six previously separate ethnic enclaves. The Jewish, Afrikaner, Greek, Portuguese, Italian and British enclaves in South Africa were all formerly discrete population groups whose members exhibited all the classic ethnic-enclave behavioural patterns. They were tightly woven cultures with long histories of reciprocity inherent in the way they transacted with other members. They had various historical events that brought them together in a manner representing bounded solidarity. They were self-sufficient communities. They each had their own banks, lending almost exclusively to their own members, lived separately in concentrated areas segregated from others, and schooled their children separately with culturally calibrated curricula. Even separately, these six enclaves had all been among the most successful ethnic enclaves by global standards. They commanded vast economic interests with huge financial resources and well-educated sources of human capital. Most importantly, over time, they each had cemented all three dimensions of social capital.

These ingredients, turbocharged by explicit 'white empowerment' government policies under apartheid, spawned successful institutional vectors through which these ethnic groups could entrench themselves as dominant forces in the South African economy. They were fiercely competitive with each other and cooperated hesitantly. A common threat, in the form of BEE, changed all that, starting in the late 1990s (after years of debate and lobbying, BEE was formally put into law in 2003). 'Whiteness' became their primary identity, as it represented the common basis upon which their socio-economic privileges were to be defended. The segregation that had been the hallmark of these enclaves gave way to large-scale integration, where possible, and widespread cooperation across industries. The creation of this amalgamated European ethnic enclave has proven to be an obstacle to further integration with indigenous South Africans.

One reason for this success may be that the social glue that cemented bounded solidarity among European ethnic minorities was a reinforcement of their perceived superiority relative to indigenous South Africans. This may just have reinforced the Western European tendency of sorting by identifying sameness and differences, choosing to gravitate to that which is most like you and move apart from that which is not. At face value, the experienced utility of so-called white South Africans confirms what was initially a less pronounced notion of the superiority of European ethnic groups.

Some people would argue that European ethnic minorities in South Africa perform so much better, and are consequently so well remunerated, because they are more disciplined, work harder and are better educated. *The Triple Package*, by Amy Chua and Jeb Rubenfeld, makes just such a case for Asian Americans, and favourably compares them to 'similarly' disciplined minority ethnic groups relative to white Americans. According to Chua and Rubenfeld, the three factors that make up the triple package, and that therefore determine success, are insecurity (outsiderdom), a sense of superiority and good impulse control.[19] Together these factors constitute a kind of Puritan mindset long abandoned by white Protestant America. Chua and Rubenfeld contend that immigrants from certain parts of the world these days tend to possess such a mindset, which represents an advantage. Much of 'white' superiority in South Africa rests on a very similar fallacy.

A similar line of argument has been used (less openly after 1994) to explain the success of Afrikaners in South Africa. Many people view the Calvinist work ethic as key to the ability of Afrikaners to drive economic development. 'Afrikaner Calvinism kept to its primitive roots because the liberalising influences of the European Enlightenment were not able to reach the isolated Boers in South Africa. As a direct result of the dominant Old Testament theology, the belief became entrenched that the Afrikaners were superior to the "obviously damned" Bantu and other indigenous peoples such as the Hottentots and the Bushmen.'[20] Through a long series of conflicts with native peoples, a bond arose within the Boer society, strengthened by the claim of being a sanctified, chosen people of God. These factors led Afrikaner Calvinism, though theologically similar to European Calvinism, to affect Boer society significantly differently from comparable societies in Europe. The belief in Afrikaners' being a 'chosen people' facilitated a blunter display of racial superiority in South Africa than was the case anywhere in Europe (with the exception of Hitler's Germany).

Prior to Afrikaners' taking control of government, there was no sign of higher productivity or economic performance based on a unique Afrikaner work ethic. The mining industry, agriculture and manufacturing, even the much-vaunted infrastructure built during the apartheid era, were all built disproportionately on the back of cheap indigenous labour. In fact, Afrikaner nationalism birthed the idea of apartheid in the 1930s largely because the white electorate thought Afrikaners were being out-competed at school by English-speaking kids, and missionary-educated indigenous people were beginning to threaten their access to work opportunities. Their feeling of superiority was a faith-based sense of entitlement, not an observed reality based on any empirical research on interracial productivity and work-ethic differences. Ethnic intellectual superiority as a hypothesis just does not hold up as a reason for the distribution of wealth in any society.

The theory underlying *The Triple Package* has been challenged by psychologists Joshua Hart and Christopher Chabris, who counter that intelligence, conscientiousness and economic advantage are the most likely elements of success, regardless of race or ethnicity.[21] As we will shortly see, conscientiousness is not an easy virtue to live by when your surroundings and those of your school do not affirm your identity. In fact, when critically confronted, all of the myths underpinning 'white' superiority are similarly unconvincing.

White supremacy rests on four faulty intellectual pillars. First, there is the theologically and historically false premise that Jesus was a 'white' man with blond hair and was created by God, his father, in his image. With the help of anthropology and science, it has been established with some certainty that any man with the family, geographical and ethnic background of Jesus was in fact much more likely to be a brown-skinned man with curly hair. Today, he would certainly be more likely to be considered 'black' than 'white'.[22] This has not stopped the European-dominated Catholic and Anglican churches from continuing to portray Jesus as blond-haired and 'white', even in the many African countries where their missionary work has taken them.

Second, the 'white' superiority myth rests on the fallacy that the Greeks and Romans were the founders of modern civilisation. Historians propagating this fallacy go on to draw a direct line between the great Greek and Roman civilisations and most things modern in our world. The invention of mathematics, law, astronomy and the modern state, among others, are deemed proof that the heritage of 'white civilisation' points to a cognitive superiority that is unmatched. The work of polymath Cheikh Anta Diop and his contemporaries has disproved this fallacy. In his seminal works, Diop has proven that, on the contrary, Egyptians were dark-skinned Africans whose civilisation owes its origins to the Nubian people of Sudan and modern Ethiopia.[23] That Egyptians were robbed of their knowledge systems by their Greek colonial masters is no longer an issue of great controversy.

Historians as far back as Herodotus have confirmed that it was the Egyptians who were the founders of the modern state, and the founders of geometry, astronomy, medicine and academia. Egyptian priests and their scribes wrote many of the books that were in the Library of Alexandria. The conquest of Egypt by Alexander the Great facilitated the oldest and most significant intellectual property transfer, from the Egyptians to the Greeks and Romans, by pillaging the collections of that original Egyptian library. The work of Diop and others has shown that Greek thinkers such as Plato and Pythagoras were actually standing on the unacknowledged shoulders of Egyptian intellectual giants.

Third, through both constant repetition and personification, the words 'white' and 'black' have slowly taken on positive and negative connotations as Anglo-Saxons gained global power and influence. In early versions of the Old Testament (the first Latin version, for instance), the words 'black' and 'white' had subtly different connotations. Over time, as Europeans began injecting race into scripture, public discourse and the media of the day, these words were politicised until they took on the one-sided stereotypes, with white representing purity and black representing evil and darkness.

Diop has shown that, in fact, Egyptians held the colour black in high esteem, and in their art painted their gods the darkest black available. They depicted members of the higher class as darker and slaves as lighter, a perception of colour and privilege that is the inverse of the modern view. In fact, the fertile, pitch-black soil along the banks of the Nile River encouraged the Ancient Egyptians, who were also the world's first imperialists, to associate blackness with fertility, wealth and prosperity. The use of the words 'white' and 'black' today is ever pregnant with meaning and innuendo that both create and reinforce stereotypes.

Fourth, the 'white' supremacy fallacy rests on the deeply held belief that the Anglo-Saxon culture, values and belief systems are the essential ingredients for the sustainable modernisation of societies around the world. Many history books cite the correlation between imperialism, colonialism and slavery, and modern political and economic liberalism, which came on the heels of the Enlightenment. The failure of communism around the world has been touted by many as the final proof of the superiority of Anglo-Saxon institutions and the values that underpin them. The work of political economist Francis Fukuyama – famous for his 'end of history' thesis – illustrates the inverse relationship between European influence in China and the functionality of the Chinese state. In *The Origins of Political Order*, Fukuyama shows how advanced China was long before Europe moved away from the doomed city-state model,[24] hinting that, if anything, the positive influence was the other way around. A critical reading of history provides no support for the myth of white institutional supremacy.

There must therefore be other reasons, beyond racial categories, for the continued collective economic success of those regarded as whites in South Africa, and for their belief in their ethnic supremacy. The disproportionality and sheer scale of their success, and its resilience to policy changes more than 25 years after the fall of apartheid, warrants exploration and discussion.

It turns out that there is no single reason, but rather a combination of factors, such as long periods of monocultural insulation, educational reinforcement of a superiority complex, cultural control of popular media and greatly reduced transaction costs, facilitated by high social capital. These have been the springboard for economic prosperity and the maintenance of ethnic minorities' advantages in modern-day South Africa.

Psychosocial bias

Some readers may be aware of the Pygmalion effect, which was mentioned earlier in the chapter. This predicts that those learners identified by their teachers as potential high performers will largely perform according to those expectations. Essentially, the policy of Bantu education was a giant Pygmalion experiment driven by low expectations on the part of society at large of black learners, producing predictable results. What is less well known is the Pygmalion effect's opposite, the Golem effect, which shows how low expectations are triggered and conveyed. Just as high teacher expectations propel learners' high achievements, low teacher expectations impel learners down a slippery slope of underperformance. Bantu education's effect on indigenous children was an unprecedented giant Golem effect. It has led to generations of underperformance, due primarily to lower expectations combined with a lack of access to educational resources and social cues. All these combined to trigger the stereotype-threat phenomenon in indigenous people. The toxic combination of the Pygmalion and the Golem effects, when extended to the workplace, set the stage for what impedes transformation in South Africa today.

The forms of unconscious bias I discussed earlier are crucial to examining how bias in the workplace can extend the advantage of a dominant class. Given that European ethnic-minority employees occupy 73 per cent of management positions in South Africa, bias can only be unidirectional. Positive bias plays out between members of an in-group in the workplace, eliciting feelings of warmth and help towards each other. This facilitates senior management's helping those in need, smoothing their path towards professional ascension by choosing key assignments for them, and by pairing them with fellow high performers. Negative bias obviously has the opposite effect.

Positive bias in the workplace is facilitated by value attribution. Psychologists DM Taylor and JR Doira observe: 'Research has found that we often exhibit attribution biases when interpreting the behaviour of others, and specifically when explaining the behaviour of in-group versus out-group members. More specifically, a review of the literature on inter-group attribution biases noted that people generally favour dispositional explanations of an in-group member's positive behaviour and situational explanations for an in-group's negative behaviour. Alternatively, people are likely to do the opposite when explaining the behaviour of an out-group member, ie, to attribute positive behaviour to situational factors and negative behaviour to disposition.'[25] This has a fundamental effect on how professionals justify promoting some colleagues while firing others. What is worse is that when out-group members recognise these factors at play in the workplace, it paralyses them. They often internalise this bias, becoming completely ineffective and unproductive, and thereby confirming a self-fulfilling prophecy. Eurocentric cultural benchmarks for what makes reliable and productive managers and/or employees in corporate South Africa effectively alienate African professionals.

Indigenous people have to live in a world where the norm is to speak English or Afrikaans, wear business suits, eat European food and assess each other according to European standards. This makes it difficult for indigenous professionals both to be themselves and to be successful. For those attempting to preserve privilege, this dilemma conveniently shrinks the pool of potential managers of enterprises and leaders in society, and has created immovable obstacles for the transformation of South Africa's socio-economic system.

Inverting the psychosocial ethnic-enclave hypothesis

Carl Gustav Jacob Jacobi, a German mathematician living in the 1800s, once said, 'Man must invert, always invert.'[26] Jacobi believed that the solution for many difficult problems in mathematics could be found if the problems were expressed in the inverse. In that spirit, I have attempted to invert the logic of ethnic-enclave theory, social-capital theory and identity economics so that we can analyse them from the opposite point of view.

One of the challenges in choosing which lens to look at a problem with is that the problem and the likely solution always look slightly different depending on your perspective. One of South Africa's most basic challenges is creating shared perspectives through which actors can better judge the actions of others. Because of the ethnic-enclave history and how it has metamorphosed today, different 'racial' groups have different ideas of why history and politics play out in the ways they do. A question some European ethnic minorities often ask is why indigenous South Africans have been outperformed over the last 25 years when government was under their control. Looking at this question purely against the backdrop of ethnic immigrants competing for scarce resources with the local ethnic majority yields predictable stereotypical responses.

However, it is instructive to answer this question through an inversion of the principles of identity economics and of the ethnic-enclave argument. One could guess that, first, indigenous people in South Africa have failed to build productive social capital. Second, indigenous South Africans also lacked African-owned or African-controlled enterprises and the expertise to build or use institutions in a way that allowed their social capital to become a national phenomenon. Third, and perhaps most importantly, indigenous people lack sufficient sources of economic opportunities to create sustainable wealth at the scale required to become a national force to be reckoned with.

These are well-known deficiencies in indigenous communities, and there are many different viewpoints about how to address them. What is less well understood is the role of identity, working in tandem with a lack of social capital, in perpetuating the status quo. Identity economics holds that, in trade-offs between financial rewards and dignity, dignity often wins. If people feel that they have to face the choice of adopting an outsider identity and risk unemployment, or adopting an identity that is incongruent with their core beliefs in order to stay employed, they will often choose the outsider identity. Over time, those outsiders begin to take pride in an oppositional identity. Outsider groups, as indigenous people in South Africa are, can actually become bound together by their exclusion from the mainstream.

Identity economics posits that it is rational to preserve one's 'identity utility' even though it comes at a steep economic cost. The emerging counterculture of rule-flouting, corruption and criminality is one such expression of 'outsiderdom' but by no means the only one. The majority of South Africans have opted out of participating in what they view as a rigged system. Some live on the welfare system. Most are marginalised in the informal economy, which condemns them to a hand-to-mouth existence to protect their identity utility. A lucky few indigenous people become truly independent entrepreneurs.

A minority of indigenous South Africans have adopted the emerging rule-flouting culture to their benefit. These perpetrators of actions counter to the norms espoused in the Constitution or in the codes of conduct of many enterprises, both public and private, are opting out of a system they do not identify with. They gain affirmation, or identity utility, from the ability to subvert the system in a way that gives them some power and helps them take ownership of their life circumstances. For example, the destruction of institutions has an affirming effect on the out-group's identity through the added identity utility it creates.

This phenomenon plays out in similar ways in the classroom. The internalisation of years of low expectations results in underperformance. Given that many learners come from homes where the adults raising them were victims of the same education system, these low expectations are reinforced in the household. What is difficult to observe is the long-term impact on the individuals concerned through what are called 'identity contingencies' and how they function.

In his book *Whistling Vivaldi*, the celebrated social psychologist

Claude Steele describes identity contingencies as cues in a social environment that signal particular stereotypes attached to an aspect of one's identity. In an experiment first run at university campuses in the United States, Steele's research demonstrates how the concerns students face as a result of these stereotype threats affect a wide range of educational outcomes.[28] Steele uses several experiments and analyses their results to explain how the threat of a stereotype, and the extra effort required of students who try to dispel them, interferes with student performance. It is not difficult, once one understands how stereotype threat works, to use it to explain indigenous people's underperformance in the current South African context.

Stereotype threat is a central identity contingency. In an academic paper on diversity cues for African Americans, the authors assert, 'People who belong to stigmatised groups may question whether their group is valued in mainstream settings, for example, in workplaces, schools, religious settings, especially in those in which their group has been historically discriminated against or stereotyped. We use the term "social identity contingencies" to refer to a range of vulnerabilities and opportunities a person expects to face based on settings' response to one or more of the person's social identities.'[28]

Group-based stigmatisation, of the kind that South Africa has had for centuries, creates what psychologists call 'chilly climates'. These are environments within which a certain group's performance is held in suspicion. In these types of environments, the stigmatised group struggles to outperform the non-stigmatised group out of fear of confirming a stereotype.[29] These social contingencies suppress the yield that the affected party gets from their own intellectual talents. This is the central injustice of identity contingencies: they rob individuals of the ability to create much-needed self-efficacy.

In an attempt to overcome stereotype threat, two overcompensating mechanisms kick in before stereotype threat overcomes its victim and leads them to give up trying to accomplish whatever activity they are failing to achieve. 'Over-efforting' and 'undue displays of self-sufficiency' are often caused by stereotype threat. Both mechanisms make those affected difficult to work with in teams. Being seen as difficult to work with is a long-term economic disability.

A critical impediment caused by this type of identity-threat-triggered anxiety is a reduction in working memory. People going through stereotype threat are constantly aware of how they are being viewed. They are riddled with self-doubt and constantly monitor their own performance relative to the expectations of others. They retain large volumes of data related to people's approval or disapproval of their performance. This clogs up their short-term working memory. Claude Steele's research shows that these are all contributing factors to momentarily diminished cognitive capacity for higher-order tasks. This reduces indigenous people's competitive capacity in the classroom and in the workplace. Over-efforting makes someone an inefficient and unproductive scholar or professional. Making all this even more perverse, research has shown repeatedly that the more members of a stigmatised group care about high performance, the more vulnerable they are to stereotype threat.

A central aspect of identity contingencies is that they are triggered by the stigmatised person's recognition that they are operating in a chilly climate. The act of categorisation across the warmth and competence dimensions can severely impair the work experience. How we are perceived by our peers is critical to our performance. When we have warm feelings, often elicited by a feeling of fellowship with or sameness to others, we find ourselves trusting people's motives and assigning to their actions innate competence and work ethic. The opposite is true about those we feel to be 'other' than us.

When learners or professionals feel themselves being judged by their peers or superiors across these warmth and competence dimensions, they automatically expect to fail the snap tests or evaluations. Their fear is also based on a legitimate expectation, based on their peers' propensity to categorise, that they will end up being unfairly placed on a lower starting place across each axis (warmth and competence) than they would rate themselves, or than a fellow out-group member would rate them.

The reality for indigenous South Africans, in particular in the workplace or at school, is that these identity contingencies matter when it comes to what groups people are placed in for work and school assignment. Placements into certain teams at work or access to opportunities for upward mobility are highly dependent on both these contingencies. The bias of people in power within these organisations has a major impact on an individual's career prospects. The fact that more than 70 per cent of managers are from European ethnic minorities, and that close to 70 per cent of university professors are from this minority group, seems to suggest that corporations and universities remain chilly climates for indigenous people. They are saturated with cues that trigger stereotype threat. The result is that it is more difficult for indigenous people to succeed in these institutions.

This is the backdrop against which indigenous South Africans fail to break through the managerial layers in corporate South Africa. From a seemingly trivial thing such as who we choose to sit next to in a room or who we pick to join our group in a work setting, warmth and competency assessments are the major factors underlying the gut instincts we form about people. The feeling of belonging or connectedness to the group elevates and submerges different people to perform above or below their natural abilities. Having understood how difficult it is to work against both the burden of low expectations and the debilitating effects of stereotype threat at an individual level, we can begin to appreciate how high the social barriers to entry are to the upper echelons of a society, thus allowing the impact of racial categorisation to persist unchecked.

Conclusion

This case study has attempted to show that three fundamental human desires have combined to shape South Africa's political economy. These are: the desire to categorise information for sense-making purposes; the desire to draw oneself towards those most similar to oneself; and the desire to preserve the privileges one has. These desires have resulted in plunder, enslavement and exploitation, leading to an economy controlled by European ethnic minorities and their surrogates. The modern locus of this control is in the norms, values and codes of conduct formed over many years within European ethnic enclaves. These norms, values and codes of conduct are now encoded in South Africa's institutional architecture. They are used as filters to determine which members of society qualify as insiders. They determine which entrepreneurs deserve the support of capital providers. They determine how talent is compensated for within various industries. Indigenous South Africans face institutionalised stereotypes that signal their 'outsiderdom' in the country of their birth.

Turning indigenous South Africans into outsiders has shrunk the group of available professionals for each job. It has lowered the probability of smart indigenous children prospering through the educational system. It has significantly reduced the chances of good indigenous entrepreneurs succeeding. Rendering indigenous people outsiders has made South Africa an anti-meritocratic society.

Indigenous individuals have not taken commercial ostracism lying down. Some have completely opted out of the system and are thriving in the informal economy or surviving on grant payments. A minority has chosen largely to maximise their identity utility over their economic utility by propagating a counterculture of rule-flouting and anti-institutionalism, which superficially confirms the stereotype. This has left a trail of institutional decay along the way. I have come to the conclusion that racial categorisation is the single biggest cause of the inequality of opportunities faced by South Africans today.

We are all entitled to our own self-expression. We are all free to have whatever primary and secondary identities we desire. Identity is an intensely personal possession that we should guard jealously. It becomes a national imperative, however, when an individual community's identity leads to statistical discrimination. South Africa exhibits statistical discrimination against indigenous South Africans because of a form of aversive racism born out of the culture of ethnic enclaves. Aversive racism is facilitated by identity contingencies built up by years of discrimination. These identity contingencies, particularly in the form of stereotype threat, conspire to repress indigenous scholastic and professional development.

Removing statistically significant discrimination will take a powerful social movement. The catalyst for this movement has to be what South Africans consider their primary identities. For as long as South Africans of European descent are monolithically referred to as 'white', they will retain hegemony over privileged positions in the socio-economic structure. Indigenous South Africans will not be able to shake the identity contingencies that haunt them for as long as 'blackness' is their primary identity. Identity economics predicts that the South African status quo, characterised by high income inequalities, low socio-economic trust and low productivity, will continue for as long as the majority of employees, voters and students do not identify with the ideals, norms and objectives of the institutions they are asked to function within. They will choose to maximise their identity utility over economic incentives even if it means losing out financially. The perpetuation of the status quo will ensure that in-group members of the European ethnic enclave and the 'black' elite political enclave will continue to prosper at the expense of ordinary South Africans.

South Africa's leaders have to realise the divisiveness of attributing all the current ills of indigenous people to racism, or, perversely, to lack of effort or skills shortages. Leaders are failing in their most basic job of providing direction towards better solutions by not acknowledging the lack of social capital, the presence of stereotype threat and the inability to build enterprises that support indigenous wealth creation. The promise of skills development, more state support or get-rich-quick mechanisms through state tenders are not sustainable remedies to the significant challenges discussed above. Nor is a mechanistic reliance on a state-led development plan going to do the trick.

South Africa's future prosperity hinges on the ability to ignite individual maximisation of talent. This requires leaders to address what is holding individuals back and to remove those constraints. My research has found that one of the biggest inhibiting factors to South African individuals' economic progress is race-based categorisation and the resulting stereotype threat and chilly climates created both at work and within educational environments. A focus on removing these barriers to talent maximisation could facilitate the beginning of a journey down the discovery path to a more positive national identity and both bonding social capital and bridging social capital.

Anthony Appiah sums up the dangers inherent in societies retaining race as a primary form of identity: 'The truth is that there are no races: there is nothing in the world that can do all we ask race to do for us ... The evil that is done is done by the concept, and by easy – yet impossible – assumptions as to its application.'[30] What we miss through our obsession with the structure of relations of concepts is, simply, reality.

The belief that one can erase years of racism by legislating alternative means of race-based reparations fails to understand the mechanics of South Africa's European ethnic-minority privilege-preservation system. 'White' privilege in South Africa is perpetuated by a myth that there is a biological difference between races. Years of intense indoctrination have successfully convinced both European immigrants and indigenous South Africans of this fallacy. For as long as race is part of South Africans' primary identities, the stereotypes will persist. That white equals successful, intelligent, productive stereotypes and that black equals the opposite will continue to have self-fulfilling manifestations. Forcing South Africans to own all of the successes and failures within the country by taking away race-based psychological crutches will open the path towards an accountable, active citizenry.

In trying to shape South Africa towards a more unified, less racially stratified nation-state, its leaders should consider how the

19th-century French historian Ernest Renan answered a question he posed in the essay 'What is a Nation?': 'Man is a slave neither of his race, his language, his religion, the course of his rivers, nor the direction of his mountain ranges. A great aggregation of men, in sane mind and warm heart, created moral conscience that calls itself a nation. As long as this moral conscience proves its strength by sacrifices that require subordination of the individual to the common good, it is legitimate and has the right to exist.'[31] A nation is about belonging in the widest possible sense. It must therefore be a task taken up by all leaders to explore how to make people feel that they belong in all parts of the country.

Leaders in all spheres of life within South Africa have to learn to use both economic utility and identity utility to incentivise individuals in the modern economy, to align their interests with the organisations they work for. Making employees feel that they belong to the institutions within which they work requires a connection between their identity and the mission and values of the organisation. This bond is what facilitates true intrinsic motivation, which research has proven to be far more effective as a tool to motivate people.

The future prosperity of South Africa rests on the individual decisions 55 million South Africans make, namely, what they choose as their primary identities. To the extent that most people choose an alternative primary identity over a racial one, identity alignment between them and key national institutions can take place, leading South Africa towards prosperity. If the large majority continues to use a primary racial identity, then the status quo will prevail.

The key lessons from years of prejudice in South Africa are twofold. First, at an individual level, human beings are what they pay attention to. Identity is one of the best conduits for attention Mother Nature has given us. If we embrace race as part of our primary identity, we grow to obsess over it. It drives our behaviour. We pay detailed attention to everything affirming and denying that identity. Second, expectations are what makes us both socially functional and socially dysfunctional human beings. The more likely we are to expect people to follow an agreed set of rules, the better we can cooperate with them. The opposite is also true. When you step back from these two critical sources of path dependency, you realise the danger of building a country where identity puts citizens on a collision course, and a lack of trust makes them brace for impact as opposed to steering away from danger.

Ultimately, South Africans need to ask themselves why it is not enough for them to just be referred to as Africans. Anchoring their identity in the continent of their origin will have the effect of unlocking a set of bonds that have been formed over thousands of years with neighbouring countries, bonds that their oppressors have successfully severed. If it was necessary to sever these bonds for the oppression to be complete, logic suggests that the restoration of these bonds is the key for liberation to be complete. South Africans will not be completely free until they re-establish and nurture their African identity.

8

Liberating human capital

IN 1996, I HAD THE GREAT FORTUNE to meet an individual who would change my life forever. His name is Jeremy, an African American professor from California. At the time of our meeting, I was in danger of becoming a cliché in the form of a university dropout. I had settled firmly into a mediocre academic performance level in my first year of university, and was doing the same in the beginning of my second year when we met. But, when I heard Jeremy's personal story, his consciousness and Pan Africanism opened my eyes to how important it was for an African with access to education to work hard in order to succeed. The excuses I had developed in my own mind about the relevance and content of the curriculum we were being asked to study and the whiteness of our professors didn't matter to Jeremy. He had overcome far steeper odds to get to where he was, so no excuse was acceptable to him as an impediment to education.

Growing up in the famously dangerous Compton neighbourhood of Los Angeles, Jeremy had to skate a very thin line between fulfilling his tremendous talent at high school and giving in to the pull of gang life. Despite these challenges, Jeremy chose the academic route, going on to earn a top-class undergraduate degree, a master's degree in Law and then a PhD at Cambridge University. What made Jeremy exceptional was not the fact that he had a world-class education, despite coming from one of the poorest neighbourhoods in the US. It was his supreme appetite for and patience in mentoring and challenging young minds. In this particular year, he was at the University of Cape Town (UCT) doing some research when he met me and a friend named Luswazi Vokwana.

Jeremy spent the first few meetings engaging us in conversation about all things to do with Pan African politics, history and economics. He gently but firmly exposed just how ignorant we were. He couldn't believe how little we knew about African history, even though I was majoring in History at UCT. I was, with respect, being taught by a very nice British professor who knew little about life in Africa before his ancestors came to the continent. Luswazi, who was better educated than myself, having gone to private schools and completed his A levels in the UK, was equally shaky on ancient African history.

It was then that Jeremy first introduced us to Cheikh Anta Diop. I began to understand the proper historical context within which to put Ancient Egyptian society, ancient Sudan, Ethiopia, the Mali Kingdom of Mansa Musa and the achievements of great men and women like Shaka Zulu and the Queen of Sheba. Suddenly, with this context and a newfound fact base, my own history was enlivened and stripped of the subtle shame I felt at the way my British professor used to describe my ancestors. From the vantage point of a growing comfort within my cultural identity, I was able to launch myself into life as a student, operating on an equal footing with my classmates. Though many fellow Africans, particularly those educated outside South Africa, may have had the benefit of a deeper connection with ancient African history earlier than I did, not all Africans are lucky enough to have a teacher like Jeremy who cared enough about the empowering nature of the mentor-mentee connection to invest the time in inspiring young minds.

Learning to make connections between the achievements of the ancients and those of present-day heroes and heroines is a necessary foundation of critical thinking. Critical thinking depends on in-ternalised heuristics (processes or methods) that connect at a deep level within those Africans on a learning path. These heuristics, or shorthand developed by old wisdom, come from all over the world. The ones that are home-grown ring especially true. Those of us who were robbed of the opportunity, at high-school level, to learn about the Egyptian source of Pythagoras's theorem, invented hundreds of years before the Greeks became literate, or to understand Africa's contribution to the Christian faith, missed opportunities for our learn-ing to crystallise. Understanding that trial and error on the African continent has led to more than its fair share of scientific and math-ematical breakthroughs is critical to building an identity-affirming learning environment for African children. Children who grow up with African identities that are not overtly affirmed by the history they study or the language they speak have a harder time becoming both successful and themselves.

Africans, like people the world over, share a set of aspirations for their continent to become prosperous, productive, economically powerful and politically stable. The natural resources and the youth-ful human capital that this continent possesses could help make that dream come true. To do this, Africans have to figure out how to make the African continent feel more like their own. This will re-quire that Africans create a set of institutions that are aligned with their cultures. Specifically, these institutions need to support rules and laws that have the legitimacy to commit the actions of their citizens towards productive means. Africans often speak of needing, wanting or longing for a level of autonomy in managing their own affairs. 'African solutions for African problems' is a phrase we hear often. What exactly does it mean? Why is it important? How does it lead to meaningful change?

If one asks what is meant by 'African solutions for African prob-lems', it has become common practice for Africans to use words such as freedom, liberty, autonomy and true independence. To uncover what this desired condition could potentially look like, I would like to unpack the meaning of these words. The word 'liberty', for instance, comes from the Latin word *libertatem*, which means 'freedom' or 'condition of a freeman'. It was introduced into the English language through the old French word *liberté*, which means 'freedom'.[1] Freedom and liberty are, therefore, interchangeable words.

Understanding freedom seems to be a matter of looking at it from different perspectives. One definition of freedom is 'the power or right to act, speak, or think as one wants'.[2] As simple and elegant as this definition is, its implications are profound. It presents a state of mind that is perhaps elusive to achieve. Indeed, for reasons I shall describe, it is an achievement to which few Africans can lay claim.

A second definition of freedom, from the Merriam-Webster dictionary, is 'the absence of necessity, coercion, or constraint in choice or action'.[3] This difference in nuance introduces the idea that freedom and liberty have positive and negative definitions. The difference between the two is the perspective from which freedom is viewed. The first definition represents an internal and deeply personal perspective of freedom. The second views freedom through an external lens focused on a removal of constraints to the exercise of one's liberty.

A third definition of freedom brings social obligations into the equation: 'Freedom stands for something greater than just the right to act however I choose; it also stands for securing to everyone an equal opportunity for life, liberty, and the pursuit of happiness.'[4] This is a more universal definition of freedom, requiring us to consider whom we view as the people with whom we have a duty to share our freedom.

These three perspectives will be the lenses through which I investigate the subject of this chapter – liberation. The first perspective is temporally oriented, internal, intimate and personal. The second is institutional, communal and cultural. The third perspective is global, philosophical and timeless.

We need to understand why liberation has positive and negative connotations. According to the *Stanford Encyclopedia of Philosophy*: 'On the one hand, one can think of liberty as the absence of obstacles external to the agent. You are free if no one is stopping you from doing whatever you might want to do ... On the other hand, one can think of liberty as the presence of control on the part of the agent. To be free, you must be self-determined, which is to say that you must be able to control your own destiny in your own interests.'[5] These perspectives on freedom are driven by how you conceive yourself and the world around you to be. Indeed, the point of pursuing the designation of being a conscious or free-thinking person is to know oneself and to freely exercise that knowledge in the lifestyle one chooses.

These three lenses interact with each other to bring into focus our actual state of being. Freedom is very much a combination of subjective and objective ideas.[6] It is a concept that is malleable depending on our perspective and the influences that drive this point of view. What we perceive around us dominates our view of what is conceptually possible, and therefore what to *expect* from fellow citizens. This can either be a limiting factor, through poor self-image created by a dominance of foreign symbols of superiority, or, as we have seen for immigrants living in ethnic enclaves, it can be an enabling factor based on a constant stream of external validation from one's community. External validation allows individuals to organise themselves around a strong self-narrative that is inherently reaffirming. In a normal society – to the extent that there is such a thing – there is some balance between positive and negative signals depending on your performance that day, who was around to observe you and what particular tasks you were attempting to complete.

The philosopher David Hume explains this distinction as follows: 'All the perceptions of the human mind resolve themselves into two distinct kinds, which I shall call *impressions* and *ideas*.'[7] Impressions happen to us as we react to the events of the day (we are shaped by those impressions that enter our minds with the greatest force); ideas are formed over time, even though they may reveal themselves to us in a flash. According to Hume's logic, the impressions that have entered African people's minds with the greatest force and violence over the last 300 to 400 years are those sharp distinctions between them and the way foreigners look, dress, transact, organise communities, talk, write and pay homage to their God. From these impressions, those affected Africans have created an *idea* or, more precisely, *ideas* of modernity, which has put the African continent on a cultural treadmill, chasing a state of development it will never attain.

Perhaps, for Africans, much of our perspective has to do with how we see ourselves in history and what we perceive to be our people's lack of contribution to modern life. What would happen if Africans developed the confidence to claim aspects of modern African life as extensions of initiatives begun in ancient African society (Ethiopian, Sudanese or Egyptian), copied by Greeks and Romans and institutionalised in Western Europe, only to be returned to them through colonialism? Young Africans have organically begun such a movement around the concept of being 'woke'. Reimagining Africa in this way demands an understanding or acceptance of how African ideas have metamorphosed over time, leaped borders, changed languages, experienced intellectual refinement and thus been repackaged through social reproduction and learning. It requires turning 'woke-ness' from a vanity project on social media, which defines a privileged few, into a popular movement.

Free societies the world over are forced by circumstances to learn to sift through social history to find hidden cultural gems that help inform their people's present-day attitudes towards traditional norms and values. Africans have to be able to buttress their norms and values within a historical understanding of their culture. Waiting for external permission to do so is futile. We have to give ourselves this permission to embark on a journey to locate ourselves in the modern world on our own terms.

This journey will show that freedom is a complex idea that can be simplified and privatised to fit an African agenda. According to David Hume, freedom, like other complex ideas, must be derivative of a set of simple impressions. These impressions are themselves sub-jective and thus dependent on the particular perspective we carry as we observe them. As differentiated as many African countries' colo-nial and post-colonial experiences are, the material reality of a large majority of Africans is remarkably homogeneous. Many aspects of this material reality reflect a lack of basic economic freedoms re-quired to build successful societies. This lack of economic freedom, compounded by a lack of political freedom (in the hands of ordinary citizens) to shape society even at the most local of levels, undermines the capacity of future generations to outperform their parents.

A statistic captured by an Afrobarometer study, suggesting that 74 per cent of Africans are struggling with poverty and its effects, is indicative of the size of the problem.[8] Though we often discuss poor Africans as statistics, their lived reality is often lost in the numbers. This means that close to three-quarters of all Africans' impressions of life are of struggle. Their lives are constrained by a chronic lack of time and by the lack of the physical, social and human capital resources required to impose control over their lives for long enough to imagine being free.

Freedom escapes ordinary Africans from the moment they open their eyes and does not return until they are back home fast asleep, free to dream about what they would like. Over 74 per cent of Af-ricans live in circumstances that impose massive constraints on the preservation of their dignity, as they wake up every day to a fami-ly sleeping in cramped, uncomfortable quarters. In many cases, the freedom to nourish family members is compromised by the absence of enough food, forcing fathers and mothers to rotate who eats throughout the week and older kids to scavenge. The statistics paint a grim picture. According to UN Food and Agriculture Organization estimates, 233 million people in Africa are hungry or under-nourished. Unicef data confirms that one in three children in Africa experiences symptoms of stunted growth based on malnourishment.

For the minority of salaried Africans, the freedom to dress as they choose eludes them from the moment they leave their baths.

Those lucky few Africans who have a steady job have to suffer the indignity of being forced to dress according to the cultural constraints placed on them by their employers.

According to a UCT study, it is only in South Africa that the majority of workers have the peace of mind of a steady (small as it may be) salary. The Pan African average is that only 20 per cent of workers in sub-Saharan Africa get a reliable salary.[9]

Nor is freedom available to these Africans, when they get to work or school, to choose to speak in their mother tongue. They are instead asked to address their colleagues and superiors in the language of their former oppressors. In 2014, an article by the writer Bwesigye bwa Mwesigire described how children in Uganda are being punished in schools for speaking their mother tongue. The most common punishment documented was for the child in question to wear a dirty sack until he or she came into contact with another child speaking mother tongue so the sack could be passed to them! This may not happen in all schools but it epitomises an attitude to one's own language that reflects self-hate.[10]

All through the day, the freedom to optimise their God-given talents is withheld by the stereotype threat many Africans are forced to work under in the office, factory or farm field. Many of those going to school are robbed of the freedom to learn their own history. They are instead forced to deal with the biased presentation of their history, which reflects the inferiority of their ancestors, robbing them of the basic freedom to be proud of their ethnic heritage. The adoption of a foreign standard, the Cambridge School Certificate syllabus, has in many African countries created the norm of limited teaching of African literature, history and art.

Africans' freedom to go straight home after a long day at work is constrained by spatial planning and public-transport networks, which involve two- to three-hour daily commutes in cramped, stuffy trains or taxis. After a long day at work, labourers in cities such as Maputo have to queue, sometimes for hours, before they can get into a train that will take them home. The indignities of the workday rob these Africans of the freedom of parenthood, arriving home as they do, too tired to think, let alone to have the patience required for child-rearing. Children are robbed of the freedom to enjoy the assurances of maternal and paternal love required for them to be the productive people they have the potential to become.

The indignity of unemployment robs more than a third of this group of Africans of the ability to be affirmed by earning an honest living. They are forced, by circumstance, to become thieves, beggars or a combination of both. In doing so, they unwittingly impinge on the freedom of movement of fellow Africans, who are afraid of being victims of robbery. Out of 115 countries that gather crime statistics, the African countries for which statistics are known rank among the top 50 most dangerous countries in the world.

Freedom evades the 10 per cent of lower-class and middle-class Africans as well. For them, freedom is constrained by the incongruity of who they are versus who they are asked to be in order to successfully function in a society where most of the rules are misaligned with their internal value system. Freedom not to participate in morally questionable transactions in a society beset by systemic corruption eludes them if they care to provide for their immediate and extended families. 'Middle class' in Africa is a nebulous concept. One hundred million African people, excluding South Africans, fit this category. This number may sound impressive but closer examination by researchers, led by Professor Haroon Bhorat, found that the average African middle-class wage earner receives $17 a day. Roughly 35 per cent of the middle class earned less than $10 per day. Only half of this group has an indoor sink; less than 42 per cent of them have running water.[11]

For these 'middle class' Africans, the freedom to organise their workday as they please, to speak in the manner that comes most naturally, to be at ease in the company of fellow employees at their place of work, is almost completely absent. They are robbed of the freedom to speak freely to figures of authority, who often spew bigotry or are patronisingly dismissive. The authoritarian institutional framework that defines public and private professional life in Africa constrains their freedom. Their inability to self-actualise, by narrowing the gap between who they are and who they want to be, often robs them of the freedom to return home proudly to be a moral compass to their children. Less than 32 per cent of them own a car. Yet everything they and their children see on television indicates that they are falling behind by not owning a vehicle. Their aspirations are well ahead of their ability to achieve material change. Worse still, many of these middle-class citizens face violations of their rights by their own governments. Freedom House estimates that just 12 per cent of all Africans live in politically free societies.[12] They are, as a result, as un-free as so-called poor Africans. The only difference lies in the degree of the daily assaults on their dignity.

Many of the top one per cent of Africans also find freedom elusive. The legitimacy of their capital base is constantly questioned. Given how corrupt and un-transparent many African countries are, it is often difficult to discern when and how wealth has been created. Freedom eludes them due to their failure to attain a lifestyle in their home countries framed by a mental mirage of affirmation in a desert of Western cultural superiority. According to Oxfam, Africa loses $14 billion in tax revenues through the use of tax havens by Africa's super-rich. They travel to Davos, Washington and Aspen, to conference after conference, where, as caricatures, they are asked to participate in order to reduce the pressure on global elites to be seen to be listening to the voices of poor people. Ironically, their freedom to speak for 'their people' is compromised by being deemed to be out of touch with the masses they represent.

The African super-rich return to their constituencies as subjects of a global system without the freedom to exercise policy choices at odds with the advice from global elites. For some in this group, the internalisation of Western orthodoxy blinds them to their inability to grant their people freedom of movement, both internally and externally. Their inability to view themselves as leaders of nations, as opposed to leaders of political parties, factions or narrow corporate interests, denies them the freedom to unite their people. On the contrary, some of these leaders seem to be driven by a compulsion to divide in order to stay in power and continue to enrich themselves.

This has to change. African societies need to liberate themselves. This starts with a different way of thinking. What follows is an outline of an approach to personal, professional and communal liberty, underpinned by cultural regeneration and a redefinition of the concept of active citizenship. This way of thinking entails a total commitment by society to reorient itself towards African cultural values and embrace old African wisdom as an essential element of modern education. The approach to learning, teaching and working needs to be completely transformed into one that is unapologetic in its placing of the African perspective at the heart of all decision-making. Adjusting the standard against which our society's norms and values are judged would be freedom-maximising. It would restore African people's ability to be, authentically, both themselves and successful.

A freedom-maximising approach to human capital

The central message in this book is that African institutions matter. They create the rules of the game that leaders could use to manufacture sufficient predictability in the lives of citizens. They would enable Africans to operate with a road map to enhance their contributions to their personal development and to national economic development. Human capital development in Africa is undermined by uncertainty about the rate of return on the investment of time and money in training and education that Africans can expect in the job market. Counselling their leaders to make a conscious decision to construct societies on a merit-based system would be freedom-maximising for young people in Africa.

It is important, though, that we recognise some major positives in relation to African human capital development. There has been some astounding progress in getting young Africans to start their learning journeys. According to a report published in 2018 by the World Bank, since 1990 'sub-Saharan Africa's progress toward universalising primary education has been nothing short of stupendous. The region's average primary gross enrolment ratio (GER) rose from 68 per cent in 1990 to 98 per cent in 2015 and enrolments grew from 63 million students to 152 million, with 78 per cent of primary-school-age children enrolled.'[13] The central challenge now for policy-makers on the African continent is how to make good on the implicit promise that primary school education offers to these 152 million children. If the current status quo remains, and only 12 million of these children make it to tertiary education (including vocational schools), then a major promise to African families will be broken. Leaders have primed these families to expect a drastically different future for their children but cannot yet deliver on that promise. We cannot expect these children to sit idly waiting for opportunities while the system fails them. This is the opposite of how trust within society is built.

Human beings are learning creatures. We are constantly deciphering and remodelling concepts and their associations. Members of society continuously test the rules of the game to establish what the boundaries of behaviour are, or could be. In recent years, stimulus/response theories (made famous by Pavlov's dog experiments) and cognitive theory have combined to help to explain how learning results from events that reinforce psychological drivers that activate our behaviour. As a result, the more we learn, the more automated responses we develop to things we encounter in society.[14] Building automatic responses that *reinforce merit-based rules* will take time and the patient building of trust within both urban and rural African communities.

It will take deliberate and intentional effort to affect people's expectations of each other. Central to this mission is trust-building. African citizens, and more importantly their leaders, need to be convinced that a merit-based society infused by African customs is the choice that maximises freedom for the greatest number of people. Their identity utility would be maximised through a lived experience in which their actions, efforts and professional endeavours have a reasonable expectation of being fairly compensated. Aesthetically, employers and those in charge of learning institutions have to make a concerted effort to transform work and school spaces. The more culturally affirming the learning and working environments in Africa become, the more self-actualised her people will feel.

Humans are socially primed to avoid certain actions and repeat others. For example, when it comes to punishment, behaviour that avoids punishment is learned through memory of the pain of having been punished in the past. In a similar way, colonial authoritarianism, followed by post-colonial authoritarian governments, has built an instinctive response by Africans to fear authority and avoid challenges to its legitimacy. Africans often choose to subvert rather than confront authoritarianism. This has contributed significantly to Africa's approach to education. *Unlearning authoritarianism and the instinct to subvert African institutions* is the most crucial single action that can enhance Africans' free thinking. We need to be diligent about building educational cultures that place the learner at the centre, and pay attention to creating learning habits that encourage free thinking and problem-solving. Confident free-thinking Africans are more likely to confront than subvert authoritarian systems.

It cannot be emphasised strongly enough that, like other formal institutions, educational institutions need to align themselves to informal knowledge systems to enhance their effectiveness. Teaching Africans about themselves and the world they live in, from the point of view of other Africans, needs to start with a thorough *understanding of their own history* and what their ancestors' global contributions have been. This has to be combined with an improvement in teaching the hard skills like mathematics and science a lot better than many African states are currently able to. For example, 'Knowledge capital drives economic growth and enables countries to harness the world's storehouse of information to improve the well-being of their citizens …

However, for knowledge capital to catalyse socio-economic transformation, more people need skills and competencies at levels of sophistication that are required for modern economies ... On tests of knowledge and application of different mathematical concepts, for example, eighth graders in Botswana, Ghana and South Africa underperform compared with their peers in other regions.'[15] Interestingly, all three of these countries are rated by the World Bank as having the most established education systems with the least visible challenges. This has to point to the learning and teaching cultures and invisible informal norms as the source of their underperformance. Something has to be changed in the educational institutions of these three countries to improve learning outcomes. As Africans reimagine the cultural settings within which they want future generations to learn, it is critical that learners are taught by Africans who look like them, and that their African identities are celebrated as part of the learning experience.

Many African leaders have spoken about the need to *regenerate African culture*, and to infuse the education system with it. Aesthetically, some leaders have chosen to lead by example, through the reintroduction of traditional cultural clothing, language and certain symbols and ceremonies into modern African life. It is not enough that the aesthetics be changed; the curriculum has to be the subject of a major overhaul in many African countries. Former British and French colonies suffer the hangover of curricula that were put in place to create learning outcomes that reflected a belief in a class-based society with the elites receiving a world-class education and the large majority of the population being trained to serve these elites. The regeneration of the African learning culture requires a different way of thinking about knowledge systems. A focus on aligning this cultural regeneration through a revival of old knowledge systems has to be based on enhancing the learning environments that the average child in each country is subjected to, and on changing the expectations signalled by their teachers. Few countries have attempted to systematically track the implementation and correlation of African cultural regeneration to robust formal African educational institutions with the objective to measure an increase or decrease in the quality of learning outcomes.

Achieving this will require coaxing, championing and active campaigning for African cultural regeneration, and the declaration of an all-out war against its displacement by foreign popular culture while simultaneously tracking the improvement in the quality of teachers and their ability to transmit hard skills. It will involve rethinking how both teaching and learning work in an African context to make learning local cultures cool again in the minds of the younger generation. Most importantly, it will require the nurturing of a positive learning frame of mind. Teaching has to become the sacred profession it once was in African society.

Our understanding of how learned or observed impressions shape individuals makes a strong case for *positive role-modelling by African leaders*. At an individual level, the impressions that David Hume observed as combining to create ideas also create an idea of self. African teachers have to be restored to the highest possible status in African societies. We have to rethink what teachers are paid, how they are trained and the level of investment society makes in them. These teachers are most likely to be the first role models African children will ever have. Positive role models across leadership in society are vital for a positive self-image that is essential to effective human capital development in Africa. The idea of who we are is largely shaped by aspirational qualities we see in others and subsequently identify in ourselves.

Culturally transformed work environments are equally critical. Where possible, social stigmatisation should be stamped out, even if it entails making it a criminal offence or a basis for civil lawsuits. We have to protect the self-image of all learners and workers, especially those lower down in the socio-economic hierarchy. They are the most vulnerable members of society. The individual's self-image is particularly vulnerable to the feeling of standing out in a group or crowd in a negative light. As we search the groups within which we socialise for virtues and vices that we can relate to, we tend to be highly conscious of the question of agency in this social process.[16] We want to be able to relate to virtues, and to shun vices. We do not want to be stereotyped into a group whose vices are socially disqualifying. We do not want to be stereotyped into a group bereft of virtues we deem socially desirable.

Human beings are wired to constantly assess difference as a way of enhancing learning and ensuring survival. In so doing, we develop shorthand patterns of recognition to make sense of our assessments. Georg Simmel explains this phenomenon as follows: 'Man is a creature whose existence is dependent on differences, ie, his mind is stimulated by the difference between present impressions and those which have preceded. Lasting impressions, the slightness in their differences, the habituated regularity of their course and contracts between them, consume, so to speak, less mental energy than the rapid telescoping of changing images, pronounced differences within what is grasped at a single glance and the unexpectedness of violent stimuli.'[17]

African people's impressions of the differences of culture, language, style of dress, manner of speaking and other general codes of conduct that have surrounded them over the centuries of colonial cultural domination have been internalised to produce an insatiable longing for all things foreign. This longing is inherently unsustainable. Unlike other ethnic immigrants, indigenous Africans have not sufficiently built an intra-African trust base and models of success to create the foundations for a bias towards sameness to be sustained. Urban Africans seem to have rewired themselves towards a bias in favour of difference. Anecdotes of West African elites getting their laundry done in Europe, or buying their groceries overseas, show this foreign preference most acutely. Africans tend to prefer trade with foreigners above that with their own indigenous African counterparts.

The profound reorientation towards anything that is decidedly not African is the result of a highly successful process of cultural and mental deconstruction. It is a self-protection mechanism against perceived negative stereotyping indicative of self-hate. The resulting predilection for all things foreign makes some modern urban Africans feel like hostages to their heritage, instead of seeing their heritage as a resource to free them from mental bondage.

If true freedom is the power to act, speak or think as one wants, then some may argue that if Africans want, and in fact need, modernity at the expense of their own culture, then so be it. The implication here is that this is part of African people's exercising their freedom to choose who they are. The question I would ask in response is this: can one be free while not being true to oneself?

The philosopher Rodger Beehler frames his response to this question as follows: 'As I conceive authenticity, a person can live authentically even if his or her life is deliberately conducted very much like that of other persons (as a monk's life is very much like that of other monks or a ballerina's very much like that of other artists whose art is that of ballet). The determining factor in whether a person lives authentically is that the life lived be what he wants and chooses.'[18] Does this bias for all things foreign reflect a modern authentic African expression of freedom?

At face value, answering 'yes' to the above proposition is perfectly sensible. It is only when we pick up the second lens, which focuses on the absence of constraints through which we have chosen to look at freedom, that this answer is unsatisfactory. Can Africans genuinely say they currently seek to forgo their culture in 'the absence of necessity, coercion, or constraint in choice or action'? My suspicion is that they cannot. Coercion can be embedded in day-to-day life and sense-making in such a way as to become unrecognisable.

The theory of social learning holds that there is an interaction that produces reciprocal feedback loops between three elements: behaviour, internal personal factors and environmental factors. These are critically shaped by two other variables, expectations and incentives, which ultimately drive behaviour in society.[19] Through both expectations and incentives, Africans are coerced by upper-class societal norms to be other than themselves. Critically understanding what the last 400 years of history has done to Africans' expectations and incentives is obligatory for those interested in building African institutions of the future. The social cues seen by Africans on a daily basis at work, school and church indicate an environment that reflects the superiority of Anglo-Saxon culture. These reinforce the belief that without following Western leadership models, progress is unattainable. Unlearning this internalised deference to Anglo-Saxon culture is essential.

Happiness, liberty and 'skin in the game'

John Stuart Mill, the father of utilitarianism, argued that everyone's happiness matters and that each person's happiness matters equally. The word 'utility' underlying 'utilitarianism' has an interesting background. It is used by utilitarians to invoke a principle that approves or disapproves of every action depending on whether it has augmented or diminished the happiness of the party whose interest is in question. According to Mill, 'Utilitarianism assesses actions and institutions in terms of their effects on human happiness and enjoins us to perform actions and design institutions so that they promote – in one formulation, maximise – human happiness.'[20] Mill and his followers have placed a heavy emphasis on the notion that individuals will act according to their self-interest. Mill believed that democracy would work because it aligned the political interests of citizens with those of leaders.

The problem with this belief is twofold: individuals express their self-interests or preferences in a divergent fashion. The two biggest ways that preferences can be classified are *economic preferences* and *identity-affirming (or -disaffirming) preferences*. So the dimensions of individual liberty are complicated by how individuals observe these two types of preferences and how they affect the decisions they make.

Economists have for many years attempted unsuccessfully to measure the value that individuals or groups place on certain preferences by thinking about the additional utility generated by consuming a particular product or service. In the same way, identity economics, discussed extensively in Chapter 7, attempts to do this by looking at additional identity affirmation generated by acting on a preference. This attempt at quantifying human utility is less useful than understanding that costly signalling of preferences should be taken more seriously than costless signalling.

The universal orientation of utilitarianism ties together the happiness and liberty of individuals with that of the broader society. In the book *Skin in the Game*, Nassim Nicholas Taleb offers a simple but highly sophisticated way of judging the signalling of both identity-affirming preferences and economic preferences: one should not trust actors, agents and leaders who offer advice or direction when they have nothing to lose if that advice or direction turns out badly.[21] Taleb's insistence on 'skin in the game' is underpinned by the idea that 'the ethical is always more robust than the legal. Over time, it is the legal that should converge to the ethical, never the reverse.'[22] This point is pivotal to our conversation on the failure to successfully democratise liberty in Africa.

Taleb reminds us that humans can signal their preferences either costlessly or with some degree of cost. His advice is that nature has set up the rules within the process of evolution to support and be supported by costly signalling.[23] He recommends that this process be mimicked in the construction of socially complex systems. The majority of Africa's institutional mechanisms are not user-friendly, because those drawing up the institutional rules have too much social distance from the users. Users are thus not in a position to more closely monitor how much skin in the game the leaders have.

Those who led Africans prior to colonialism were distinguished by their skin in the game. Modern African leaders have mimicked skin in the game by citing their contributions to or their relationship with those who made contributions to the liberation of the particular African country in question. Given that it has been between 25 and 60 years since liberation was achieved, this just doesn't represent tangible skin in the game. Conversely, the lack of legitimacy of these leaders, and of the rules and laws they are supposed to represent, brings into question African citizens' ability to trust in the enforcement of these laws, and therefore in the need to follow the laws operating within their home nations.

Many of the rules we are bound by as citizens do not work as a deterrent to defective or malicious actions to subvert or break them. The idea of an active citizenry with costly preference signalling – ranging from voting with your conscience at a minimum to, ideally, active participation in protests and strikes – represents real skin in the game. The next layer of skin in the game we can grow as citizens is to invest our culture, customs, ethics and norms in the broader laws that govern how we interact with our community, fellow employees and fellow citizens. We need to demand that the teachers in our children's schools look like us and allow our children to express themselves freely in their home language. We need to demand that local politicians send their children to the same public schools that they are in charge of. Healthcare bureaucrats should be forced to have themselves and their friends and family use local primary healthcare centres. We need to stop paying taxes to corrupt local and national governments as a form of protest action. We need to vote corrupt political parties out of office, with no regard for their so-called struggle credentials. Such costly signalling would get the attention of our leaders and indicate our requirement for their skin in the game.

We can only do so by being informed, demanding, active citizens, participating in the amendment of unfair laws and the upholding of laws we hold dear. African leaders have failed to affirm the voting public's identity utilities, while also ignoring or underperforming in their duty to deal with African people's economic utility. We have let them get away with these home-grown failures.

The key question is, can Africans find strong alternative mechanisms around which civic learning can be built? These alternative civic-education mechanisms have to be anchored by values, norms and beliefs that reconnect Africans with positive communitarian ethics that foster long-term-oriented free thinking. Formal education (pre-primary to tertiary) and informal education (religious, oral history, traditional ceremonies and African popular culture) are key cornerstones for transforming behaviour, changing expectations while impacting incentives.

Africa is leapfrogging the rest of the world in education innovations. The well-documented scarcity of education opportunities has attracted multiple entrepreneurs to dedicate themselves to thinking differently about education. The result is an explosion of hundreds of new charter schools offering high-quality education, enabled in many instances by technology. Online higher-education tools are beginning to become popular around the continent. These efforts need to be supported by government programmes to think differently about the teaching profession, knowledge management, education technology and the role of civic and values-based education in the curriculum. Citizen expectations of acceptable learning outcomes need to be upped and signalled to politicians in the costliest way possible. African citizens need to tie their voting patterns to local issues that affect their families' human development.

Reimagining African human capital has to be informed by the third definition of freedom and measured by skin in the game: securing for all Africans an equal opportunity for life, liberty and the pursuit of happiness. This definition of freedom compels communitarian Africans to make good on the values of Ubuntu by not forgetting to ensure the prosperity of others.

In summary, democratising freedom in Africa requires that the following specific programmes be introduced:

- **Reinforce merit-based rules:** African citizens have to demand a normalisation of talent aggregation in our societies. A return to the pre-colonial ideal of meritocracy is the surest way to pull Africans from poverty, by matching people's skills to roles they should play in the economy. As much as constitutions on the continent are focused on people's right to vote, an equally important right that needs to be constitutionally enshrined is the right for the talents of people to be the sole determinant of employment both in public- and private-sector Africa.

- **Unlearning authoritarianism** is critical to ensuring that economic opportunities can be democratised. It is assumed that parliamentarians or members of senates in Africa are well versed in civic education. This is sadly not the case. The large majority of African politicians act as if they are account-able only to senior members of their political parties. This will change only when African citizens demand that it does. Ultimately, only when politicians are directly accountable to the specific communities that put them in power will they operate as agents of change on behalf of these community members.

- **Curriculum redesign focused on Africans' under-standing of their history and culture** is an essential free-dom-maximising tool. Schooling at every level should be in-tentional in creating a positive historical context for African learners. This should include both written and oral history. Injecting old wisdom into the public debates about where Afri-can society is to go is critical to lasting change. The specific out-put should be to instigate, at both the national and Pan African levels, a conversation about how to regenerate African culture and adapt it for modern times. A programme stimulating this debate through the arts, television shows and online media has to be nationally driven to promote public consciousness. This initiative would help transform the negative African stereo-types that drive Africans towards foreign preferences.

- **Positive role-modelling by African leaders** is the surest way to drive behavioural change for the future. In this context, the word 'leader' is applicable in the widest possible sense. Any-one in any context who is followed by people is a leader. The old wisdom of mentoring, coaching and apprenticeship needs to be reapplied in the modern era. We all need working models for how to take the next step in life, whether in a professional or personal context. The old adage that good leaders have to first become good followers is important to emulate. Africans should entrench this principle in all phases of the education process. Importantly, this should include the spiritual education needed to live and lead ethically.

- **Skin in the game:** In as much as this book is a call for scalable Pan African federalism, its accompanying call for active citizenship, particularly at the local government level, needs to be recognised as an essential element. Allowing citizens to have skin in the game, through taking an active part in the direct election of their representative leadership, should be accompanied by strong civic-education programmes heavily influenced by community elders and an increase in joint legal actions to enforce and oppose unfair laws.

These programmes are already being initiated by civil society in many African countries. Providing them with budgetary support and a high social-priority status is paramount. Democratising human development in Africa will take the concerted work of a generation. The global community will enjoy the fruits of this effort, because, in two decades' time, Africa will be home to the world's largest labour force. For Africa to fulfil the prophecy of giving the world a more human face, the human faces on the African continent have to have their dignity restored. This is the ultimate African solution for a 400-year-old African problem.

9

Banking social capital

As an investor in private and publicly owned companies over the last 18 years, I have had to learn and relearn the key principle that corporate social capital often trumps the possession of investment capital in determining business outcomes. I have been fortunate enough to be part of more than 20 business transactions that involved the purchase or sale of a company from one shareholder (or group of shareholders) to another. None has illustrated the value of social capital like a manufacturing transaction I was recently involved in.

Our company spent 24 months unsuccessfully trying to buy a cheese manufacturing business based in South Africa. Aside from the obvious disappointment of not being able to close this transaction, I have no regrets and consider the time well spent. I learned some powerful lessons in the commercial application of social capital. The experience opened my eyes to a different way of evaluating profit pools that tend to be hidden in value chains when an industry is dominated by a handful of players.

I came away from this experience astonished by how instrumental the commercial use of social capital for certain segments of the South African business community is. The South African dairy market is enormous, employing 45 000 workers and milking 671 000 cows to produce just over three billion litres of milk per year. Changing weather patterns, increased imports and increased costs of feeding cattle have had a material impact on the nature of the dairy industry. This has resulted in a tremendous reduction in the number of dairy farms, decreasing from 50 000 in 1997 to just under 1 600 today.[1]

Our team learned just how tightly knit the commercial dairy farming and agro-processing community is. The 1 593 farmers that dominate this R15-billion industry are close to the manufacturers of cheese, yoghurt, butter and cream, who are in turn extremely close to supermarkets and family grocers, the retailers of pizza, pasta and other high-dairy-consuming outlets. As a result, the major players in the industry operate without the need for contracts, with the entire value chain confident that social capital in the industry is sufficient to secure trust that weekly supply agreements worth tens of millions done by handshake will be honoured. While this particular feature is laudable, it essentially means that outsiders to the industry like ourselves have no hope of paying fair value for a business that is worth one price in the hands of insiders who can enforce handshake contracts and another to those who can't. Needless to say, everyone we met in this industry, across the entire value chain, belonged to a European ethnic enclave in some or other corner of South Africa. This dynamic of economic insiders and economic outsiders raises interesting long-term questions for indigenisation policies across the continent.

To illustrate how different South Africa is from another large dairy-producing market like Kenya, one again has to follow the numbers. Kenya is an even larger producer of dairy than South Africa, producing over five billion litres a year. The industry accounts for roughly 14 per cent of Kenya's GDP, translating to roughly $2 billion.[2] In contrast to the number of South African farmers, Kenya has one million dairy farmers. Its industry generates one million jobs at farm level, another 500 000 in direct wage employment and 750 000 upstream jobs in support services. In South Africa, by contrast, the dairy industry employs only 45 000 people directly and another 70 000 indirectly.[3] What has allowed Kenya to achieve such scale without huge upfront investment (dairy plants can cost over $15 million to set up) has been the adoption of a cooperative system called the New Kenya Co-operative Creameries. The system is responsible for the marketing of 60 per cent of all milk produced. Some 84 per cent of this milk is collected in small shared storage facilities to be sold raw to customers.[4]

The different approaches by South Africa and Kenya illustrate an interesting developmental crossroads. The paths policy-makers choose have massive long-term implications for the structure of the African economy as a whole. Going the South African route brings with it better quality, higher productivity and international competitiveness. Going the Kenyan route brings with it higher employment levels, broader distribution of economic outcomes, lower barriers to entry, higher social stability and lower pricing power in the hands of producers. The advantages of one route point to the disadvantages of another. The core principles in this example apply for most industries.

Cooperative models have existed in various guises throughout the African continent over the last 100 years. For example, the Kilimanjaro Native Planters' Association of Tanganyika (modern Tanzania), formed in 1925, was the first-ever indigenous association of African coffee growers. This association protected African subsistence farmers from opposition from the European coffee planters. Despite starting just before a global economic depression, this cooperative helped create a vibrant coffee industry in Tanzania that today employs more than 400 000 people, the majority of them small-scale indigenous farmers. Another example is the more decentralised model of communal life insurance in Ethiopia called Idir, which was established about a century ago. The purpose of an Idir is to form a voluntary mutual agreement between community members to ensure collaboration when members face an unexpected event (death, disability or serious illness). It is estimated that, depending on geography, between 70 and 90 per cent of all Ethiopians enjoy social security through membership of an Idir.

These cooperative models were the target of structural adjustment policies introduced in Africa throughout the 1980s. Bad advice given to African governments recommended their dismantling based on the efficient free market hypothesis. Those cooperatives that did survive this period have proven how wrong the advice to dismantle them was. Each of the examples cited above represent ways to solve collective cooperation challenges. In the South African dairy example, members use specialisation and consolidation as a mechanism to keep those remaining members of the industry sufficiently prosperous and efficient. They achieve this objective by annually negotiating prices up and down the value chain in a way that allows everyone to stay in business, and to earn consistent margins. These negotiations are informal and thus hard to regulate. The same can be said for Tanzanian coffee growers or Kenyan dairy farmers. They have a formal framework of agreement that allows for healthy localised competition and cooperation to be balanced.

The key challenge is how one gets a group of people to simultaneously act collectively and individually, in a manner that is in keeping with their society's norms while adding value to the economy. Human beings have a hard time organising successful cooperation with each other in large numbers. Collective action problems stem from the inherent trust deficits that arise when humans deal with other humans who are not kin. The above points of emphasis are important in understanding social capital. They also point to the economic benefits derived from solving challenges related to trust deficits.

The creation of financial tools, such as global currencies, stock markets, insurance companies (to pool and disperse risk), global credit rating agencies and so on, point to humanity's capacity to harness social capital for the purpose of maximising profits by reducing the frictional costs of transacting with each other. Humans make up mythical institutions that become norms, which are then translated into laws that are enforced by governments to establish and maintain order.

We could argue that the entire purpose of capitalism is to develop mechanisms of monetising social capital. In more developed African countries, this monetisation has been harnessed by a few select innovators, with the majority serving as customers (as opposed to beneficiaries of innovation). These innovations have succeeded in increasing trust, easing transaction costs and elevating human capacity to transact. They have enabled those who are allowed into the formal sector to enjoy the luxury of pursuing self-efficacy. As a collective, humanity is the richer for all the innovations that make transacting easier. But the disparity in the benefits flowing from these innovations has to be bridged. This bridging capacity is particularly important on the African continent.

Depending on the availability of data, it should be possible, in every human ecosystem, to measure social capital by the efficiency with which human beings are able to transact with each other. The lower the cost, the more seamless the interaction, the less red tape between the actors, the more transparent the exchange of value, the higher the social capital in that particular environment. The intellectual dishonesty within this debate to date lies in the assumption that free-market-based capitalism, as practised in predominantly Anglo-Saxon countries, is the only way of achieving low transaction costs. China's state-directed capitalism has proved that there are vastly different ways of successfully bridging collective cooperation problems. After seeing China successfully taking over the global manufacturing of everything from cellphones to solar panels, even the most hardened economic conservatives have had to open themselves to the possibility that China's culturally specific practice of capitalism is a positive force in the world.

Economic theory posits that environments with high transparency and low frictional costs, accompanied by high trust, should exhibit increased competition as more and more competitors clamour to enter the market, thereby reducing returns in the long run. Yet almost all African states have unwittingly created dual economies operating at two different levels of equilibrium, which allow economic returns for insiders to stay consistently high over the long run.

The formal economy is usually dominated by a private sector that exhibits relatively high transparency and high trust, facilitating seamless transactions. This market is usually dominated by non-indigenous Africans who operate in homogeneous ethnic enclaves. Each major industry typically has just a handful of oligopolies, which have the lion's share of the market. The social capital inherent in these ethnic enclaves is so high that it compensates for any market inefficiencies and thrives even in a low-growth, high-inflation environment.

The other market is the informal sector, typically, but not necessarily, dominated by indigenous entrepreneurs. While statistics on the informal sector are difficult to obtain, it seemingly exhibits high transaction costs (relative to the formal economy), high frictional costs and rampant mistrust, combined with the inherent inefficiencies that result from a lack of scale. The operators in this economic segment have continued to make profits despite these deficiencies – a tribute to their skill and grit. This market is severely hampered by slow growth in both GDP and wages.

Looking around the world, we can see that there is a correlation between how inclusive and efficient economies are, and how large or small the informal markets are. Without these informal markets, poor people who do not have a strong credit history, working capital, access to corporate social networks and credible work experience would be completely locked out of the economy.

The informal sector contributes 55 per cent of the GDP of sub-Saharan Africa, while generating a staggering 80 per cent of jobs for the labour force.[5] The size of the informal economy in countries such as Mauritius and South Africa ranges from 20 to 25 per cent.[6] In countries such as Benin, Tanzania and Nigeria, the private sector's contribution to GDP is between 50 and 75 per cent. According to Deloitte's African Powers Retailing report, 90 per cent of retail transactions in Africa occur through informal channels.[7]

These extraordinary statistics tell the economic story of how those locked out of the formal economy have chosen to transact with each other. In addition to creating alternative channels for consumption, informal savings networks in Africa reflect old customs that have been modernised. Three savings instruments – rotating savings and credit associations, village savings and loans associations, and alternative savings and credit associations – collectively involve more than 50 per cent of the adult African population. More than half of national savings in the overwhelming majority of African countries are mobilised by one of these three instruments. Through these mechanisms, Africans who are not sufficiently banked have created some social security for themselves. Though these savings instruments mobilise capital independently, they almost always turn it over to large established 'formal economy banks', which offer them paltry returns in exchange for their money.

Although there are some fundamental differences between the approaches taken by each instrument towards aggregating people's savings, all three are trying to solve two basic problems: *chronic lack of trust* and *lack of sufficient cash flow*. The majority of Africans are just not trusted by the banks, insurance companies and asset management corporations operating in their communities. These firms deem the majority of Africans to represent too high a credit risk to transact with. Participants in these three instruments also have learned not to trust themselves or their relatives and friends not to spend excess cash. Most importantly, given their limited cash flow, these participants don't trust that they will have enough money available in the event of an emergency, wedding, funeral or urgent need for school tuition. They tap into their social capital in small familiar circles, to form clubs, associations or credit unions to remedy the trust and cash-flow deficits.

By attempting to solve their individual trust and cash-flow problems in this way, Africans achieve the short-term objective of aggregating savings and creating access to cash flow on a rotational basis. Even though these were, historically, entirely sufficient ways of communally saving, modern times demand a wider social network within which one is trusted and higher returns on one's capital to keep up with rising costs of living.

These existing instruments do not fundamentally deal with the core inefficiency at the heart of the problem facing at least half of Africans, namely, periodic access to cash but no consistent cash flow. They don't belong to large enough social networks within which their credibility alone is their social currency. Collectively, they are huge buyers of all manner of consumer goods and services but lack individual buying power. They have overwhelming needs for insurance but are often uninsurable. They have huge needs for banking products but find themselves deemed unbankable. When they are grouped together in disparate savings or insurance schemes such as the Idir, they are unable to profit from the scale and buying power of pooling their assets.

These dichotomies illustrate much more clearly the problem of the lack of a conceptual framework as the root cause of post-liberation Africa's impoverishment. There is no existing theory I could present to the reader to capture this complexity. Failing to think collectively at a large enough scale about both trust and cash-flow deficiencies undermines Africans' capacity to address these deficiencies. This has led to the false assumption that their savings will only be safely aggregated within small networks of trusted friends and family. This in turn ensures that these small networks very rarely get access to good managers who can make their capital grow.

Even though the informal economy is responsible for 50 per cent of Africa's savings, by comparison with the banks, insurance and asset management companies operating in the formal sector, African informal savings schemes generate paltry returns. In this respect, a report from the World Bank on youth unemployment states, 'Even the larger and more sophisticated savings and credit cooperatives (SACCOs) may struggle with profitability, as their membership base may never be large enough for them to spread out the basic overhead costs of facilities, management, and security and achieve lower unit costs than other financial institutions, especially in sparsely populated rural areas (5 000 clients is often considered a minimum efficient size for MFIs).'[8]

African leaders have sought to respond to this challenge by finding ways to coax the existing banks operating in the formal economy to bank the unbanked. Doing this, either by nationalising banks or by legislating the modification of their credit policies, won't sustainably address the core problem. Formal-economy banks think incorrectly about the banking risk posed by indigenous African customers. They look at them individually when they should be trying to aggregate them. They ignore their informal income when they should be trying to incorporate it into their credit-scoring processes. They think about their thin urban-asset base without taking into account their share of family-owned rural assets. They punish non-payment caused by temporary cash-flow shortages by downgrading credit ratings – just as if it were fraud.

If somehow the savings operations of these informal credit unions could be formalised and run by professional managers, using very large pools of capital, the economies of Africa could be completely transformed. Aggregating savings through newly created, mutually owned financial-services entities is an achievable task. By merging smaller savings and credit cooperatives, Africans can create an entirely new capital base from which members can claw their way into the formal sector.

Even more importantly from a consumption point of view, though indigenous Africans are by far the largest spenders in their respective economies in aggregate, they often pay more for their goods and services because of the logistics networks necessary to overcome generally poor infrastructure. The premium placed on consumer products is also as a result of buying consumer goods in small quantities, on credit and through multiple channels. According to World Bank data for 2010, Africans spend just under $90 billion on the purchase or building of houses in a single year. They spend $65 billion buying grain, $60 billion buying fruits and vegetables and roughly $50 billion on meat and fish per year. A large portion of this money is enjoyed by the shareholders of the foreign companies that provide the goods and services purchased. Instead of being resigned to current patterns that keep African entrepreneurs in the shadows of the informal sector, new innovative partnerships are needed to unlock the hidden opportunities of collective action.

By way of example, a partnership between the United Nations Industrial Development Organization (UNIDO) and a network of small enterprises in Ethiopia's leather industry has shown what is possible. Ethiopia is the world's tenth-largest producer of livestock, and generates 2.7 million hides, 8.1 million sheepskins and 7.5 million goatskins annually. In a typical leather business, these raw hides and skins constitute 55 to 60 per cent of all manufacturing costs. Using their competitive advantages of cheaper hide procurement and lower cost of labour, UNIDO has worked with government to create an enabling environment to cluster a total of 377 enterprises employing 4 000 workers.[9] This has propelled these enterprises into a scalable, internationally competitive unit with buying power.

African governments can play a critical part in creating enabling regulations geared to promote a form of broad-based social capitalism that can radically transform Africa's economic landscape. This will require the adoption of a form of collectivised procurement on a scale previously untested by indigenous people in Africa. A report from the African Development Bank highlights the opportunity represented by the continent's burgeoning urban agglomerations: 'According to the UN there are 53 urban agglomerations in Africa with a population of more than one million people. By 2025, the UN expects there to be 84 agglomerations in Africa of at least one million, 17 of which are in Nigeria.'[10] Setting up two competing procurement firms per agglomeration, owned by members of the community, who give them the mandate to procure goods on their behalf in exchange for their shareholding, would be a significant transformative mechanism to maximise the economic purchasing power of urban Africans.

Massive gains in economic value can be created by allowing

middle-, lower- and non-income-generating Africans to use these newly created corporations to pool their resources, thereby exercising collective savings, insurance, pensions, burial schemes and rotating savings and credit associations and collective buying at scale. This would enable poor people to access cellphone data, education, healthcare, housing, grain, alcohol, banking services, and so on. These gains can be consolidated by handing these newly created resources to high-quality indigenous management teams with industry-specific knowledge and experience.

These management teams could harness the scale and buying power of the majority of people, while benefiting from efficient, transparent markets with deep capital pools in search of high returns. These firms would instantly become large corporations operating in all sectors of the economy, offering competition to incumbents. The profits generated by these corporations could become the seed capital needed to create community-based banking, insurance and asset management corporations specifically designed to lend, insure and manage the money of the unbanked. This would lower the cost of capital for poor Africans, and lead to lower price inflation at the bottom of the economic pyramid, increased savings rates, greater access to capital, accelerated transformation and a rebalancing of economic power across Africa's ethnic groups.

Deliberate regulation by government should be targeted at laws discouraging the collectivisation of savings, at the ability to pool capital for essential consumption and at anti-competitive behaviour by members of the incumbent oligopolies prevalent across Africa's major industries. Competition commissions across Africa have to understand the value-add of these new procurement firms, and their capacity to enhance competition for all market players. These firms should not be allowed to sell equity or merge with incumbent operators. Incumbents will always act in an oligopolistic fashion. The best way to change their behaviour is to facilitate competition with them.

Civil society will have a role to play to help conscientise Africans at the bottom of the pyramid about the hidden power of their own social capital networks. Conscientised citizens alive to the commercial opportunities unlocked by these collective purchasing arrangements would be better able to take advantage of the gaps in the market for entrepreneurial activity. This is a crucial intervention to help those living in poverty to move from survival mode towards an abundance mentality that feeds off inherent social capital networks and will be the key to their achieving prosperity. A clear understanding of their agency will need to be created through financial literacy education. This will be an enormous step towards self-efficacy.

I illustrate how this new system of social capitalism can work by means of two case studies. The first looks at South African financial services giant Sanlam, demonstrating how just one company has been able to consolidate an ethnic group's power and change its people's bargaining position in society over a period of a few decades. Sanlam's use of consolidated savings as a mechanism to amplify their stakeholders' economic power has since been replicated by groups such as the Royal Bafokeng in the North West province of South Africa. The second case study examines the DHAN Foundation in India, which has shown the power of stimulating social capital in neighbourhoods previously ravaged by poverty. Africa can learn from these two case studies about how to create strength in the ties that bind masses of poor people and how to turn those ties into formidable wealth-creation machines.

Case study 1: Sanlam – consolidating savings to create empowerment

In 1918, when the South African National Trust and Assurance Company Limited (Suid-Afrikaanse Nasionale Trust en Assuransie Maatskappij Beperk, the predecessor to Sanlam) was founded, the political and economic climate was not dissimilar to that prevailing today. According to a PhD thesis by Simone Halleen: 'The prevalence of foreign companies in the insurance industry at the beginning of the 20th century was a reflection of the state of the rest of the economy. British companies dominated all sectors of the South African economy except agriculture. Positions in the mainstream economy were mostly dominated by foreigners.[11] In 1916 the number of 'poor whites' living in South Africa was estimated at 106 000. The Carnegie report published in 1932 put the number of poor whites at closer to 300 000, most of them Afrikaners.[12]

The spirit of Afrikaner nationalism at the time was so great as to warrant the convening of an Economic People's Congress in 1919, to engage with the plight of poor Afrikaners.[13] The congress concluded that the solution lay in the creation of industry-specific finance houses that could play a vanguard role in establishing footholds in each industry on behalf of Afrikaner investors, or in the government acting as their conduit. The government insisted that every public employee bank, insure and transact through a Sanlam-linked company. This had the effect of aggregating capital and channelling it through a directed set of vehicles (state-directed capitalism).

Shortly after the congress, Sanlam began a gradual process of seeding other finance companies: Federale Volksbeleggings Beperk, Bonuscor, Federale Mynhou, Central Finance Corporation and Sanlam Investment Corporation Limited. These companies opened the door for Sanlam to invest in property development, commerce, financial services, mining and manufacturing: 'By the 1980s Sanlam had expanded into a diverse conglomerate with investments in almost all sectors. By 1985 the distribution of Sanlam's investments on the JSE was as follows: mining R912 million, the financial sector, R380 million, the transport sector R158 million, electronics R146 million, engineering R34 million, industrial holdings R301 million, and the retail sector R94 million.'[14]

This vast array of investments would not have been possible were it not for the asset-gathering capacity that Sanlam developed. Because of the raw nationalism that created bounded solidarity among Afrikaners, few objected to the creation of a norm that required the exclusive use of Sanlam insurance if you were an Afrikaner.

This was later expanded to require the exclusive use of savings banking, home mortgage finance and stock brokerage. This norm created the financial muscle that was necessary to enter new market segments and to train or attract talented management. This aggregation of resources was the linchpin in Afrikaner empowerment, along with the careful development of capable, highly skilled managers to run it. Because of the success of Sanlam, firms like Remgro and PSG were able to follow suit. These firms supported many cooperatives owned by Afrikaner farmers throughout the country to grow to great scale.

Taking a cue from Sanlam, Africans should look to create a consolidation of savings assets in densely populated areas. This could be achieved by aggregating informal savings and credit organisations. Similar to the role Sanlam played for Afrikaners in the 20th century, these newly consolidated savings pools could then be used to grant access to new funding opportunities, lowering transaction costs and giving access to community banking and insurance products.

Setting up firms in large urban agglomerations gives them a chance to become instantly large. Using this newly acquired scale, these organisations could then look to providing the same services in neighbouring townships, rural areas and peri-urban centres. The premise of the banking and insurance business model is simple enough. It is an extension of the delayed gratification principle that Africans practise each time they participate in a rotating credit and savings group.

By postponing individual consumption in exchange for collective social security at a large enough scale, these community banking and insurance firms could become formidable financial intermediaries. They would finally be capable of connecting ordinary Africans with stock markets and international debt markets that could transform their returns on savings.

Banking as a business model is only sustainable when three key attributes are in place. First, a proprietary product is needed to accelerate asset gathering in the form of deposits or equity. Second, there must be an underwriting system that can generate a high-quality loan book. Third, there needs to be effective credit controls capable of efficiently pricing risk to protect the quality of the loan book.

I believe that community banking run by high-quality indigenous management teams using existing social capital can tick all of the boxes outlined above. To understand why, one has to grasp the fact that, like all good products, this idea simultaneously turns a pain point into a profit centre while saving prospective customers significant amounts. Poor people generally have the multiple burdens of having to travel long distances for quality products, poor credit history, low disposable income, no access to financial services advice, high costs of capital, weak bargaining power and high transaction costs.

To alleviate these pain points we need to start by signing community-based collective purchasing agreements that will serve as the catalyst for the gathering of capital. South Africa is further along the path than most African countries because of the presence of a national body that has taken it upon itself to register all informal savings and credit organisations. Similar institutions should replicate the National Stokvel Association of South Africa across the continent as a regulating body that can help guide how these informal savings organisations can be transformed into community banks.

In each case, a community bank holding company should be created. One share in each community bank holding company should be traded in exchange for a long-term commitment to deposit savings, receive salaries and procure all shareholders' goods and services through the procurement systems to be set up by these companies. The massive savings generated by collective procurement will create a pool of equity that the community bank can use as seed capital upfront, and as operating income going forward.

Another pain point this concept can address is the burden of transportation costs, by outsourcing the delivery of goods through a third-party delivery mechanism. Africans spend 30 to 35 per cent of their income on transportation. Some of that is to get to work and school, but a significant part is also for transportation for individual family members to buy groceries and do other forms of shopping. Collective purchasing of groceries and consumer goods would make it possible also to tap into delivery and storage firms that only contract with those moving products at scale. This would achieve a lower cost of transport and effectively put more free cash flow in the pockets of those participating in this collective purchasing model.

The lending side of the community bank will largely service informal retailers and traders. Modern underwriting technology, in the form of point-of-sale-based lending, can be tapped into to manage risk appropriately. Organisations are sprouting up around Africa that use point-of-sale technology to advance capital to retailers in exchange for a deduction facility that takes a percentage of each transaction. This mechanism, referred to as merchant cash advance, can help these informal retailers with working capital, stock purchase and the capacity to create better-looking storefronts to enhance the customer experience. This model can also help to give seed capital to those wanting to get into new franchising concepts. The aim is to circulate cash flow within the community.

On top of deploying the best available credit scoring software, a key feature of reducing underwriting risk is having a transparent lending platform that allows members to see who the borrowers are online and how they are meeting their repayment terms. This transparent credit model induces the appropriate level of social pressure to honour agreements and reduces the risk of moral hazard or beggar-thy-neighbour strategies. The explosion in the use of blockchain technology allows small transactions between individuals to be tracked using a unique electronic fingerprint (which condenses the full transaction details and stores them as a permanent public record for future reference).

The collective procurement initiative can radically transform communities by unleashing dead capital trapped in consumption. This can apply across the purchasing spectrum, embracing bread, childcare products, toiletries, flour, fruit, veg, airtime, home appliances, building materials, beverages and much more.

The key point is that the capital generated from these savings is not used to fund further consumption but rather to fund local entre-preneurship, education, agro-processing, healthcare and insurance. Each area would see a single product aimed at facilitating personal empowerment and improving community members' quality of life. The entire activity would be for profit, distributing annual profits to community members at the end of each year. If full national aggregation is achieved, each community could be a branch, but the members would be able to leverage each other's purchasing power on a national scale.

Case study 2: The DHAN Foundation – harnessing social capital for poverty reduction

The primary aim of the DHAN Foundation – the initials stand for Development of Humane Action – is the mothering of develop-ment innovation for poverty reduction. The foundation started with a community banking model, then tackled the difficult challenge of access to water. By 2000, four clear development themes had emerged: micro-finance, rain-fed agriculture techniques, information technology for poor people and democratising civic participation.

Over time, the foundation's strategy has been to create localised comprehensive development capacity that can work with govern-ment to increase the quality of life for poor people in India. The DHAN Foundation has institutionalised the lessons learned from its development work to create an academy that upskills community organisers and helps them prepare for a career in local community work. This structured apprenticeship programme, which initially took place over 12–15 months, is focused on the skills needed to help local informal institutions working with communities of 3 000 to 5 000 people towards the accomplishment of development goals. After the apprenticeship period, each new graduate picks a com-munity to work with, jointly decides on a key intervention with that community, and spends the next three to five years dedicating themselves to its success. This is real skin in the game. As a consequence of their commitment to these communities, these leaders are trusted and their objectives are widely supported.

Large organisations such as the Tata group have partnered with the DHAN Foundation to expand its poverty reduction activities throughout India. Tata has formalised the educational activities of the DHAN Foundation by creating the Tata-DHAN Academy. This has allowed the expansion of programmes in development education to two or three years. Tata has fully funded the tuition in exchange for a commitment from the graduates to work in recognised NGOs for a minimum of three years after graduation.

Today, more than 25 years after it was founded, the DHAN Foundation works in 51 districts in India, and has reached close to 850 000 families.[15] Many of its programmes have been adopted by the Indian government to become national poverty alleviation schemes. For example, the government has led a financial inclusiveness drive, housed in the Ministry of Finance and championed by the Indian prime minister. Despite India's having 300 banks, operating across 75 000 branches, 400 million Indians were unbanked in 2014. The Pradhan Mantri Jan-Dhan Yojana (PMJDY, the Prime Minister's People's Wealth Scheme) is India's primary financial inclusion drive. By February 2017, after just three years of operation, over 270 million bank accounts had been opened under the scheme, injecting $10-billion worth of savings into the formal economy. Account holders are provided with bank cards, overdraft facilities (limited to one member per family), mobile banking and accident insurance.

The DHAN Foundation and its pioneering work can teach Africans a tremendous amount about how to achieve development that is community-centred, inclusive and focused on initiatives that are of highest local priority and that tackle poverty at great scale. When combined with the for-profit community banking model proposed earlier, this could have a powerful long-term impact on uprooting poverty in Africa. There is no shortage of capable champions of community development on the continent. The willingness of business elites and government officials to partner with them in the execution of successful poverty eradication is the missing first step in a long journey. India shows us what is possible when this willingness is encouraged simultaneously top-down and bottom-up. Ultimately, it is up to individual Africans to realise the empowering possibilities latent in these development strategies, and to lobby for elites to adopt freedom-maximising, customised versions to transform their local communities for the better.

The achievements of the DHAN Foundation in India show that external interventions led by local community organisers who are guided by the needs of the community help unlock individual self-efficacy to become sustainable. Based on data provided by the World Economic Forum, 13 African countries could implement the recommendations made in this chapter without much difficulty.[16] The citizens of Ethiopia, Rwanda, Tanzania, Kenya, Côte d'Ivoire, Morocco, Botswana, Uganda, Mauritius, Senegal, Mali, Ghana and Cameroon are fortunate to be led by pioneering leaders who support the development of this self-efficacy in their respective countries. As they build their nations, these leaders are succeeding in balancing the formation of formal and informal institutions with the promotion of bottom-up community development. If they manage to set their sights higher by building large indigenous savings facilities and commit themselves to bottom-up initiatives for inclusive growth, they will quickly prosper.

The citizens of these 13 countries are reaping the rewards of human development programmes that have successfully introduced skilled workers to their national workforces. According to the World Economic Forum (which excludes Ghana and Cameroon because their political economies are deemed to be unstable), these countries produce one-fifth of the continent's GDP. This is significant, given that three of Africa's giant economies, Nigeria, Egypt and South Africa, are not included in this group. Most of the countries building strong institutions have real GDP growth in excess of five per cent.[17]

Notwithstanding the performance of these 13 outstanding institution-building countries, the balance of 42 African countries are under-performing in their duty to create economic opportunity for their citizens. Citizens in these 42 African countries need to advocate for the type of community interventions that are currently transforming India. Elites in these countries need to advocate for a Sanlam-like model to transform their economies. Sadly, these 42 countries are the ones in which the social distance between communities most in need and the elites is at its widest.

Conclusion

African business and political leaders in these 42 countries need to connect the dots between ownership, accountability and productivity in order to find ways to entrench these three pivotal elements in the architecture of their societies. Ownership in this context goes beyond legal ownership to embrace what is called psychological ownership. According to an academic study of this concept, 'More precisely, psychological ownership has been described as a cognitive-affective construct deemed as, "the state in which individuals feel as though the target of ownership or a piece of that target is theirs", and reflects "an individual's awareness, thoughts, and beliefs regarding the target of ownership" ... Like other psychological resources, psychological ownership can be measured, invested in, developed, and managed for performance impact and competitive advantage.'[18]

Measurement of the developmental impact and investment opportunity of anything is predicated on its value. The value of psychological ownership has been deliberately hidden from African society. Colonialism and imperialism were designed to actively obliterate any feelings of psychological ownership indigenous people had. Reimagining the African political economy as one that embraces social capitalism would have an enormous impact on Africa's working-age population. Controlling more than half the continent's savings and more than 80 per cent of its spending in newly created indigenously owned organisations would transform the way Africans think about who owns their economies.

If you do not feel the burden of ownership, you cannot be a good custodian, citizen or employee, because you don't have skin in the game.[19] As discussed in the previous chapter, when socio-economic actors have skin in the game, they are better trusted by their fellow citizens. This new social capitalism will change the burden of accountability in African societies. Psychological ownership of a country, and ultimately feeling a sense of patriotism about the land where one comes from, begins with an emotional connection to a symbol. A flag, an anthem, sports teams representing those symbols – all are meant to be a gateway to a commitment to abide by a set of laws and codes of conduct. This is strengthened by an alignment of individual identity to that of a group, which eventually leads to an internalisation of certain group values and guiding principles. This is a precondition for the collective cooperation problems in African countries to be solved at scale. Social capitalism offers an African solution to large-scale African problems.

10

Ten figments of reimagination

AFRICAN SUPERPOWER. These two words, sitting side by side, are an assault on the senses. The term 'superpower' was popularised during the Cold War, and was clearly meant as a description of the United States and its Soviet nemesis, reflecting what must have felt at the time as a permanent status quo. I use the term to reflect the wish for Africa to qualify as a superpower, defined as 'a state that cannot be ignored on the world stage and without whose cooperation no world problem can be solved'.[1]

Imagine for a moment that there has just been a major global shift in political and economic power. It is the year 2030, five years since the monumental Kinshasa Conference that led to the creation of the African Union Federal Government. Of the 55 African countries, 40 have chosen to join together in a Pan African government structure modelled on Swiss decentralised federalism.

The world has moved from a unipolar world, where the United States of America was the sole dominant actor, to a multipolar world. China is now a dominant global force, its rise to the summit of global power having been accelerated by years of US recession. This recession was the result of the years of quantitative easing and the incoherent protectionist policies of the Trump presidency. The other superpowers are the EU (kept together by the measured leadership of German chancellor Angela Merkel and French president Emanuel Macron and the economic platform they mapped out), India, Russia, Japan and Africa.

Since the founding of the AU Federal Government, the incumbent President Kamaria Annan (now going into her second term) has defied the odds to create a coherent, well-functioning and fast-growing African political economy. Supporting her are five governors, from Southern Africa, East Africa, Central Africa, West Africa and North Africa. With over seven per cent GDP growth for the sixth year running, Africa has attracted more than $100 billion in FDI this year. New modern buildings are popping up everywhere on the continent. Tower cranes dominate city skylines. Road construction continues to connect cities to the agro-processing centres that are springing up in rural Africa. The African currency, the rand, has hit a five-year high on the back of general market confidence in the sensible way that the AU Federal Government has managed Africa's economic integration.

The faster-than-expected GDP growth is still largely urban-centred, and Africa's ten largest cities are growing faster than municipal service delivery can possibly keep up with. Rural economies need ever more resources to remain economically competitive. President Annan is having a hard time convincing local government to work with her on the tax reform necessary to reallocate enough resources from cities to fund rural areas. A Fiscal Equalization Fund is mooted to generate sufficient resources to be deployed towards both urban service delivery and rural development. This initiative cannot come fast enough as growing civic unrest threatens to be a major obstacle for the AU Federal Government. In addition to these budgetary pressures, the young, impatient population is demanding entrepreneurial support so that they can take their economic future into their own hands.

A merger between Ethiopian Airways, Air Mauritius, Air Kenya, Nigerian carrier Air Peace and South African Airways has transformed air travel. New airports are being built every few months and new routes added on almost a daily basis, making travel easier for African businesspeople and tourists, both domestic and internation-al. Ironically, this boom in travel is powered by supersonic jet engines built in South Africa by Elon Musk.

Africa is now home to the world's largest mining company in the form of a rejuvenated Anglo American, the company having returned to its African home base powered by a massive investment from Africa's new sovereign wealth fund. Anglo's focus on local refining and value-add of minerals has created hundreds of thousands of jobs, complemented by those generated by a diamond exchange based in Luanda. A joint venture between a new Pan African oil company, African Oil, and PetroChina has led to new oil discov-eries, providing energy security even as Africa rolls out the world's largest solar plants in the Sahara and Kalahari deserts. The DRC's giant Congo River hydroelectric complex has emulated China's Three Gorges Project to create a utility that has lowered the price of electricity in Africa to make it among the most competitive in the world. Solar and wind projects are closing the gap on traditional energy sources, continuing the trend of meteoric renewable energy growth in Africa.

These projects are underwritten by a new insurance network based in Mauritius and modelled on Lloyd's of London. Through this mechanism, a consortium of African financiers have been able to competitively price risk on African projects and the underwrit-ing of commodity sales, building up an impressive book, powered by blockchain technology, that has so far managed to escape major catastrophe.

East Africa has become the African technology hub, with both MIT and Cambridge University having built campuses there to benefit from the high demand for tertiary education and learn from local biotech specialists, who have unlocked medicinal value from previously unknown African flora. The world now looks to East Africa for major breakthroughs in tackling cancer and the chronic depression epidemic that has ravaged developed economies.

With the youngest workforce in the world, Africa has become the manufacturing hub for nanotechnology and computer equipment now exclusively driven by artificial intelligence. The use of 3D printing centres has given those Africans inclined towards design and manufacturing the freedom to become tinkerers and hobbyists who can build small enterprises to supply growing market segments. Consistently high internet penetration has been facilitated by President Annan's effort to build a virtual internet blanket connecting every African city and village to high-speed fibre-optic/satellite internet.

The Nigerian and Johannesburg stock exchanges have merged and are now based in Lagos. This has created a powerful financial market that rivals the London, Frankfurt, Beijing and New York exchanges for liquidity and sophistication. In terms of commodities trading, the Afro Exchange now ranks number one in the world, thanks largely to the BRICS countries' throwing their weight behind it. The emergence of the petro-yuan has facilitated non-dollar-denominated oil transactions. The fast African GDP growth over the last five years has attracted 20 million expatriates back home. They have come from sophisticated global markets and have brought with them the capital, networks, know-how and intellectual property to make Africa globally competitive in financial services. President Annan is currently on a continent-wide anti-corruption campaign that is transforming African governance systems. She was elected outside of a political party on the strength of her own governance track record and policy proposals, granting her the political capital to lead referendums in the African Parliament. Legislative changes have been enacted to make it difficult for political parties to abuse their power. President Annan has used a coalition of government whistle-blowers, faith-based leaders and civic organisations to root out corruption, starting at the local level. These efforts are beginning to change African people's expectations of their leaders. A new culture of resignations of officials implicated in impropriety serves as proof that Africa is internalising formal institutional rules.

The federal leadership, in their wisdom, have outlawed racial categorisation in any shape or form. The introduction of ancient African history to the educational syllabus is helping to transform how African children see themselves. Together with a plethora of podcasts and YouTube videos dramatising oral history, this has led to a resurgence of overt displays of African cultural heritage preservation. Streets, monuments and buildings all over the continent are being renamed to pay homage to fallen leaders. Language instruction in schools has changed to mother tongue, owing to Google translation technology that has made cross-language communication effortless. Academics around the continent attribute this as the major reason for surging academic test scores, unearthing hidden talent, particularly in urban slums and rural areas.

Slow progress is being made in health- and education-sector reform. The incorporation of African traditional healing into the healthcare profession has increased the numbers of professionals available to provide healthcare, and changed the way clinics see themselves relative to African communities. Cross-pollination of knowledge systems has begun taking place at healthcare training centres, bringing to the fore old medicinal wisdom that was until recently only being informally practised in large cities. Integrated teaching has become the African mantra. Cross-disciplinary education is feeding into an apprenticeship system that has drastically reduced unemployment.

The AU Federal Government has used funds seized from the proceeds of corruption to successfully commission the building of 500 new clinics, as well as tripling the total number of high schools and committing to doubling the number of universities over the next five years. As a result, life expectancy across Africa has reached 65 years for the first time, and the number of new graduates entering the job market is expected to rise to 50 million over the next five years.

A primary driver of job creation has been the new cooperative movement championed by the AU Federal Government's finance minister. This has allowed small and medium enterprises (SMEs) to come together to create shared services (procurement, financial management, human resources and legal) to formalise their operations. Tax receipts have risen to above $1.5 trillion. Unemployment has been reduced to 16 per cent across the continent. Africa's total GDP has more than doubled in the last seven years.

Surprisingly, the cooperative model has kept inflation within globally acceptable levels, as collective bargaining for individual purchases has limited the pricing power of suppliers. The Pan African Reserve Bank now balances inflation targeting, job creation and the competitiveness of the African currency as its joint mandates. The scale of local markets has allowed Africa to corner the market in electric car manufacturing. Based on three hubs around the continent, electric car manufacturers have become centres of excellence that are integrated with the global supply chains of motor manufacturers.

Agriculture has been dramatically transformed by the creation of the AU Federal Government. Rural employment has risen thanks to a focus on subsistence farmers, who have a shared service model that allows them world-class access to price-sensitive information, equipment financing, reasonably priced input costs and training techniques. The heavy investment in locally relevant agro-processing facilities and port and rail infrastructure necessary to access global markets has stemmed the tide of urbanisation. African agriculture is for the first time in decades seeing an increase in its share of GDP.

Making the future as reimagined above a reality is in the hands of African voters. Their insistence not to have their prosperity subverted by the greed and hunger for power of national leadership is essential to achieving this future. Business as usual is not an option. The world continues to become more and more competitive. Scale, responsive governance, expertise and social capital are the critical components of global competitiveness. Africa has to drastically reduce its poverty. A new socio-economic model has to be adopted to achieve this.

Back to reality

Recent events are bringing Africa a step closer to this imagined future. Though we still live in an era in which a fractured continent wages a governance and economic transformation war on 55 fronts, close to 44 of these 55 countries have proven themselves alive to the challenges of fighting for global market share in a disparate fashion. The actions taken by these countries indicate that there is hope that our leaders are moving in the right direction. The monumental announcement, on 21 March 2018, of the signature of the African Continental Free Trade Agreement, is evidence of this commitment.[2] The agreement represents the largest free trade area created since the World Trade Organization was established in 1995. If all African countries join the new area by 2030, its market size is expected to include 1.7 billion people, with over \$6.7 trillion cumulative consumer and business spending.[3]

There has never been a better time to be African. At the time of writing, Africa remains the world's second-fastest-growing region. By 2034, Africa is set to have a working population of 1.1 billion people. This will give it both the largest and youngest working-age population in the world. Household consumption in Africa is projected to reach an annual figure of \$2 trillion by 2025. By 2050, the relatively sparsely populated continent will be home to 2.4 billion people,[4] and Africa's demographic advantage will continue to grow. Young Africans will outnumber young Europeans by ten to one. If today's trends continue, the majority of this youth will be technologically savvy.

Africa has the most to gain by investing in its people, and yet the continent underperforms in its most important task. In many African countries, it remains a sad reality that ethnicity, religion, sex or 'race' will define the type of education you get. This is a major limiting force for African economies, and also retards the culture of productivity. By attempting to predetermine who gets the best education, African societies remove the incentive to promote merit-based performance.

In the absence of merit, people resort to alternative means of social value extraction as a way out of poverty and underdevelopment. High crime rates, corruption and uncontrolled emigration are the social costs of the inability to develop the talents of Africa's citizens. This book has attempted to make the case that it is much more productive to redouble people's efforts towards both their formal and informal education and to get them started on a journey to self-affirmation. This will help change their expectations of each other and create the basis for law and order. Human development requires a shift in mindset towards sustained national prosperity, as opposed to short-term individual opportunism. The expectation of domain excellence (being fully competent in your area of work), and an uncompromising commitment to reward mastery when it is achieved, needs to be re-established as part of Africa's cultural readjustment. In societies where post-liberation social capital has been weakened by a culture of impunity in corruption and other abuses of power, the incentives for individuals to invest in mastery are low. Too many African political economies reward influence peddlers who are generalists. Rebuilding social capital and creating a culture that enhances professionalism is a massive but necessary task.

There is much at stake. According to the African Development Bank, Africa now collects $500 billion in taxes annually.[5] In addition, the continent receives $50 billion in foreign aid and another $120 billion split between remittances and FDI flows.[6] With stronger, more entrenched institutions creating a high-trust-based African economy, much more capital could be unlocked. To put things in context, the Chinese government collects $2 trillion in tax revenue alone each year.[7] This point is made even stronger when we recall that 40 to 50 per cent of African GDP comes from an informal sector that by definition goes largely untaxed. What could Africa do with an additional $300–500 billion if the informal economy were to be coaxed out of the shadows and appropriately taxed?

I've used the term 'reimagining Africa' to indicate that Africans need to have an open mind to dream boldly about where our continent can and should go. The reimagination that is called for needs to be accompanied by the empowerment of African citizens to develop historical consciousness that promotes self-efficacy.

Africans can continue to believe the myth that it is essential to their well-being to defend the existence and independence of 55 African states. Or they can take the alternative path chosen by the United Arab Emirates and Switzerland to strengthen their federal bonds while retaining their local identities. Taking this step requires the firm belief that there is tremendous value in our African identity. That value can be enhanced by a sense of local government ownership by citizens. If citizens are allowed to lead this discussion, taking Africa to the next step in its long regional integration journey, Africa's youth will be the dominant voice. It is incumbent on this youth to look to the future and imagine what Africa could be like if it operated as one labour market, one set of financial markets, one economic trade zone and one massive retail market. Africa's future 1.1 billion-strong labour force will only maximise their talent and opportunities if they are free to seek jobs in an Africa that regulates itself as a single labour market. This talent aggregation will make up for some of the massive skills deficiencies in certain key African countries. Because of a lack of opportunity in their home markets, Africa has lost millions of scholars and newly qualified professionals. A Pan African labour market won't necessarily retain all these talented individuals, but many could be enticed home by the opportunity to contribute to their continent's development. Africa would represent the biggest wealth creation opportunity anywhere in the world for these expats.

Supporting a single capital market will greatly enhance liquidity, facilitate deeper Pan African investment pools and ultimately lessen dependence on international investors. The large single African market will support manufacturing at a scale that can facilitate gaining global footholds in key supply chains. African firms would need to be dominant in key market segments in order to generate sufficient employment opportunities to employ new graduates. Job creation and human capital development are matters of life and death for the continent's politicians. Peace, security and law and order will not be possible on the continent if young people anticipate a future that forces them to live with large-scale unemployment.

With 55 out of the total 196 countries in the world, isn't it time for Africa to take advantage of its scale? Should it not combine this with a process of cultural readjustment to align its formal and in-formal institutions while accelerating its human capital investments? The economic argument for this intervention alone should dwarf the complexities of executing the creation of an African Union Federal Government. As much as there are no guarantees for success, Africa will remain un-free for as long as it remains splintered into 55 con-stituent parts. Pan African integration would be the catalyst for new formal institutional design and implementation. It presents a do-over opportunity for a continent in desperate need of a fresh start.

Inevitably, the integration will be more of a top-down process than people would like to see. There will be ethnic, cultural and bud-getary fallout. The risk is certainly worth taking for this long-term opportunity. The framework question that stares us in the face has never been more compelling: would this be a freedom-minimising or freedom-maximising move for the large majority of Africans? From an economic point of view, the freedom-maximising aspect of regional integration was first explained by the economist Paul Krugman, who received the Nobel Prize in Economics in 2008.

Krugman showed that for US and later for South East Asian firms, it was commercial scale that facilitated single-product specialisation, which in turn created the operational excellence that eventually allowed local firms to be globally competitive. Krugman's work has gone a long way to explain why countries with (or with access to) large populations, who are able to establish relatively high domes-tic demand in a few key products, have managed to become more and more globally competitive by exporting within these niches. This finding holds much promise for an integrated African economy, offering the potential benefits of global trade liberalisation while building deep expertise in the manufacturing of products in high demand both in home and international markets. When combined with the development of a social-capitalistic economy that can successfully aggregate the buying and saving power of previously marginalised indigenous people back into the formal economy, regional integration can be a very powerful development tool indeed.

There is an obvious tension that will play itself out whenever one looks at freedom or liberty outside of the individual perspective. A human being's right to be able to pursue whatever path he or she likes may be, and often is, at odds with the right of an organisation or state to act in the collective interests of a community or broader society.

Living in societies with low human capital accentuates the need of Africans for alternative beliefs about the role of education, work, cooperation and leadership in general. Racism, religious intolerance, ethnic violence, tribalism, corruption and predatory criminal activism by default become part of mainstream values. These alternative values undermine African human capital development by reducing the incentive of any one citizen to remain committed to such broken societies and to invest in their own development.

A belief that society is there to be gamed by takers, who take from the timid, creates alternative African subcultures that have proven resilient to reform. In this alternative reality, nepotism is justified, bigotry is a means to an end, shirking is a natural response, and corruption is par for the course. Such a broken society is not likely to attract the best talent nor the most creative people to invest in shared prosperity.

To reverse this negative snowball effect, I have attempted to pull together lessons from both the African continent and abroad. Adopting these lessons will help make this the African century. Many of these suggestions are borrowed from the case studies of successful African leadership. Some are borrowed from fellow African academics seeking new solutions to old African problems. In many cases, the suggested changes aren't new and have been discussed for decades by leaders and followers alike. What would make these ideas new would be a commitment to collective regional implementation.

Summarised below are the ten principles that I consider to be non-negotiable core proposals for a continent in search of a turnaround strategy. Together, these ten principles form a shorthand for a new philosophy on Africa's future direction.

Ten African fundamentals required for a reimagined future

1. Transform the way we think about African history

How history is recalled, documented and passed on to the next generation is the sacred work of African elders. The value we place on certain current mythical beliefs is heavily impacted by our location of these myths within a historical context. This will only be transformed if Africans digitise their oral history, amplify their written account of ancient history and make the resulting syllabus mandatory for primary, secondary and tertiary education.

A true reflection of African history, beginning in ancient times (at least 3000 BCE), would transform Africans' self-perception by enabling them to locate themselves within a global historical context. This is an important first pillar in teaching both the positive contributions Africans have made to global civilisation and the horrific mistakes made over time by African leaders and citizens alike. Understanding this history would build a foundation for a positive self-image that is essential for the long-term task of generating self-efficacy.

2. A return to a philosophy of abundance

For thousands of years before colonialism, Africa's primary belief system was a form of holism informed by an understanding that everything is connected to everything. This holism facilitated a long-term outlook that created a sense of abundance of time and a belief in the enduring power of the human spirit. A better understanding of the historical and cultural impetus driving African people's attitudes to work and play over time is crucial. One cannot understand modern African attitudes to work, productivity and efficiency without a cultural context from which these attitudes evolved. This is a critical first step towards achieving what some African scholars call 'a cultural readjustment'.

This book is a contribution to a deeper understanding of who we are and what we can become. We need to better understand the history of what I have termed 'the sources of African cultural fragility'. This analysis is an attempt to add to the literature of why Africa's failure to adapt to the modern world has a cultural context and what some of the most obvious points of cultural weaknesses have been. The ultimate aim is to find the best way to maximise people's sense of productivity while not impinging on their natural bent towards leisure-oriented collectivism. How this plays out in practice will be through a localised grassroots expression of preferences that will balance people's identity and economic enhancing needs.

3. *Understand our psychological baggage*

Identity contingencies are to be understood as the essential personal 'baggage' that drives our emotional reactions to everyday occurrences. This could be something as obvious as superiority or inferiority complexes that make us choose in-groups and out-groups on the basis of predetermined criteria. Or it could be something more subtle, such as an aversion to numerical subjects based on a preconceived notion that we cannot solve mathematical problems. These social contingencies are triggered by social cues that can have a powerful effect on our impulses.

African social attitudes to women are driven by identity contingencies that need to be unpacked in order to create societies that don't exhibit hostility to gender equality. African men have been plunged into an identity crisis as a result of patriarchal power relationships, in which racist notions of superiority and inferiority create structural impoverishment of indigenous people that deny them the ability to fit the male stereotype. The crisis of emasculated men translates into vicious cycles of violence and abuse against women and children, as well as violence between men, that undermines African social capital.

Ethnic biases that pigeonhole certain ethnicities to narrow types of work need to be fought against to give life to existing anti-tribalism, anti-sexism and anti-racism legislation. It needs to be understood that these identity contingencies drive negative counterproductive attitudes that ultimately retard productivity. I have used South Africa as a case study to show in practice how this works.

4. Value rural Africa and its development

In Chapter 5, I identified three threats to Africa's development: urbanisation, unemployment and migration. These three threats have complex causes and even more complex implications for African societies. The genesis of these threats is identity contingencies derived from what modernity means. The preconceived notion of modernity is dislocated by its emphasis on matters urban, totally undermining the value of rural life and its vital contribution to national sustainable development. This results in the erosion of investment in rural social, financial and human capital. The failure to invest in rural development and to secure its role in national prosperity has led to people giving up on rural life, resulting in a surge in migration to search for jobs and economic opportunities in the cities. This surge has fuelled an urbanisation process that is far ahead of the ability of African cities to create jobs and dignified human settlements.

Many of Africa's major cities have become transit centres for migrants headed abroad. The result has been that transient, opportunistic social environments flourish in cities such as Johannesburg, Lagos and Cairo. These barely liveable metropoles are places of especially low social capital levels and offer low quality of life, exemplified by poor healthcare, education and social security. The resulting high crime rates are a reflection of what is lacking in these urban centres. Africans have to rededicate themselves to reclaiming the urban centres as safe places to raise families and redouble efforts at investing in rural development to address imbalances that drive forced urbanisation.

5. Adopt a direct, non-political-party form of government

Africa needs to circumvent factional, political-party-dominated democracy. The alternative is to remove any barriers between the voting public and the political representatives that they choose. This is a fundamentally different form of democracy, one that is closer to the ideals that Africans fought for during their liberation struggles. Much of the analysis of African democracy over the years has failed to explain why political parties do not operate in the national interests of African citizens. Analysts have taken the political party's role in African democracy as a permanent feature. There is a critical need for a robust critique of the very essence and misplaced role of political parties in the modern African state.

The history of political parties in Africa is intertwined with liberation politics. This has created an absence of interethnic harmony, incessant class categorisation and a low sense of citizenship underpinned by patriotism. What is tragic is that almost all political parties, however well-meaning they may have been at their founding, have over time become toxic vessels for social divisions in post-liberation democracies. This is not a uniquely African problem, but the continent's lack of institutions strong enough to rein in political parties has made the problem more acute. It is time for Africans to choose a different form of representation, one that places Africans' future in their own hands.

6. Africa needs psychological liberation

The liberation I describe is cognitive liberation that frees Africans to experience an unfiltered sense of ownership of their households, their communities and their broader society. This type of freedom requires skin in the game. The African cognitive revolution needs to start within the realm of self-perception. It has to divorce self-worth from external validation to create a more sustainable internal spiritual base on which people can strive to become the best independent version of themselves.

Coming, as many do, from a communitarian cultural outlook, Africans have struggled to define themselves within the context of modernising societies that deliver disaggregated economic opportunities for them and their social circles. Africa needs to adopt a framework that enables freedom-maximising choices, to mediate between some of these tensions. This outlook is fundamental to Africans' ability to become free-thinking and thus economically competitive.

Making freedom-maximising choices is critical to taking personal ownership of our individual contribution towards increasing social capital. Individual freedom is maximised by the strength of our immediate community. That strength is gauged by the level of trust within society, the degree to which members of that society conduct themselves with integrity and the bounded solidarity that they display to each other. This trust is further strengthened by institutionalised rules and norms. When rules and norms are embodied in organisations that carry this value system within their DNA, then trust is assured. Making social capital travel beyond geographical locations of networks is an essential mechanism for unlocking the power of human cooperation in Africa.

7. *Africans need to bank their social capital*

Africa needs to dismantle the gap between the formal and informal economy. Of paramount importance is a move away from the Pan African romance with the myth that SMEs will solve Africa's future employment needs. The answer to future African employment generation lies in a consolidation of the saving power, purchasing power and entrepreneurial capacity of large concentrated settlements of African people. Out of the ashes of this dismantled informal economy will come the large, employment-generating companies of the future. These companies will by definition be owned and managed by indigenous people. Their orientation will do much to change Africa's economic landscape.

8. Develop a shared view of success

A shared view of success creates the basis upon which the members of society can calibrate their ambitions and judge their leaders' ability to deliver human development tools to them. Once African societies have started on a path towards more nurturing conditions for human capital development, they will have to spend a significant amount of energy promoting the socialisation of a shared view of success. Success will never be the same for everyone, but Africans need to agree on their own version of 'the house with a white picket fence and a dog' that frames success in Western societies.

Africans don't have a dominant view of what aspirant middle-class lifestyles should look like. Neither has Africa learned to deal comfortably with extreme wealth. Without this shared view, people feel perpetually unsatisfied, as they have no choice but to judge themselves according to the lifestyles of society's rich and famous. A society that is unable to agree on this 'middle-class vision' will not be able to form adequate social compacts to create incentives for people to aspire to and live by.

9. Embrace meritocracies

Meritocracies work differently in China, the United States and Singapore. But, once established, meritocracies affirm norms, reward adherence to commonly agreed values and encourage law-abiding, conscientious behaviour. This is the basis on which successful societies are constructed.

Human capital development is predicated on an implicit understanding of the returns on capital spent on education and training that an individual is able to earn. Such returns are a direct consequence of the social contract that binds people together. This social contract explicitly promises a middle-class future to the majority within society in exchange for an individual's dedication to personal development. Getting Africa to actively support those citizens who have the patience to achieve professional mastery is critical to making the continent globally competitive.

10. Now is the time to realise the dream of a United States of Africa

African leaders have, over decades, laid the foundations for a realisation of the dream of a united Africa. What is still required is sufficient bottom-up pressure from African citizens for a politically integrated continent. When asked about regional integration, in an Afrobarometer survey, a majority of Africans responded that it would have tangible benefits for them. A large majority voiced high expectations regarding the flow of those benefits from integration and how these could impact their lives.[8] What has not been presented is a unified vision for an integrated African continent that could offer Africans a future that captures their imagination and ignites their passion to propel the continent out of poverty.

Africans have to overcome their biggest blind spot of all – their inability to let go of borders erected to divide them. As we all know, in the early 1800s Africa was a single continent made up of multiple societies that lived together without borders. A deal executed in Berlin by European states led to borders that eventually created 55 separate countries. This has created 55 separate governments, 55 national development strategies, 55 different sets of trade agreements and 55 different approaches to human development. To be successful Africa has to have 55 good governments capable of picking talented bureaucrats. It will also need 55 well-functioning meta-institutions that correspond well with local informal institutions. The probability of this being accomplished is incredibly low. That was the point of divide and rule, to sow the seeds of mistrust and tribalism that would make independent governance impossible.

Africa has spent close to six decades creating a multinational organisation called the African Union. Over time, the AU has become the custodian of Africa's vision to function as an integrated continent. The AU has developed multiple institutions that all combine to attempt to resolve the major cooperation challenges covering almost all areas of the continent's political economy. As an outcome of this process, Africa has the makings of an African Central Bank, an African Development Bank, the African Continental Free Trade Area, an African Investment Bank, an African Parliament, an African passport and an African Constitutional Court.

It is time for African citizens to breathe life into these institutions by occupying the foreground in the conversations to determine their future. I have presented a model of African federalism, based on the Swiss model, to bring together two seemingly opposing objectives as a potential African political solution. The first objective, that key industries and capabilities that are best unlocked with the benefit of scale, should be the domain of the federal government. The second objective is that governance challenges that are highly localised should be the domain of directly elected local governments, allowing citizens to take back control of the interaction with the agents they pick to represent them in government. This will require the transition of the AU from a loose membership to a fully integrated federation. The vision I present attempts to balance state power and local authority while allowing for the construction of a new African federal political economy.

These ten African fundamentals are offered here to stimulate productive conversations to promote the realisation of a reimagined Africa. In proposing them, I am part of a long African intellectual relay race that has been run over multiple generations. I hope my contributions will allow those who pick up this baton to take this conversation closer to the finish line.

Notes

Foreword

1 Graduation address, Wesleyan University, 3 June 1984.

2 Freely translated by Phyllis Ntantala-Jordan.

3 Steve Biko (1978), *I Write What I like: a selection of his writings*. Edited by Aelred Stubbs CR. Heinemann, Oxford, p 99.

Introduction

1 MR Leary and JP Tangney (2012), *Handbook of self and identity*, Guilford Press, New York, p 69.

2 N Pratt (2005), 'Identity, culture and democratization: the case for Egypt', *New Political Science*, 27(1), pp 69–86.

3 According to the definition adopted by the United Nations in 1981, 'indigenous' refers to communities, peoples and nations that have a historical continuity with pre-invasion and pre-colonial societies that developed on their territories, and that 'consider themselves distinct from other sectors of societies now prevailing on those territories, or parts of them'. See United Nations (no date), 'Indigenous peoples at the UN', UNDESA Division for Inclusive Social Development: Indigenous Peoples, homepage. Available at www.un.org/development/desa/indigenouspeoples/about-us.html, accessed on 30 August 2018.

4 A Bandura (2012), 'On the functional properties of perceived self-efficacy revisited', *Journal of Management*, 38(1), pp 9–44.

5 A term popularised in the South African context by Dr Mamphela Ramphele.

6 DP McAdams (2001), 'The psychology of life stories', *Review of General Psychology*, 5(2), pp 100–122.

7 CM Steele (2011), *Whistling Vivaldi: and other clues to how stereotypes affect us*, WW Norton & Company, New York, pp 3–5.

8 The *Cambridge Dictionary* defines productivity as 'the rate at which a company or country makes goods, usually judged in connection with the number of people and the amount of materials necessary to produce these goods'.

9 YN Harari (2014), *Sapiens: a brief history of humankind*, Vintage, London.

10 CA Diop (1989), *The African origin of civilization: myth or reality*, Chicago Review Press, Chicago.

11 Ibid.

12 C Winters (2012), 'Dravidian is the language of the Indus writing', *Current Science*, 103(10), pp 1220–1225.

13   I van Sertima (2003), *They came before Columbus*, Random House, New York.

14   I van Sertima (1992), *Golden age of the Moor*, Transaction Publishers, Piscataway, NJ.

15   Edward W Said (2003), *Orientalism*, Penguin, London.

16   CA Diop (1991), *Civilization or barbarism: an authentic anthropology*, Lawrence Hill Books, Brooklyn, New York.

Chapter 1

1   M Emirbayer (2008), *Emile Durkheim: sociologist of modernity*, Wiley-Blackwell, Hoboken, NJ.

2   CA Diop (1989), *Civilization or barbarism: an authentic anthropology*, Lawrence Hill Books, Brooklyn, New York, p 211.

3   Q Huy (2011), 'How collective emotions and social identities influence strategy execution', *Strategic Management Journal*, 32(13), pp 1387–1410.

4   RA Stebbins (1992), *Amateurs, professionals and serious leisure*, McGill-Queen's University Press, Montreal, p 2.

5   Plato (2008), *The Republic* (ebook). Digireads.com, Lawrence, KS.

6   D McLean and A Hurd (2014), *Recreation and leisure in modern society*, Jones & Bartlett Learning, Burlington, MA, p 25.

7   I van Sertima (1992), *Golden age of the Moor*, Transaction Publishers, Piscataway, NJ.

8   YN Harari (2015), *Sapiens: a brief history of humankind*, Vintage, London.

9   M Weber (2002), *The Protestant ethic and the spirit of capitalism*, Penguin, London, p 18.

10   Ibid, p xi.

11   M Griaule and G Dieterlen (1986), *The pale fox*, Continuum Foundation, Chino Valley, AZ, p 58.

12   CA Diop (1988), *Precolonial Black Africa*, Chicago Review Press, Chicago, p 4.

13   Ibid, p 6.

14   Harari, *Sapiens*, pp 19–29.

15   PL Berger and T Luckmann (2011), *The social construction of reality: a treatise in the sociology of knowledge* (ebook reprint), Open Road Media, New York (originally published 1967).

16   Harari, *Sapiens*, pp 30–35.

17   E Kain (2011), 'The Dalai Lama is wrong', Forbes.com, 12 October 2011. Available at /www.forbes.com/sites/erikkain/2011/10/12/the-dalai-lama-is-wrong/#787eb6d4671a, accessed on 28 August 2018.

18   MK Asante (2000), *The Egyptian philosophers: ancient African voices from Imhotep to Akhenaten*, African American Images, Chicago, p 31.

19   Ibid, pp 167–169.

20 JH Clarke (1991), *New dimensions in African history: the London lectures of Dr Yosef Ben-Jochannan and Dr John Henrik Clarke*, Africa World Press, Trenton, NJ.

Chapter 2

1   JJ Macionis and L Marie (2011), *Sociology*, Prentice Hall, Toronto, p 24.

2   R Rashidi (1983), 'The Kushite origins of Sumer and Elam', *Ufahamu: A Journal of African Studies*, 12(3), pp 215–233.

3   GO Cox (1974), *African empire and civilization: ancient and medieval*, African Heritage Studies Publishers, New York.

4   B Gascoigne (no date), 'History of writing', Historyworld.net. Available at historyworld.net/wrldhis/PlainTextHistoriesResponsive.asp?historyid =ab33, accessed on 28 August 2018.

5   EA Havelock (1986), 'The alphabetic mind: a gift of Greece to the modern world', *Oral Tradition*, 1(1), pp 134–150.

6   Gascoigne, 'History of writing'.

7   Ibid.

8   'Medieval papermaking & printing', Going Medieval: a BOSP 2015 Summer Seminar, Stanford University, 2015. Available at sites.stanford. edu/medievalfreiburg/medieval-papermaking-printing, accessed 25 October 2018.

9   DH Pink (2006), *A whole new mind: why right-brainers will rule the future*, Riverhead Books, New York.

10 Ibid.

11 According to Joseph Campbell, these archetypes include the (Great) Mother, the Father, the Hero, the Eternal/Miraculous Child, the Youthful Maiden, the Seductress, the Wise Woman, the Old Man, the Crone and the Shadow. See J Campbell (2008), *The hero with a thousand faces*, New World Library, New York.

12 EJM Witzel (2013), *The origins of the world's mythologies* (ebook), Oxford University Press, Oxford.

13 AL Kroeber (1940), 'Stimulus diffusion', *American Anthropologist (New Series)*, 42(1), pp 1–20.

14 AS Saakana (ed) (1986), *African origins of the major world religions*, Karnak House Publishers, London.

15 Ibid.

16 Ibid.

17 H Wellendorf (2008), 'Ptolemy's political tool: religion', *Studia Antiqua*, 6(1), p 35.

18 P Nabarz (2005), *The mysteries of Mithras*, Inner Traditions, Rochester, VT.

19 Witzel, *The origins of the world's mythologies*.

20 TC Oden (2011), *The African memory of Mark: reassessing early church tradition*, InterVarsity Press, Westmont, IL.

21 Ibid.

22 Ibid.

23 N Etherington (2008), *Missions and empire*, Oxford University Press, Oxford.

24 Ibid.

25 JK Olupona (2001), *African spirituality: forms meanings and expressions*, The Crossroad Publishing Company, New York.

26 Pew Research Center (2010), 'Tolerance and tension: Islam and Christianity in Sub-Saharan Africa', Pew-Templeton Global Religious Futures Project. Available at www.pewforum.org/2010/04/15/executive-summary-islam-and-christianity-in-sub-saharan-africa/, accessed on 28 August 2018.

27 Ibid.

28 YB Jochannan (1996), *The need for a black Bible: the black man's religion*, Africa World Press, Trenton, NJ.

29 NF Hoggson (1926), *Banking through the ages*, Dodd, Mead & Company, New York, p 8.

30 T Wilkinson (2013), *The rise and fall of Ancient Egypt* (ebook), Random House, New York.

31 G Simmel (2004), *The philosophy of money*, Psychology Press, London, p 151.

32 Ibid.

33 M Zimmerman (2014), 'Intrinsic vs extrinsic value', Stanford Encyclopedia of Philosophy, 24 December 2014, available at plato. stanford.edu/entries/value-intrinsic-extrinsic/, accessed on 28 September 2018.

34 Simmel, *The philosophy of money*, p 57.

35 Ibid, p 60.

36 Plato (2008), *The Republic* (ebook), Digireads.com, Lawrence, KS.

37 Simmel, *The philosophy of money*, pp 62–63.

Chapter 3

1 SB Biko (1978), 'Steve Biko on death', *The New Republic*, 7 January 1978. Available at newrepublic.com/article/122784/biko-death, accessed on 26 October 2018.

2 GGM James (2012), *Stolen legacy: the Egyptian origins of western philosophy* (ebook), Start Publishing, New York.

3 C Williams (1974), *The destruction of black civilization: great issues of a race from 4500 BC to 200 AD*, Third World Press, Chicago, p 134.

4 Aristotle (1999), *Nicomachean ethics* (T Irwin, ed), Hackett Publishing Company, Indianapolis.

5 Ibid.

6 JL Kincheloe (1999), 'The struggle to define and reinvent whiteness: a

pedagogical analysis', *College Literature*, 26(3), pp 162–163.

7   JF Blumenbach (1969), *On the natural varieties of mankind*, Bergman Publishers, New York (original edition 1775).

8   NI Painter (2003), 'Why white people are called "Caucasian"', conference paper, Proceedings of the Fifth Annual Gilder Lehrman Center International Conference, Yale University, 7–8 November.

9   T Jefferson (1918), 'Thomas Jefferson's thoughts on the Negro: part 1', *The Journal of Negro History*, 3(1), pp 55–89. Available at www.jstor.org/ stable/2713794?seq=1#page_scan_tab_contents, accessed on 28 August 2018.

10 K Haltinner (2014), *Teaching race and anti-racism in contemporary America: adding context to colorblindness* (ebook), Springer, New York.

11 Ibid.

12 D Jordan and M Walsh (2007), *White cargo: the forgotten history of Britain's white slaves* (ebook), New York University Press, New York.

13 Ibid.

14 S Manning (2013), 'Britain's colonial shame: slave-owners given huge payouts after abolition', *Independent*, 24 February 2013. Available at www. independent.co.uk/news/uk/home-news/britains-colonial-shame- slave-owners-given-huge-payouts-after-abolition-8508358.html, accessed on 25 September 2018.

15 Ibid.

16 National Park Service (1995), 'Bacon's Rebellion', Historic Jamestown website, November 1995. Available at www.nps.gov/jame/learn/history- culture/bacons-rebellion.htm, accessed on 14 August 2018.

17 Kincheloe, 'The struggle to define and reinvent whiteness', p 164.

18 A Hossain (2000), '"Scientific racism" in enlightened Europe: Linnaeus, Darwin and Galton', Serendip Studio, 16 January 2008. Available at seren- dipstudio.org/exchange/serendipupdate/scientific-racism-enlightened- europe, accessed on 28 August 2018.

19 Ibid.

20 Ibid.

21 M Shermer (2016), *The moral arc: how science makes us better people*, St Martin's Griffin, New York.

22 JC Venter et al (2007), 'The diploid genome sequence of an individual human', *PLOS Biology*, 5(10). Available at journals.plos.org/plosbiology/ article?id=10.1371/journal.pbio.0050254, accessed on 28 August 2018.

23 T-N Coates (2017), *We were eight years in power*, Oneworld, London, pp xv– xvii.

24 BJ Flagg (2005), 'Foreword: whiteness as metaprivilege', *Washington University Journal of Law & Policy*, 18, pp 1–11.

25 F Fanon (2009), 'The fact of blackness', in L Back and J Solomos (eds), *Theories of race and racism: a reader*, Routledge, London.

26   ON Saracho and B Spodek (1998), *Multiple perspectives on play in early child-hood education*, SUNY Press, Albany, p 296.

27   A Mazama (2002), *The Afrocentric paradigm*, Africa World Press, Trenton, NJ, pp 4–6.

28   Ibid.

Chapter 4

1   CL Griswold, Jr (1999), *Adam Smith and the virtues of enlightenment*, Cambridge University Press, Cambridge, p 15.

2   A Powell (2016), 'Young continent, old leaders: the aging face of African governance', VOA Africa, 30 December 2016. Available at www.google.co.za/amps/s/www.voanews.com/amp/3657215.html, accessed on 28 August 2018.

3   S Griggs, AJ Norval and H Wagenaar (2014), *Practices of freedom: decentred governance conflict and democratic participation*, Cambridge University Press, New York.

4   AA Yengoyan (2006), *Modes of comparison: theory and practice*, University of Michigan Press, Ann Arbor.

5   F Boas (1932), *Anthropology and modern life*, Routledge, New York.

6   K Wiredu (1997), *Cultural universals and particulars: an African perspective*, Indiana University Press, Bloomington.

7   WC Hamblet (2008), *Savage constructions: the myth of African savagery*, Lexington Books, Lanham, MD, p 76.

8   Kwaai City (2016), 'Rare 1993 interview with Nelson Mandela, episode 5: collective leadership of the ANC', YouTube, 10 February 2106. Available at https://www.youtube.com/watch?v=6VvFwGGF8QY, accessed on 26 October 2018.

9   CC Udeani (2008), 'Traditional African spirituality and ethics – a panacea to leadership crises and corruption in Africa', *Phronimon*, 9(2), p 65. Available at docplayer.net/50770375-Traditional-african-spirituality-and-ethics-a-panacea-to-leadership-crisis-and-corruption-in-Africa.html, accessed on 28 August 2018.

10   J Mohanty and W McKenna (1989), *Husserl's phenomenology: a textbook*, University Press of America, Washington, DC, p 147.

11   C Sanderson (2010), *Social psychology*, Wiley, Hoboken, NJ.

12   P Ikuenobe (2006), *Philosophical perspectives on communalism and morality in African traditions*, Lexington Books, Lanham, MD, pp 5–6.

13   South African psychologist Nhlanhla Mkhize explains Ubuntu in the following way: 'The African view of personhood denies that a person can be described solely in terms of the physical and psychological properties. It is with reference to the community that a person is defined. The importance of the community in self-definition is summed up by Mbiti "I am because we are, and since we are, therefore I am" ... It is this rootedness of the self-in-community that gives rise to sayings such as "Umuntu

ngumuntu ngabantu" (Nguni) and "Motho ke motho ka batho" (Sotho). These roughly translate to: "It is through others that one attains selfhood."' See R Nicolson, ed (2008), *Persons in community: African ethics in a global culture* (ebook), University of KwaZulu-Natal Press, Pietermaritzburg.

14 MJ Manala (2014), 'Servant leadership: a required leadership model for efficient and effective service delivery in a democratic South Africa', *Studia Historiae Ecclesiasticae*, 40(Supplement), pp 255–256.

15 Gwyneth McClendon (2012), 'The politics of envy and esteem in two democracies', unpublished doctoral dissertation, Princeton University, June 2012.

15 S Pejovich (1999), 'The effects of the interaction of formal and informal institutions on social stability and economic development', *Journal of Markets & Morality*, 2(2), p 166.

16 See N Schofield, G Gaballero, A Greif et al (2011), *Political economy of institutions, democracy and voting*, Springer-Verlag, Berlin and Heidelberg.

17 Pejovich, 'The effects of the interaction of formal and informal institutions', p 171.

18 NN Taleb (2014), *Antifragile: things that gain from disorder*, Random House, New York, pp 68–69.

19 J Netshitenzhe (1998), 'The media in the African Renaissance', presentation, African Renaissance Conference, session 6, 28 November 1998. Available at www.gcis.gov.za/content/newsroom/speeches/ceo/joel-netshitenzhe-african-renaissance-conference-session-6, accessed on 15 August 2018.

20 MC Campbell and SA Tishkoff (2008), 'African genetic diversity: implications for human demographic history, modern human origins, and complex disease mapping', *Annual Review of Genomics and Human Genetics*, 9, pp 403–433. Available at www.ncbi.nlm.nih.gov/pmc/articles/pmc2953791/, accessed on 28 August 2018.

21 P Kreager, B Winney, S Ulijaszek and C Capelli (2015), *Population in the human sciences: concepts, models, evidence*, Oxford University Press, Oxford.

22 LR Andersen and T Björkman (2017), *The Nordic secret: a European story of beauty and freedom*, Fri Tanke, Stockholm, pp 72–74.

23 H Wubie and Z Tsegaw (2012), 'Historical background of the African Union', Abyssinia Law, 29 February 2012. Available at www.abyssinialaw.com/study-on-line/item/377-historical-background-of-the-african-union, accessed on 28 August 2018.

24 DC North (2016), 'Institutions and economic theory', *The American `Economist*, 61(1), pp 72–76.

25 African Development Bank (2013), 'Africa is now the fastest growing continent in the world', 11 July 2013. Available at www.afdb.org/en/news-and-events/africa-is-now-the-fastest-growing-continent-in-the-world-12107/, accessed on 28 August 2018.

26 The World Bank (2015), 'Deepening African integration: intra-Africa trade for development and poverty reduction', media statement, 14 November

2015. Available at www.worldbank.org/en/news/speech/2015/12/14/deepening-african-integration-intra-africa-trade-for-development-and-poverty-reduction, accessed on 28 August 2018.

Chapter 5

1   African Union (no date), 'What is Agenda 2063?'. Available at au.int/en/agenda2063, accessed on 29 August 2018.

2   D Acemoglu and J Robinson (2013), *Why nations fail: the origins of power, prosperity, and poverty*, Currency, New York, pp 42–44.

3   CR Williamson and RL Mathers (2011), 'Economic freedom, culture, and growth', *Public Choice*, 148(3), pp 313–335.

4   Ibid.

5   Ibid.

6   Definition according to the *Collins Dictionary*.

7   A Giddens (1971), *Capitalism and modern social theory: an analysis of the writings of Marx, Durkheim and Max Weber*, Cambridge University Press, New York.

8   EO Wright (2002), 'The shadow of exploitation in Weber's class analysis', *American Sociological Review*, 67(6), pp 832–853.

9   N Lin, K Cook and RS Burt (2001), *Social capital: theory and research*, Transaction Publishers, Piscataway, NJ.

10   Ibid, p 4.

11   R Pitso (2017), 'A degree and deep desire to work isn't always enough in SA', *Business Day*, 11 March 2017. Available at businesslive.co.za.

12   Ibid.

13   P Bourdieu, C Calhoun, E LiPuma and M Postone (1993), *Bourdieu: critical perspectives*, University of Chicago Press, Chicago.

14   Lin, Cook and Burt, *Social capital*, p 11.

15   The World Bank (2012), 'African diaspora', FAQs, April 2012. Available at siteresources.worldbank.org/INTDIASPORA/Resources/AFR_Diaspora_FAQ.pdf, accessed on 29 August 2018.

16   The World Bank (2013), 'Remittances create safety net for African households', feature story, 26 June 2013. Available at www.worldbank.org/en/news/feature/2013/06/26/remittances-create-safety-net-for-african-households, accessed on 29 August 2018.

17   International Organization for Migration (2014), 'Regional Strategy for Southern Africa 2014–2016'. Available at https://reliefweb.int/sites/reliefweb.int/files/resources/Regional_Strategy_2014_web.pdf, accessed on 29 October 2018.

18   A Portes and RD Manning (1986), 'The immigrant enclave: theory and empirical examples', in S Olzak and J Nagel (eds), *Competitive ethnic relations*, Academic Press, Orlando, Fl, p 61.

19   South African Institute of Race Relations (2017), 'What will South Africa

lose if all immigrants are sent home?', press release, 13 March 2017. Available at irr.org.za/media/media-releases/what-will-south-africa-lose-if-all-immigrants-are-sent-home/view, accessed on 29 August 2018.

20 African Development Bank (2012), *African Economic Outlook 2012: promoting youth employment*, OECD Publishing, Paris. Available at www.undp.org/content/dam/rba/docs/Reports/African%20Economic%20Outlook%20 2012%20En.pdf, accessed on 8 February 2019.

21 P Zak and S Knack (2001), 'Trust and growth', *The Economic Journal*, 11(470), pp 295–321.

22 LR Andersen and T Björkman (2017), *The Nordic secret: a European story of beauty and freedom*, Fri Tanke, Stockholm. pp 181–191.

23 M Sow (2015), 'Foresight Africa 2016: urbanization in the African context', Brookings Institution, 30 December 2015. Available at www.brookings.edu/blog/africa-in-focus/2015/12/30/foresight-africa-2016-urbanization-in-the-african-context/, accessed on 29 August 2018.

24 J Bararofsky, E Siba and J Grabinsky (2016), 'Can rapid urbanization in Africa reduce poverty? Causes, opportunities and recommendations', Brookings Institution, 7 September 2016. Available at www.brookings.edu/blog/africa-in-focus/2016/09/07/can-rapid-urbanization-in-africa-reduce-poverty-causes-opportunities-and-policy-recommendations/, accessed on 29 August 2018.

25 African Development Bank (2016), *African Economic Outlook 2016*, OECD Publishing, Paris. Available at www.afdb.org/fileadmin/uploads/afdb/Documents/Publications/AEO_2016_Report_Full_English.pdf, accessed on 29 August 2018.

26 E Glaeser (2016), 'Managing the challenges and opportunities of urbanization in Africa', address to conference, World Bank, 13 June 2016. Available at www.youtube.com/watch?v=37O58T4Jyx4&feature=youtu.be&t=10m07s, accessed on 16 August 2018.

27 J Abel, I Dey and T Gabe (2011), 'Productivity and the density of human capital', Federal Reserve Bank of New York Staff Papers, Staff Report no 440, March 2010 (revised September 2011). Available at www.newyorkfed.org/medialibrary/media/research/staff_reports/sr440.pdf, accessed on 29 August 2018.

28 H Bhorat et al (2014), 'Foresight Africa: Top priorities for the continent in 2014', report, Brookings Institution, January 2014. Available at www.sub-sahara-afrika-ihk.de/wp-content/uploads/2014/01/Foresight-Africa_Full-Report.pdf, accessed on 29 August 2018.

29 International Labor Organization (2016), 'Facing the growing unemployment challenges in Africa', press release, 20 January 2016. Available at www.ilo.org/addisababa/media-centre/pr/WCMS_444474/lang--en/index.htm, accessed on 29 August 2018.

30 J Bulow and L Summers (1986), 'A theory of dual labor markets with application to industrial policy, discrimination and Keynesian economics', *Journal of Labor Economics*, 4(3, part 1), pp 376–414.

31 ML Baldwin, RJ Butler and WG Johnson (2001), 'A hierarchical theory of occupational segregation and wage discrimination', *Economic Inquiry*, 39(1), pp 94–110.

32 African Center for Economic Transformation (2016), 'Unemployment in Africa: no jobs for 50% of graduates', press release, 1 April 2016. Available at acetforafrica.org/highlights/unemployment-in-africa-no-jobs-for-50-of-graduates/, accessed on 29 August 2018.

33 Forbes Insights (2015), 'Job creation in sub-Saharan Africa: entrepreneurs, governments, innovation', report. Available at images.forbes.com/forbesinsights/StudyPDFs/Djembe-jobcreationinSubSaharanAfrica-REPORT.pdf, accessed on 29 October 2018.

Chapter 6

1 Times Staff (2017), 'Special report: Inside Zuma's battle to the bitter end as ANC rebels', *Business Day*, 5 April 2017. Available at www.businesslive.co.za, accessed on 29 August 2018.

2 Transparency International (2018), 'Corruption Perception Index 2017 shows high corruption burden in more than two-thirds of countries', press release, 21 February 2018. Available at www.transparency.org/news/press-release/corruption_perceptions_index_2017_shows_high_corruption_burden_in_more_than, accessed on 29 August 2018.

3 ZT Sirna (2012), 'Ethiopia: when the Gadaa democracy rules in a federal state. Bridging indigenous institutions of governance to modern democracy', unpublished PhD dissertation, University of Tromsø, Norway, May 2012. Available at munin.uit.no/bitstream/handle/10037/5080/thesis.pdf?sequence=2, accessed on 29 August 2018.

4 A Jalata (2012), 'Gadaa (Oromo democracy): an example of classical African civilization', *The Journal of Pan African Studies*, 5(1), pp 121–152.

5 Ibid.

6 Transparency International, 'Corruption Perception Index 2017'.

7 K Boafo-Arthur (2003), *Ghana: one decade of the liberal state*, University of Chicago Press, Chicago, p 12.

8 AA Mazrui and F Wiafe-Amoako (2016), *African institutions: challenges to political, social, and economic foundations of Africa's development*, Rowman & Littlefield, Lanham, MD.

9 P Bourdieu and J-C Passeron (1990), *Reproduction in education, society and culture*, translated by Richard Nice, 2nd ed, Theory, Culture and Society series, Sage Publications, London, p 213.

10 Republic of South Africa (2018), Ministry of Rural Development and Land Reform, 'Land Audit Report 2017', 5 February 2018. Available at www.ruraldevelopment.gov.za/publications/land-audit-report, accessed on 29 August 2018.

11 *Forbes* (2018), 'Real Time Net Worth', 22 April 2018. Available at Forbes.com, accessed on 29 August 2018.

12 Ibid.

13 SP Huntington (1991), *Democracy's third wave: democratization in the late twentieth century*, University of Oklahoma Press, Norman, p 15.

14 Ibid.

15 RD Putnam (2002), 'Community-based social capital and educational performance', in D Ravitch and JP Viteritti (eds), *Making good citizens: education and civil society*, Yale University Press, New Haven.

16 MC Brinton and V Nee (eds) (1998), *The new institutionalism in sociology*, Russell Sage Foundation, New York.

17 M Mamdani (1996), *Citizen and subject: contemporary Africa and the legacy of late colonialism*, Princeton University Press, Princeton, NJ, pp 16–25.

18 Ibid.

19 Ibid, p 13.

20 Ibid, p 16.

21 Ibid.

22 B Zewde and S Pausewang (2002), *Ethiopia: the challenge of democracy from below*, Nordic Africa Institute, Uppsala.

23 Afrobarometer and Transparency International (2015), *People and corruption: Africa survey 2015. Global corruption barometer.* Available at afrobarometer. org/sites/default/files/publications/Joint/partner%20publications/ab_joint_pubs_people_and_corruption_africa_survey_2015.pdf, accessed on 29 August 2018.

24 Ibid.

25 See 'United Arab Emirates's Constitution of 1971 with Amendments through 2004', Constitute Project, 17 January 2018. Available at www.constituteproject.org/constitution/United_Arab_Emirates_2004.pdf, accessed 28 September 2018.

26 B Berger (2013), 'Breaking the hold of two-party politics', *US News & World Report*, 2 May 2013. Available at ww.usnews.com/opinion/articles/2013/05/02/why-the-two-party-political-system-is-failing-the-united-states, accessed on 17 August 2018.

27 JE Lane (2001), *The Swiss labyrinth: institutions, outcomes and redesign*, Frank Cass, London.

Chapter 7

1 G Akerlof and R Kranton (2011), *Identity economics: how our identities shape our work, wages and well-being*, Princeton University Press, Princeton, NJ, p 15.

2 Ibid.

3 CM Steele (2011), *Whistling Vivaldi: and other clues to how stereotypes affect us*, WW Norton & Company, New York.

4 R Brown (2000), 'Social identity theory: past achievements, current

problems and future challenges', *European Journal of Social Psychology*, 30(6), pp 745–778.

5   R Rosenthal and L Jacobson (2003), *Pygmalion in the classroom: teacher expectation and pupils' intellectual development*, Crown House, New York.

6   R Navarro (no date), 'Unconscious bias', University of California, San Francisco, Office of Diversity and Outreach. Available at diversity.ucsf.edu/resources/unconscious-bias, accessed on 30 August 2018.

7   T Piketty (2015), transcript of 13th Annual Nelson Mandela lecture, Nelson Mandela Foundation, 3 October 2015. Available at ww.nelsonmandela.org/news/entry/transcript-of-nelson-mandela-annual-lecture-2015, accessed on 30 August 2018.

8   T Piketty (2014), *Capital in the twenty-first century*, Harvard University Press, Cambridge, MA, p 27.

9   DH Pink (2010), *Drive: the surprising truth about what motivates us*, Canongate, Edinburgh, p 26.

10   A Appiah (1985), 'The uncompleted argument: Du Bois and the illusion of race', *Critical Inquiry*, 12(1), pp 21–37.

11   JF Dovidio and SL Gaertner (2000), 'Aversive racism and selection decisions: 1989 and 1999', *Psychological Science*, 11(4), pp 315–319.

12   C Tobler (2005), *Indirect discrimination: a case study into the development of the legal concept of indirect discrimination*, Intersentia, Cambridge.

13   Akerlof and Kranton, *Identity economics*, pp 10–13.

14   South African History Online (2016), 'Cape Town timeline 1300–1997', 21 July 2016. Available at www.sahistory.org.za/topic/cape-town-timeline-1300-1997, accessed on 30 August 2018.

15   Ibid.

16   Ibid.

17   P Kankonde (2013), 'The Portuguese migration to, and settlement in South Africa, 1510–2013', thematic seminar, University of Lisbon, 10 May 2013. Available at www.unescochair-iuav.it/wp-content/uploads/2014/03/Lecture-10-may-2013-Portuguese-Migration-to-South-Africa.pdf, accessed on 30 August 2018.

18   A Portes and J Sensenbrenner (1993), 'Embeddedness and immigration: notes on the social determinants of economic action', *American Journal of Sociology*, 98(6), pp 1320–1350.

19   A Chua and J Rubenfeld (2014), *The triple package: how three unlikely traits explain the rise and fall of cultural groups in America*, Penguin, New York.

20   B Williams (1991), 'Apartheid in South Africa: Calvin's legacy', *The Upsilonian*, 3. Available at www.ucumberlands.edu/downloads/academics/history/vol3/BlakeWilliams91.htm, accessed on 30 August 2018.

21   J Hart and C Chabris (2016), 'How not to explain success', *The New York Times*, 8 April 2016. Available at www.nytimes.com/2016/04/10/opinion/sunday/how-not-to-explain-success.html?_r=0, accessed on 30 August 2018.

22 J Merritt (2013), 'Insisting Jesus was white is bad history and bad theology', *The Atlantic*, 12 December 2013. Available at www.theatlantic.com/politics/archive/2013/12/insisting-jesus-was-white-is-bad-history-and-bad-theology/282310/, accessed on 30 August 2018.

23 CA Diop (1989), *The African origin of civilization: myth or reality* (ebook), Chicago Review Press, Chicago.

24 F Fukuyama (2011), *The origins of political order: from prehuman times to the French Revolution*, Farrar, Straus and Giroux, New York.

25 DM Taylor and JR Doira (1979), 'Self-serving and group-serving bias in attribution', *The Journal of Social Psychology*, 113(2), pp 201–211.

26 ZA Melzak (1973), *Companion to concrete mathematics*, 2 vols, Dover Publications, New York.

27 Steele, *Whistling Vivaldi*, p 111.

28 V Purdie-Vaughns et al (2008), 'Social identity contingencies: how diversity cues signal threat or safety for African Americans in mainstream institutions', *Journal of Personal and Social Psychology*, 94(4), pp 615–630.

29 'Ask yourself what would happen to your personality if you heard it said over and over again that you were lazy, expected to steal and had inferior blood. One's reputation cannot be hammered, hammered, hammered into one's head without doing something to one's character'; see G Allport (1979), *The nature of prejudice*, Addison-Wesley, Boston, pp 48–57.

30 KA Appiah (1992), *In my father's house: Africa in the philosophy of culture*, Oxford University Press, Oxford, p 45.

31 E Renan (1882), 'What is a nation?', text of a conference delivered at the Sorbonne on 11 March 1882, translated by E Rundell. Available at ucparis.fr/files/9313/6549/9943/What_is_a_Nation.pdf, accessed on 30 August 2018.

Chapter 8

1 CE Georges (1865), *A copious and critical English-Latin lexicon: founded on German Latin*, 8th edition, Longmans Green & Co, London.

2 M Treder (2009), 'The meaning of freedom', Institute for Ethics and Emerging Technology, 17 September 2009. Available at ieet.org/index.php/IEET2/print/3411, accessed on 30 August 2018.

3 *Merriam-Webster Dictionary*, www.merriam-webster.com.

4 R Bellamy and A Mason (2013), *Political concepts*, Manchester University Press, Manchester.

5 I Carter (2016), 'Positive and negative liberty', *Stanford Encyclopedia of Philosophy*, 2 August 2016. Available at plato.stanford.edu/entries/liberty-positive-negative/, accessed on 23 August 2018.

6 D Hume (1738), *A treatise of human nature*, Early Modern Texts/Jonathan Bennet, 2018. Available at www.earlymoderntexts.com/authors/hume, accessed on 30 August 2018.

7   Ibid.

8   Afrobarometer (2008), *The material and political bases of lived poverty in Africa*, Working Paper 98. Available at http://afrobarometer.org/sites/default/files/publications/Working%20paper/Afropaper98.pdf, accessed on 29 October 2018.

9   H Bhorat, R Kanbur and B Stanwix (2015), 'Minimum wages in sub-Saharan Africa: a primer', VoxEU CEPR Policy Portal, 6 October 2015. Available at voxeu.org/article/minimum-wages-sub-saharan-africa-primer, accessed on 23 August 2018.

10 B bwa Mwesigire (2014), 'Why are schools punishing children for speaking African languages?', This is Africa, 17 September 2014. Available at thisisafrica.me/schools-punishing-children-speaking-african-languages/, accessed on 23 August 2018.

11 Bhorat et al, 'Minimum wages in sub-Saharan Africa'.

12 Freedom House (2018), *Freedom in the world 2018: democracy in crisis*, report. Available at https://freedomhouse.org/report/freedom-world-2018, accessed on 29 October 2018.

13 S Bashir, M Lockheed, E Ninan and J Tan (2018), *Facing forward: schooling in Africa* (ebook), World Bank Group, Washington, DC.

14 IM Rosenstock, VJ Strecher and MH Becker (1988), 'Social learning theory and the health belief model', *Health Education Quarterly*, 15(2), pp 175–183.

15 Bashir et al, *Facing forward*.

16 ME Button (2016), *Political vices*, Oxford University Press, Oxford.

17 N Leach (1997), *Rethinking architecture: a reader in cultural theory*, Routledge, New York, p 70.

18 R Beehler (1990), 'Freedom and authenticity', *Journal of Applied Philosophy*, 7(1), pp 39–44.

19 W Mischel (1973), 'Toward a cognitive social learning reconceptualization of personality', *Psychological Review*, 80(4), pp 252–283.

20 C Macleod (2016), 'John Stuart Mill', Stanford Encyclopedia of Philosophy, 25 August 2016. Available at plato.stanford.edu/entries/mill/, accessed on 30 August 2018.

21 NN Taleb (2018), *Skin in the game: hidden asymmetries in daily life*, Random House, New York, pp 204–206.

22 Ibid, pp 187–189.

23 Ibid.

Chapter 9

1   C McCullough (2017), 'Why the number of South African dairy farmers has slumped from 50,000 in 1997 to just 1,600 today', FarmIreland, 23 April 2017. Available at www.independent.ie/business/farming/dairy/why-the-number-of-south-african-dairy-farmers-has-slumped-from-

50000-in-1997-to-just-1600-today-35629779.html, accessed on 30 August 2018.

2   Food Business Africa (no date), 'The dairy industry in Kenya'. Available at www.foodbusinessafrica.com/the-dairy-industry-in-kenya/, accessed on 30 August 2018.

3   Milk Producers' Organisation (2017), 'The challenges of small-scale dairy farming', 18 October 2017. Available at www.mpo.co.za/sustainability-post/challenges-small-scale-dairy-farming/, accessed on 30 August 2018.

4   Food Business Africa, 'The dairy industry in Kenya'.

5   African Development Bank (2013), 'Recognizing Africa's informal sector', blog post, 27 March 2013. Available at www.afdb.org/en/blogs/afdb-championing-inclusive-growth-across-Africa/post/recognizing-africas-informal-sector-11645/, accessed on 30 August 2018.

6   Ibid.

7   Deloitte (2017), 'African powers of consumer products 2016: the continent's home-grown Top 50 consumer products companies', report. Available at www2.deloitte.com/content/dam/Deloitte/za/Documents/Consumer_Industrial_Products/za_APCP_Brochure_Digital.pdf, accessed on 30 August 2018.

8   D Filmer and L Fox (2014), 'Youth employment in sub-Saharan Africa', research report, The World Bank, Washington, DC. Available at open-knowledge.worldbank.org/handle/10986/16608, accessed on 30 August 2018.

9   UNIDO (2012), 'Made in Ethiopia: industrial and leather products for the global market', report, United Nations Industrial Development Organization. Available at open.unido.org/api/documents/4257015/download/101072%202012%20Brochure%20Made%20in%20Ethiopia.pdf, accessed on 30 August 2018.

10 African Development Bank, 'Recognizing Africa's informal sector'

11 S Halleen (2013), 'From life insurance to financial services: a historical analysis of Sanlam's client base, 1918–2004', unpublished PhD (History) thesis, Stellenbosch University, December 2013, p 69.

12 Ibid, p 70.

13 Ibid, p 4.

14 Ibid, p 8.

15 DHAN Foundation homepage, www.dhan.org.

16 World Economic Forum (2018), 'Africa Competitiveness Report 2017'. Available at www.weforum.org/reports/Africa-competitiveness-report-2017, accessed on 30 August 2018.

17 Ibid.

18 JB Avey (2009), 'Psychological ownership: theoretical extensions, measurement and relation to work outcomes', *Journal of Organizational Behavior*, 30(2), pp 173–191.

19   C Olckers (2011), 'A multi-dimensional measure of psychological ownership for South African organisations', unpublished PhD thesis, University of Pretoria, April 2011. Available at repository.up.ac.za/bitstream/handle/2263/28730/Complete.pdf?sequence=8, accessed on 30 August 2018.

Chapter 10

1   Encyclopaedia Britannica (2018), 'Superpower'. Available at Britannica.com.

2   L Ensor (2018), 'SA remains committed to Africa Continent Free Trade Area: Davies', *Sunday Times*, 26 March 2018. Available at www.timeslive.co.za/sunday-times/business/2018-03-26-sa-remains-committed-to-africa-continent-free-trade-area-davies/, accessed on 30 August 2018.

3   L Signé (2018), 'Capturing Africa's high returns', op-ed, Brookings Institution, 14 March 2018, Available at www.brookings.edu/opinions/capturing-africas-high-returns/, accessed on 30 August 2018.

4   United Nations (2017), 'World population projected to reach 9.8 billion in 2050, and 11.2 billion in 2100', United Nations Department of Economic and Social Affairs, 21 June 2017. Available at www.un.org/development/desa/en/news/population/world-population-prospects-2017.html, accessed on 30 August 2018.

5   African Development Bank (2018), *African Economic Outlook 2018*. Available at www.afdb.org/fileadmin/uploads/afdb/Documents/Publications/African_Economic_Outlook_2018_-_EN.pdf, accessed on 30 August 2018.

6   Ibid.

7   China Daily (2018), 'China's tax revenue growth accelerates in 2017', chinadaily.com, 2 February 2018. Available at www.chinadaily.com.cn/a/201802/02/WS5a740525a3106e7dcc13a6e0.html, accessed on 30 August 2018.

8   M Olapade, EE Selormey and H Gninafon (2016), 'Regional integration for Africa: could stronger public support turn "rhetoric into reality"?', Afrobarometer Dispatch No 91, 25 May 2016. Available at afrobarometer.org/sites/default/files/publications/Dispatches/ab_r6_dispatchno91_regional_integration_in_africa_en.pdf, accessed on 29 October 2018.

Sources

Books

Acemoglu, D and J Robinson (2013). *Why nations fail: the origins of power, prosperity, and poverty*. Currency, New York.

Akerlof, G and R Kranton (2011). *Identity economics: how our identities shape our work, wages and well-being*. Princeton University Press, Princeton, NJ.

Allport, G (1979). *The nature of prejudice*. Addison-Wesley, Boston.

Andersen, LR and T Björkman (2017). *The Nordic secret: a European story of beauty and freedom*. Fri Tanke, Stockholm.

Appiah, KA (1992). *In my father's house: Africa in the philosophy of culture*. Oxford University Press, Oxford.

Aristotle (1999). *Nicomachean ethics* (T Irwin, ed). Hackett Publishing Company, Indianapolis.

Asante, MK (2000). *The Egyptian philosophers: ancient African voices from Imhotep to Akhenaten*. African American Images, Chicago.

Bashir, S, M Lockheed, E Ninan and J Tan (2018). *Facing forward: schooling in Africa* (ebook). World Bank Group, Washington, DC.

Bellamy, R and A Mason (2013). *Political concepts*. Manchester University Press, Manchester.

Berger, PL and T Luckmann (2011). *The social construction of reality: a treatise in the sociology of knowledge* (ebook reprint). Open Road Media, New York (originally published 1967).

Blumenbach, JF (1969). *On the natural varieties of mankind*. Bergman Publishers, New York (original edition 1775).

Boafo-Arthur, K (2003). *Ghana: one decade of the liberal state*. University of Chicago Press, Chicago.

Boas, F (1932). *Anthropology and modern life*. Routledge, New York.

Bourdieu, P and J-C Passeron (1990). *Reproduction in education, society and culture*. Translated by Richard Nice. 2nd ed. Theory, Culture and Society series. Sage Publications, London.

Bourdieu, P, C Calhoun, E LiPuma and M Postone (1993). *Bourdieu: critical perspectives*. University of Chicago Press, Chicago.

Brinton, MC and V Nee (eds) (1998). *The new institutionalism in sociology*. Russell Sage Foundation, New York.

Button, ME (2016). *Political vices*. Oxford University Press, Oxford.

Campbell, J (2008). *The hero with a thousand faces*. New World Library, New York.

Chua, A and J Rubenfeld (2014). *The triple package: how three unlikely traits explain the rise and fall of cultural groups in America*. Penguin, New York.

Clarke, JH (1991). *New dimensions in African history: the London lectures of Dr Yosef Ben-Jochannan and Dr John Henrik Clarke*. Africa World Press, Trenton, NJ.

Coates, T-N (2017). *We were eight years in power*. Oneworld, London.

Cox, GO (1974). *African empire and civilization: ancient and medieval*. African Heritage Studies Publishers, New York.

Diop, CA (1988). *Precolonial Black Africa*. Chicago Review Press, Chicago

Diop, CA (1989). *The African origin of civilization: myth or reality* (ebook). Chicago Review Press, Chicago.

Diop, CA (1991). *Civilization or barbarism: an authentic anthropology*. Lawrence Hill Books, Brooklyn, New York.

Emirbayer, M (2008). *Emile Durkheim: sociologist of modernity*. Wiley-Blackwell, Hoboken, NJ.

Etherington, N (2008). *Missions and empire*. Oxford University Press, Oxford.

Fukuyama, F (2011). *The origins of political order: from prehuman times to the French Revolution*. Farrar, Straus and Giroux, New York.

Georges, CE (1865). *A copious and critical English-Latin lexicon: founded on German Latin*. 8th edition. Longmans Green & Co, London.

Giddens, A (1971). *Capitalism and modern social theory: an analysis of the writings of Marx, Durkheim and Max Weber*. Cambridge University Press, New York.

Griaule, M and G Dieterlen (1986). *The pale fox*. Continuum Foundation, Chino Valley, AZ.

Griggs, S, AJ Norval and H Wagenaar (2014). *Practices of freedom: decentred governance conflict and democratic participation*. Cambridge University Press, New York.

Griswold, CL, Jr (1999). *Adam Smith and the virtues of enlightenment*. Cambridge University Press, Cambridge.

Haltinner, K (2014). *Teaching race and anti-racism in contemporary America: adding context to colorblindness* (ebook). Springer, New York.

Harari, YN (2015). *Sapiens: a brief history of humankind*. Vintage, London.

Hoggson, NF (1926). *Banking through the ages*. Dodd, Mead & Company, New York.

Hume, D (1738). *A treatise of human nature*. Early Modern Texts/Jonathan Bennet, 2018. Available at www.earlymoderntexts.com/authors/hume, accessed on 30 August 2018.

Huntington, SP (1991). *Democracy's third wave: democratization in the late twentieth century*. University of Oklahoma Press, Norman.

Ikuenobe, P (2006). *Philosophical perspectives on communalism and morality in African traditions*. Lexington Books, Lanham, MD.

James, GGM (2012). *Stolen legacy: the Egyptian origins of western philosophy* (ebook). Start Publishing, New York.

Jochannan, YB (1996). *The need for a black Bible: the black man's religion*. Africa World Press, Trenton, NJ.

270

Jordan, D and M Walsh (2007). *White cargo: the forgotten history of Britain's white slaves* (ebook). New York University Press, New York.

Kincheloe, JL (1999). *The struggle to define and reinvent whiteness: a pedagogical analysis.* Johns Hopkins University Press, Baltimore.

Kreager, P, B Winney, S Ulijaszek and C Capelli (2015). *Population in the human sciences: concepts, models, evidence.* Oxford University Press, Oxford.

Lane, JE (2001). *The Swiss labyrinth: institutions, outcomes and redesign.* Frank Cass, London.

Leach, N (1997). *Rethinking architecture: a reader in cultural theory.* Routledge, New York.

Leary, MR and JP Tangney (2012). *Handbook of self and identity.* Guilford Press, New York.

Lin, N, K Cook and RS Burt (2001). *Social capital: theory and research.* Transaction Publishers, Piscataway, NJ.

Macionis, JJ and L Marie (2011). *Sociology.* Prentice Hall, Toronto.

Mamdani, M (1996). *Citizen and subject: contemporary Africa and the legacy of late colonialism.* Princeton University Press, Princeton, NJ.

Mazama, A (2002). *The Afrocentric paradigm.* Africa World Press, Trenton, NJ.

Mazrui, AA and F Wiafe-Amoako (2016). *African institutions: challenges to political, social, and economic foundations of Africa's development.* Rowman & Littlefield, Lanham, MD.

McLean, D and A Hurd (2014). *Recreation and leisure in modern society*, Jones & Bartlett Learning, Burlington, MA.

Melzak, ZA (1973). *Companion to concrete mathematics*, 2 vols. Dover Publications, New York.

Mohanty, J and W McKenna (1989). *Husserl's phenomenology: a textbook.* University Press of America, Washington, DC.

Nabarz, P (2005). *The mysteries of Mithras.* Inner Traditions, Rochester, VT.

Nicolson, R (ed) (2008). *Persons in community: African ethics in a global culture* (ebook). University of KwaZulu-Natal Press, Pietermaritzburg.

Oden, TC (2011). *The African memory of Mark: reassessing early church tradition.* InterVarsity Press, Westmont, IL.

Olupona, JK (2001). *African spirituality: forms, meanings and expressions.* The Crossroad Publishing Company, New York.

Piketty, T (2014). *Capital in the twenty-first century.* Harvard University Press, Cambridge, MA.

Pink, DH (2006). *A whole new mind: why right-brainers will rule the future.* Riverhead Books, New York.

Pink, DH (2010). *Drive: the surprising truth about what motivates us.* Canongate, Edinburgh.

Plato (2008). *The Republic* (ebook). Digireads.com, Lawrence, KS.

Rosenthal, R and L Jacobson (2003). *Pygmalion in the classroom: teacher expectation and pupils' intellectual development*. Crown House, New York.

Saakana, AS (ed) (1986). *African origins of the major world religions*. Karnak House Publishers, London.

Said, Edward W (2003). *Orientalism*. Penguin, London.

Sanderson, C (2010). *Social psychology*. Wiley, Hoboken, NJ.

Saracho, ON and B Spodek (1998). *Multiple perspectives on play in early childhood education*. SUNY Press, Albany.

Schofield, N, G Gaballero, A Greif et al (2011). *Political economy of institutions, democracy and voting*. Springer-Verlag, Berlin and Heidelberg.

Sertima, I van (1992). *Golden age of the Moor*. Transaction Publishers, Piscataway, NJ.

Sertima, I van (2003). *They came before Columbus*. Random House, New York.

Shermer, M (2016). *The moral arc: how science makes us better people*. St Martin's Griffin, New York.

Simmel, G (2004). *The philosophy of money*. Psychology Press, London.

Stebbins, RA (1992). *Amateurs, professionals and serious leisure*. McGill-Queen's University Press, Montreal.

Steele, CM (2011). *Whistling Vivaldi: and other clues to how stereotypes affect us*. WW Norton & Company, New York.

Taleb, NN (2014). *Antifragile: things that gain from disorder*. Random House, New York.

Taleb, NN (2018). *Skin in the game: hidden asymmetries in daily life*. Random House, New York.

Tobler, C (2005). *Indirect discrimination: a case study into the development of the legal concept of indirect discrimination*. Intersentia, Cambridge.

Weber, M (2002). *The Protestant ethic and the spirit of capitalism*. Penguin, London.

Wilkinson, T (2013). *The rise and fall of Ancient Egypt* (ebook). Random House, New York.

Williams, C (1974). *The destruction of black civilization: great issues of a race from 4500 BC to 200 AD*. Third World Press, Chicago.

Wiredu, K (1997). *Cultural universals and particulars: an African perspective*. Indiana University Press, Bloomington.

Witzel, EJM (2013). *The origins of the world's mythologies* (ebook). Oxford University Press, Oxford.

Yengoyan, AA (2006). *Modes of comparison: theory and practice*. University of Michigan Press, Ann Arbor.

Zewde, B and S Pausewang (2002). *Ethiopia: the challenge of democracy from below*. Nordic Africa Institute, Uppsala.

Book chapters

Fanon, F (2009). 'The fact of blackness'. In L Back and J Solomos (eds), *Theories of race and racism: a reader*. Routledge, London.

Portes, A and RD Manning (1986). 'The immigrant enclave: theory and empirical examples'. In S Olzak and J Nagel (eds), *Competitive ethnic relations*. Academic Press, Orlando, Fl.

Putnam, RD (2002). 'Community-based social capital and educational performance'. In D Ravitch and JP Viteritti (eds), *Making good citizens: education and civil society*. Yale University Press, New Haven.

Government documents

Republic of South Africa (2018), Ministry of Rural Development and Land Reform, 'Land Audit Report 2017', 5 February 2018. Available at www.rural-development.gov.za/publications/land-audit-report. Accessed on 29 August 2018.

Journal articles

Appiah, A (1985). 'The uncompleted argument: Du Bois and the illusion of race'. *Critical Inquiry*, 12(1), pp 21–37.

Avey, JB (2009). 'Psychological ownership: theoretical extensions, measurement and relation to work outcomes'. *Journal of Organizational Behavior*, 30(2), pp 173–191.

Baldwin, ML, RJ Butler and WG Johnson (2001). 'A hierarchical theory of occupational segregation and wage discrimination'. *Economic Inquiry*, 39(1), pp 94–110.

Bandura, A (2012). 'On the functional properties of perceived self-efficacy revisited'. *Journal of Management*, 38(1), pp 9–44.

Beehler, R (1990). 'Freedom and authenticity'. *Journal of Applied Philosophy*, 7(1), pp 39–44.

Brown, R (2000). 'Social identity theory: past achievements, current problems and future challenges'. *European Journal of Social Psychology*, 30(6), pp 745–778.

Bulow, J and L Summers (1986). 'A theory of dual labor markets with application to industrial policy, discrimination and Keynesian economics'. *Journal of Labor Economics*, 4(3, part 1), pp 376–414.

Campbell, MC and SA Tishkoff (2008). 'African genetic diversity: implications for human demographic history, modern human origins, and complex disease mapping'. *Annual Review of Genomics and Human Genetics*, 9, pp 403–433. Available at www.ncbi.nlm.nih.gov/pmc/articles/pmc2953791/. Accessed on 28 August 2018.

Dovidio, JF and SL Gaertner (2000). 'Aversive racism and selection decisions: 1989 and 1999'. *Psychological Science*, 11(4), pp 315–319.

Flagg, BJ (2005). 'Foreword: whiteness as metaprivilege'. *Washington University Journal of Law & Policy*, 18, pp 1–11.

Havelock, EA (1986). 'The alphabetic mind: a gift of Greece to the modern world'. *Oral Tradition*, 1(1), pp 134–150.

Huy, Q (2011). 'How collective emotions and social identities influence strategy execution'. *Strategic Management Journal*, 32(13), pp 1387–1410.

Jalata, A (2012). 'Gadaa (Oromo democracy): an example of classical African civilization'. *The Journal of Pan African Studies*, 5(1), pp 121–152.

Kincheloe, JL (1999). 'The struggle to define and reinvent whiteness: a pedagogical analysis'. *College Literature*, 26(13), pp 162–194.

Kroeber, AL (1940). 'Stimulus diffusion'. *American Anthropologist (New Series)*, 42(1), pp 1–20.

Manala, MJ (2014). 'Servant leadership: a required leadership model for efficient and effective service delivery in a democratic South Africa'. *Studia Historiae Ecclesiasticae*, 40(Supplement), pp 249–266.

McAdams, DP (2001). 'The psychology of life stories'. *Review of General Psychology*, 5(2), pp 100–122.

Mischel, W (1973). 'Toward a cognitive social learning reconceptualization of personality'. *Psychological Review*, 80(4), pp 252–283.

North, DC (2016). 'Institutions and economic theory'. *The American Economist*, 61(1), pp 72–76.

Pejovich, S (1999). 'The effects of the interaction of formal and informal institutions on social stability and economic development'. *Journal of Markets & Morality*, 2(2), pp 164–181.

Portes, A and J Sensenbrenner (1993). 'Embeddedness and immigration: notes on the social determinants of economic action'. *American Journal of Sociology*, 98(6), pp 1320–1350.

Pratt, N (2005). 'Identity, culture and democratization: the case for Egypt'. *New Political Science*, 27(1), pp 69–86.

Purdie-Vaughns, V, CM Steele, PG Davies, R Ditlmann and JR Crosby (2008). 'Social identity contingencies: how diversity cues signal threat or safety for African Americans in mainstream institutions'. *Journal of Personal and Social Psychology*, 94(4), pp 615–630.

Rashidi, R (1983). 'The Kushite origins of Sumer and Elam'. *Ufahamu: A Journal of African Studies*, 12(3), pp 215–233.

Rosenstock, IM, VJ Strecher and MH Becker (1988). 'Social learning theory and the health belief model'. *Health Education Quarterly*, 15(2), pp 175–183.

Taylor, DM and JR Doira (1979). 'Self-serving and group-serving bias in attribution'. *The Journal of Social Psychology*, 113(2), pp 201–211.

Udeani, CC (2008). 'Traditional African spirituality and ethics – a panacea to leadership crises and corruption in Africa'. *Phronimon*, 9(2), pp 65–72. Available at docplayer.net/50770375-Traditional-african-spirituality-and-ethics-a-panacea-to-leadership-crisis-and-corruption-in-Africa.html. Accessed on 28 August 2018.

Venter, JC et al (2007). 'The diploid genome sequence of an individual human'. *PLOS Biology*, 5(10). Available at journals.plos.org/plosbiology/article?id=10.1371/journal.pbio.0050254. Accessed on 28 August 2018.

Wellendorf, H (2008). 'Ptolemy's political tool: religion'. *Studia Antiqua*, 6(1), pp 33–38.

Williams, B (1991). 'Apartheid in South Africa: Calvin's legacy'. *The Upsilonian*, 3. Available at www.ucumberlands.edu/downloads/academics/history/vol3/BlakeWilliams91.htm. Accessed on 30 August 2018.

Williamson, CR and RL Mathers (2011). 'Economic freedom, culture, and growth'. *Public Choice*, 148(3), pp 313–335.

Winters, C (2012). 'Dravidian is the language of the Indus writing'. *Current Science*, 103(10), pp 1220–1225.

Wright, EO (2002). 'The shadow of exploitation in Weber's class analysis'. *American Sociological Review*, 67(6), pp 832–853.

Zak, P and S Knack (2001). 'Trust and growth'. *The Economic Journal*, 11(470), pp 295–321.

Conference papers and presentations

Glaeser, E (2016). 'Managing the challenges and opportunities of urbanization in Africa'. Address to conference, World Bank, 13 June 2016. Available at www.youtube.com/watch?v=37O58T4Jyx4&feature=youtu.be&t=10m07s. Accessed on 16 August 2018.

Kankonde, P (2013). 'The Portuguese migration to, and settlement in South Africa, 1510–2013'. Thematic seminar, University of Lisbon, 10 May 2013. Available at www.unescochair-iuav.it/wp-content/uploads/2014/03/Lecture-10-may-2013-Portuguese-Migration-to-South-Africa.pdf. Accessed on 30 August 2018.

Netshitenzhe, J (1998). 'The media in the African Renaissance'. Presentation, African Renaissance Conference, session 6, 28 November 1998. Available at www.gcis.gov.za/content/newsroom/speeches/ceo/joel-netshitenzhe-african-renaissance-conference-session-6. Accessed on 15 August 2018.

Painter, NI (2003). 'Why white people are called "Caucasian"'. Conference paper. Proceedings of the Fifth Annual Gilder Lehrman Center International Conference, Yale University, 7–8 November.

Piketty, T (2015). Transcript of 13th Annual Nelson Mandela lecture, Nelson Mandela Foundation, 3 October 2015. Available at www.nelsonmandela.org/news/entry/transcript-of-nelson-mandela-annual-lecture-2015. Accessed on 30 August 2018.

Renan, E (1882). 'What is a nation?'. Text of a conference delivered at the Sorbonne on 11 March 1882. Translated by E Rundell. Available at ucparis.fr/files/9313/6549/9943/What_is_a_Nation.pdf. Accessed on 30 August 2018.

World Economic Forum (2018). 'Africa Competitiveness Report 2017'. Available at www.weforum.org/reports/Africa-competitiveness-report-2017. Accessed on 30 August 2018.

Other

'United Arab Emirates's Constitution of 1971 with Amendments through 2004', Constitute Project, 17 January 2018. Available at www.constitute-project.org/constitution/United_Arab_Emirates_2004.pdf. Accessed 28 September 2018.

Online

Abel, J, I Dey and T Gabe (2011). 'Productivity and the density of human capital'. Federal Reserve Bank of New York Staff Papers, Staff Report no 440, March 2010 (revised September 2011). Available at www.newyorkfed. org/medialibrary/media/research/staff_reports/sr440.pdf. Accessed on 29 August 2018.

African Center for Economic Transformation (2016). 'Unemployment in Africa: no jobs for 50% of graduates'. Press release, 1 April 2016. Available at acetforafrica.org/highlights/unemployment-in-africa-no-jobs-for-50-of-graduates/. Accessed on 29 August 2018.

African Development Bank (2012). *African Economic Outlook 2012: promoting youth employment*. OECD Publishing, Paris. Available at www.undp. org/content/dam/rba/docs/Reports/African%20Economic%20Outlook%202012%20En.pdf. Accessed on 8 February 2019.

African Development Bank (2013). 'Africa is now the fastest growing continent in the world'. 11 July 2013. Available at www.afdb.org/en/news-and-events/africa-is-now-the-fastest-growing-continent-in-the-world-12107/. Accessed on 28 August 2018.

African Development Bank (2013). 'Recognizing Africa's informal sector'. Blog post, 27 March 2013. Available at www.afdb.org/en/blogs/afdb-championing-inclusive-growth-across-Africa/post/recognizing-africas-informal-sector-11645/. Accessed on 30 August 2018.

African Development Bank (2016). *African Economic Outlook 2016*. OECD Publishing, Paris. Available at www.afdb.org/fileadmin/uploads/afdb/Documents/Publications/AEO_2016_Report_Full_English.pdf. Accessed on 29 August 2018.

African Development Bank (2018). *African Economic Outlook 2018*. Available at

www.afdb.org/fileadmin/uploads/afdb/Documents/Publications/
African_Economic_Outlook_2018_-_EN.pdf. Accessed on 30 August 2018.

African Union (no date). 'What is Agenda 2063?'. Available at au.int/en/
agenda2063. Accessed on 29 August 2018.

Afrobarometer (2008). *The material and political bases of lived poverty in Africa.*
Working Paper 98. Available at http://afrobarometer.org/sites/default/
files/publications/Working%20paper/Afropaper98.pdf. Accessed on
29 October 2018.

Afrobarometer and Transparency International (2015). *People and corruption:
Africa survey 2015. Global corruption barometer.* Available at afrobarometer.
org/sites/default/files/publications/Joint/partner%20publications/ab_
joint_pubs_people_and_corruption_africa_survey_2015.pdf. Accessed on
29 August 2018.

Bararofsky, J, E Siba and J Grabinsky (2016). 'Can rapid urbanization in Africa
reduce poverty? Causes, opportunities and recommendations'. Brookings
Institution, 7 September 2016. Available at www.brookings.edu/blog/
africa-in-focus/2016/09/07/can-rapid-urbanization-in-africa-reduce-
poverty-causes-opportunities-and-policy-recommendations/. Accessed on
29 August 2018.

Berger, B (2013). 'Breaking the hold of two-party politics'. *US News &
World Report*, 2 May 2013. Available at ww.usnews.com/opinion/
articles/2013/05/02/why-the-two-party-political-system-is-failing-the-
united-states. Accessed on 17 August 2018.

Bhorat, H, TT Deressa, V Felbab-Brown, K Gordon, C Juma, MS Kimenyi,
JW McArthur, JM Mbaku, J Page, V Songwe, A Sy and LA Warner (2014).
'Foresight Africa: Top priorities for the continent in 2014'. Report. Brook-
ings Institution, January 2014. Available at www.subsahara-afrika-ihk.
de/wp-content/uploads/2014/01/Foresight-Africa_Full-Report.pdf.
Accessed on 29 August 2018.

Bhorat, H, R Kanbur and B Stanwix (2015). 'Minimum wages in sub-Saharan
Africa: a primer'. VoxEU CEPR Policy Portal, 6 October 2015. Available
at voxeu.org/article/minimum-wages-sub-saharan-africa-primer. Accessed
on 23 August 2018.

Biko, SB (1978). 'Steve Biko on death'. *The New Republic*, 7 January 1978.
Available at newrepublic.com/article/122784/biko-death. Accessed on
26 October 2018.

Carter, I (2016). 'Positive and negative liberty'. *Stanford Encyclopedia of Philosophy*,
2 August 2016. Available at plato.stanford.edu/entries/liberty-positive-
negative/. Accessed on 23 August 2018.

China Daily (2018). 'China's tax revenue growth accelerates in 2017'. chinadaily.
com, 2 February 2018. Available at www.chinadaily.com.cn/a/201802/02/
WS5a740525a3106e7dcc13a6e0.html. Accessed on 30 August 2018.

Deloitte (2017). 'African powers of consumer products 2016: the continent's
home-grown Top 50 consumer products companies'. Report. Available at

www2.deloitte.com/content/dam/Deloitte/za/Documents/Consumer_ Industrial_Products/za_APCP_Brochure_Digital.pdf. Accessed on 30 August 2018.

Ensor, L (2018). 'SA remains committed to Africa Continent Free Trade Area: Davies'. *Sunday Times*, 26 March 2018. Available at www.timeslive.co.za/ sunday-times/business/2018-03-26-sa-remains-committed-to-africa-continent-free-trade-area-davies/. Accessed on 30 August 2018.

Filmer, D and L Fox (2014). 'Youth employment in sub-Saharan Africa'. Research report, The World Bank, Washington, DC. Available at openknowledge. worldbank.org/handle/10986/16608. Accessed on 30 August 2018.

Food Business Africa (no date). 'The dairy industry in Kenya'. Available at www.foodbusinessafrica.com/the-dairy-industry-in-kenya/. Accessed on 30 August 2018.

Forbes (2018). 'Real Time Net Worth'. 22 April 2018. Available at Forbes.com. Accessed on 29 August 2018.

Forbes Insights (2015). 'Job creation in sub-Saharan Africa: entrepreneurs, governments, innovation'. Report. Available at images.forbes.com/ forbesinsights/StudyPDFs/Djembe-jobcreationinSubSaharanAfrica-REPORT.pdf. Accessed on 29 October 2018.

Freedom House (2018). *Freedom in the world 2018: democracy in crisis*. Report. Available at https://freedomhouse.org/report/freedom-world-2018. Accessed on 29 October 2018.

Gascoigne, B (from 2001). 'History of writing'. Historyworld.net, no date. Available at historyworld.net/wrldhis/PlainTextHistoriesResponsive. asp?historyid=ab33. Accessed on 28 August 2018.

Hart, J and C Chabris (2016). 'How not to explain success'. *The New York Times*, 8 April 2016. Available at www.nytimes.com/2016/04/10/opinion/ sunday/how-not-to-explain-success.html?_r=0. Accessed on 30 August 2018.

Hossain, A (2000). '"Scientific racism" in enlightened Europe: Linnaeus, Darwin and Galton'. Serendip Studio, 16 January 2008. Available at serendipstudio. org/exchange/serendipupdate/scientific-racism-enlightened-europe. Accessed on 28 August 2018.

International Organization for Migration (2014). 'Regional Strategy for Southern Africa 2014–2016'. Available at https://reliefweb.int/sites/reliefweb. int/files/resources/Regional_Strategy_2014_web.pdf. Accessed on 29 October 2018.

International Labor Organization (2016). 'Facing the growing unemployment challenges in Africa'. Press release, 20 January 2016. Available at www.ilo. org/addisababa/media-centre/pr/WCMS_444474/lang--en/index.htm. Accessed on 29 August 2018.

Jefferson, T (1918). 'Thomas Jefferson's thoughts on the Negro: part 1'. *The Journal of Negro History*, 3(1), pp 55–89. Available at www.jstor.org/stable/ 2713794?seq=1#page_scan_tab_contents. Accessed on 28 August 2018.

Kain, E (2011). 'The Dalai Lama is wrong'. Forbes.com, 12 October 2011. Available at /www.forbes.com/sites/erikkain/2011/10/12/the-dalai-lama-is-wrong/#787eb6d4671a. Accessed on 28 August 2018.

Kwaai City (2016). 'Rare 1993 interview with Nelson Mandela, episode 5: collective leadership of the ANC'. YouTube, 10 February 2106. Available at https://www.youtube.com/watch?v=6VvFwGGF8QY. Accessed on 26 October 2018.

Macleod, C (2016). 'John Stuart Mill'. Stanford Encyclopedia of Philosophy, 25 August 2016. Available at plato.stanford.edu/entries/mill/. Accessed on 30 August 2018.

Manning, S (2013). 'Britain's colonial shame: slave-owners given huge payouts after abolition'. *Independent*, 24 February 2013. Available at www.independent.co.uk/news/uk/home-news/britains-colonial-shame-slave-owners-given-huge-payouts-after-abolition-8508358.html. Accessed on 25 September 2018.

McCullough, C (2017). 'Why the number of South African dairy farmers has slumped from 50,000 in 1997 to just 1,600 today'. FarmIreland, 23 April 2017. Available at www.independent.ie/business/farming/dairy/why-the-number-of-south-african-dairy-farmers-has-slumped-from-50000-in-1997-to-just-1600-today-35629779.html. Accessed on 30 August 2018.

'Medieval papermaking & printing'. Going Medieval: a BOSP 2015 Summer Seminar, Stanford University, 2015. Available at sites.stanford.edu/medievalfreiburg/medieval-papermaking-printing. Accessed 25 October 2018.

Merritt, J (2013). 'Insisting Jesus was white is bad history and bad theology'. *The Atlantic*, 12 December 2013. Available at www.theatlantic.com/politics/archive/2013/12/insisting-jesus-was-white-is-bad-history-and-bad-theology/282310/. Accessed on 30 August 2018.

Milk Producers' Organisation (2017). 'The challenges of small-scale dairy farming'. 18 October 2017. Available at www.mpo.co.za/sustainability-post/challenges-small-scale-dairy-farming/. Accessed on 30 August 2018.

Mwesigire, B bwa (2014). 'Why are schools punishing children for speaking African languages?' This is Africa, 17 September 2014. Available at thisisafrica.me/schools-punishing-children-speaking-african-languages/. Accessed on 23 August 2018.

National Park Service (1995). 'Bacon's Rebellion'. Historic Jamestown website, November 1995. Available at www.nps.gov/jame/learn/historyculture/bacons-rebellion.htm. Accessed on 14 August 2018.

Navarro, R (no date). 'Unconscious bias'. University of California, San Francisco, Office of Diversity and Outreach. Available at diversity.ucsf.edu/resources/unconscious-bias. Accessed on 30 August 2018.

Olapade, M, EE Selormey and H Gninafon (2016). 'Regional integration for Africa: could stronger public support turn "rhetoric into reality"?' Afrobarometer Dispatch No 91, 25 May 2016. Available at afrobarometer.

org/sites/default/files/publications/Dispatches/ab_r6_dispatchno91_
regional_integration_in_africa_en.pdf. Accessed on 29 October 2018.

Pew Research Center (2010). 'Tolerance and tension: Islam and Christianity
in Sub-Saharan Africa'. Pew-Templeton Global Religious Futures Project.
Available at www.pewforum.org/2010/04/15/executive-summary-islam-
and-christianity-in-sub-saharan-africa/. Accessed on 28 August 2018.

Pitso, R (2017). 'A degree and deep desire to work isn't always enough in SA'.
Business Day, 11 March 2017. Available at businesslive.co.za.

Powell, A (2016). 'Young continent, old leaders: the aging face of African governance'. VOA Africa, 30 December 2016/. Available at www.google.
co.za/amps/s/www.voanews.com/amp/3657215.html. Accessed on 28
August 2018.

Signé, L (2018). 'Capturing Africa's high returns'. Op-ed, Brookings Institution,
14 March 2018. Available at www.brookings.edu/opinions/capturing-
africas-high-returns/. Accessed on 30 August 2018.

South African History Online (2016). 'Cape Town timeline 1300–1997', 21
July 2016. Available at www.sahistory.org.za/topic/cape-town-time-
line-1300-1997. Accessed on 30 August 2018.

South African Institute of Race Relations (2017). 'What will South Africa lose
if all immigrants are sent home?' Press release, 13 March 2017. Available at irr.org.za/media/media-releases/what-will-south-africa-lose-if-all-
immigrants-are-sent-home/view. Accessed on 29 August 2018.

Sow, M (2015). 'Foresight Africa 2016: urbanization in the African context'.
Brookings Institution, 30 December 2015. Available at www.brookings.edu/
blog/africa-in-focus/2015/12/30/foresight-africa-2016-urbanization-
in-the-african-context/. Accessed on 29 August 2018.

The World Bank (2012). 'African diaspora'. FAQs, April 2012. Available at
siteresources.worldbank.org/INTDIASPORA/Resources/AFR_
Diaspora_FAQ.pdf. Accessed on 29 August 2018.

The World Bank (2013). 'Remittances create safety net for African households'.
Feature story, 26 June 2013. Available at www.worldbank.org/en/news/
feature/2013/06/26/remittances-create-safety-net-for-african-households.
Accessed on 29 August 2018.

The World Bank (2015). 'Deepening African integration: intra-Africa trade for
development and poverty reduction'. Media statement, 14 November 2015.
Available at www.worldbank.org/en/news/speech/2015/12/14/
deepening-african-integration-intra-africa-trade-for-development-
and-poverty-reduction. Accessed on 28 August 2018.

Times Staff (2017). 'Special report: Inside Zuma's battle to the bitter end as
ANC rebels'. *Business Day*, 5 April 2017. Available at www.businesslive.
co.za. Accessed on 29 August 2018.

Transparency International (2018). 'Corruption Perception Index 2017 shows
high corruption burden in more than two-thirds of countries'. Press

release, 21 February 2018. Available at www.transparency.org/news/press-release/corruption_perceptions_index_2017_shows_high_corruption_burden_in_more_than. Accessed on 29 August 2018.

Treder, M (2009). 'The meaning of freedom'. Institute for Ethics and Emerging Technology, 17 September 2009. Available at ieet.org/index.php/IEET2/print/3411. Accessed on 30 August 2018.

UNIDO (2012). 'Made in Ethiopia: industrial and leather products for the global market'. Report, United Nations Industrial Development Organization. Available at open.unido.org/api/documents/4257015/download/101072%202012%20Brochure%20Made%20in%20Ethiopia.pdf. Accessed on 30 August 2018.

United Nations (2017). 'World population projected to reach 9.8 billion in 2050, and 11.2 billion in 2100'. United Nations Department of Economic and Social Affairs, 21 June 2017. Available at www.un.org/development/desa/en/news/population/world-population-prospects-2017.html. Accessed on 30 August 2018.

United Nations (no date). 'Indigenous peoples at the UN'. UNDESA Division for Inclusive Social Development: Indigenous Peoples, homepage. Available at www.un.org/development/desa/indigenouspeoples/about-us.html. Accessed on 30 August 2018.

Wubie, H and Z Tsegaw (2012). 'Historical background of the African Union'. Abyssinia Law, 29 February 2012. Available at www.abyssinialaw.com/study-on-line/item/377-historical-background-of-the-african-union. Accessed on 28 August 2018.

Zimmerman, M (2014). 'Intrinsic vs extrinsic value'. Stanford Encyclopedia of Philosophy, 24 December 2014, available at plato.stanford.edu/entries/value-intrinsic-extrinsic/. Accessed on 28 September 2018.

Theses and dissertations

Halleen, S (2013). 'From life insurance to financial services: a historical analysis of Sanlam's client base, 1918–2004'. Unpublished PhD (History) thesis, Stellenbosch University, December 2013.

McClendon, Gwyneth (2012). 'The politics of envy and esteem in two democracies'. Unpublished doctoral dissertation, Princeton University, June 2012.

Olckers, C (2011). 'A multi-dimensional measure of psychological ownership for South African organisations'. Unpublished PhD thesis, University of Pretoria, April 2011. Available at repository.up.ac.za/bitstream/handle/2263/28730/Complete.pdf?sequence=8. Accessed on 30 August 2018.

Sirna, ZT (2012). 'Ethiopia: when the Gadaa democracy rules in a federal state. Bridging indigenous institutions of governance to modern democracy'. Unpublished PhD dissertation, University of Tromsø, Norway, May 2012. Available at munin.uit.no/bitstream/handle/10037/5080/thesis.pdf?sequence=2. Accessed on 29 August 2018.

Index

abundance, mentality of 6, 34–35, 41–42, 57–59, 73, 77–78, 245–246

accountability 3–4, 83, 232

Africa, history of 9–16, 22–23, 88, 190–192, 195, 197, 202, 211, 245

African Continental Free Trade Agreement 240, 252

African diaspora 113–114, 237

African National Congress (ANC) 84–85, 161–162, 163

African Union (AU) 98–101, 103–104, 115, 150–151, 252

Afrikaners 174–175, 225–226

Afrocentricity 76–78

agglomerations 120, 222–224, 226–229

agricultural sector 120–121, 124–125, 126, 213–215, 239

alphabetic languages 42–46, 52, 57

ANC see African National Congress

Ancient Egypt 11–15, 22, 24–26, 28, 35–37, 47–48, 62–63, 176–177, 192

Ancient Greece 24–26, 43, 52, 62–64, 175–176

antifragile 92–93

apartheid 7, 60–62, 158, 161–163, 173–175

attribution theory 85–87, 90, 98

AU see African Union

authoritarianism 202, 210–211

aversive racism 167, 186

banking 32, 52, 220–221, 226–227, 230

Bantu peoples 13, 66, 94–95, 97

BEE see black economic empowerment

belonging 172, 188

Berlin Conference of 1884–1885 9, 17–18, 97, 251

biases 155–158, 160–161, 167–169, 178–184, 205–207, 247

Biko, Stephen 15, 61–62, 89

'black', use of term 176–177

Black Consciousness 15–16, 60–62

black economic empowerment (BEE) 162–164, 168–169, 173

Blumenbach, Johann Friedrich 65–66, 69, 71

Botswana 77–78, 130, 142–143, 203, 231–232

bounded solidarity 139, 158, 171–173, 225, 249

capital, meaning of 107–108

capitalism 24, 27, 29–31, 55, 82, 108, 217

caste system 29, 37

categorisation 5, 156, 161–163, 184–185

race-based 14–16, 65–72, 77, 82, 159, 160–166, 185–189, 238

centrality of personhood see Ubuntu

chilly climates 182–184, 187

China 44, 113, 144–146, 177, 217, 241

Christianity 27–28, 44, 46–52, 55, 57–58, 89, 96, 108, 175, 192

cognitive dissonance 10, 70–71

cognitive revolution 19, 249

collective cooperation
   see communitarianism

collective leadership 83–85, 90, 98

colonialism

   culture and 91

   governance and 132, 135–136, 140–141, 143

   labour and 33–34

   legislation and 106–107

   ownership and 232

   psychological effects of 4, 6–7, 9–10, 14, 23

   racism and 69–70, 166

   urban areas and 116

communitarianism 4–5, 13, 24, 28–29, 33–34, 37–38, 57–58, 87–88, 210

competition 7, 217–218

conscientiousness 175

consumerism 27–28, 41

cooperative models 215–217, 239

corruption 91, 124–125, 129–130, 132–138, 141–142, 198–199, 209, 237–238, 241, 244

credit 52, 109, 122–123, 157, 218–221, 226–228